SHALOM CHURCH

SHALOM CHURCH

The Body of Christ as Ministering Community

CRAIG L. NESSAN

Fortress Press

Minneapolis

SHALOM CHURCH
The Body of Christ as Ministering Community

Cover image: Figures in a Circle © Nicholas Wilton
Cover design: Laurie Ingram
Book design: PerfecType, Nashville, TN

Library of Congress Cataloging-in-Publication Data
Nessan, Craig L.
  Shalom church : the body of Christ as ministering community / Craig L. Nessan.
    p. cm.
  Includes bibliographical references and index.
  ISBN 978-0-8006-6327-8 (alk. paper)
  1. Church—Marks. 2. Mission of the church. 3. Church work. I. Title.
  BV601.N47 2010
  262'.7—dc22

                                    2010010024

Manufactured in the U.S.A.

14 13 12 11 10 1 2 3 4 5 6 7 8 9 10

Consider the first time you conceived of justice, engendered mercy,
brought parity into being, coaxed liberty like a marten from its den to
uncoil its limber spine in a sunny clearing, how you understood the
inheritance of first principles, the legacy of noble thought, and built a
city like a forest in the forest, and erected temples like thunderheads. . . .

Do the impossible. Restore life to those you have killed, wholeness to
those you have maimed, goodness to what you have poisoned, trust to
those you have betrayed.

Bless each other with the heart and soul, the hand and eye, the head and
foot, the lips, tongue, and teeth, the inner ear and the outer ear, the flesh
and spirit, the brain and bowels, the blood and lymph, the heel and toe,
the muscle and bone, the waist and hips, the chest and shoulders, the
whole body, clothed and naked, young and old, aging and growing up.

I send you this not knowing if you will receive it, or if having received
it, you will read it, or if having read it, you will know that it contains my
blessing.

"If I Were Paul"
Mark Jarman, *Epistles*

CONTENTS

PREFACE

Two spiritual maladies cause immense harm to the church in its service of God's mission in the world. First, the church in the North American context faces the disease of a rampant individualism that conceives religiosity primarily as a matter of personal preferences rather than communal responsibility. Sociologists, such as Robert Bellah and Robert Putman, have diagnosed the nature of contemporary religion as "expressive individualism." This means that "spirituality" (not religion!—which is viewed as oppressive institutionalization) serves the individual as a therapeutic device to improve the quality of private life and as a way of expressing one's idiosyncratic proclivities. All those who serve in congregational ministry know the challenges of forging communal bonds that transcend the self-interest of individual members. Moreover, church leaders have experienced the phenomenon of "church shopping" by consumers who are looking to meet their individual needs in the most satisfactory way from the dispensers of church goods. The trend is only reinforced and accented by the individuated accessibility of all forms of electronic media, which are tailored to massage the peculiar desires of each individual. The extreme individualism of contemporary society threatens the vitality of congregational life as it has developed over the generations.

Second, the core identity of the church is at risk today due to an increasing gravitational pull toward construing its mission most ardently in relationship to those things that it opposes. A negative identity is forged by overly concentrating on those matters that the church is "against." One might not be surprised to see this development in Protestant traditions that bear the word "protest" as a central feature of their historical identity. Perhaps in these traditions the church has been predisposed to self-definition by opposition. However, the trend toward negative identity in the churches transcends all historic distinctions between Protestants and Catholics. It is the "hot button" issues of our times that are frequently used to provoke passionate reactions from otherwise passive church members: abortion, evolution, homosexuality, representational principles ("quotas"), church growth, contemporary worship, and ecumenical agreements. In the process, it may eventually prove that we are witnessing the emergence of new denominational fault lines to replace those disappearing through ecumenical rapprochement. In any case, it has become a matter of some urgency that the church define itself not primarily in relation to what it is against but what it is for!

This book in its own way addresses these critical problems in contemporary church life. It does so by proposing and articulating a constructive ecclesiology for the church as ministering community. In this project Luther's two kingdoms teaching and Bonhoeffer's interpretation of the church as "Jesus Christ existing as church-community" play integral roles. Luther's concept of the two kingdoms is here retrieved and reinterpreted as God's two "strategies" for ruling the world: the right hand strategy through the proclamation of the Gospel by the evangelizing church and the left hand strategy through the social ministry initiatives of the shalom church. The innovative proposal of Bonhoeffer regarding the sacramental nature of the church—building upon the New Testament metaphor of the church as the body of Christ—provides the theological impetus for exploring the personality or character of the church with reference to its four classical marks: one holy catholic apostolic.

These threads of the theological tradition are woven together with strong interconnections to the fiber of the biblical narrative into a constructive ecclesiology for the church as ministering community. The rampant individualism of contemporary church life is countered by the strong medicine of defining membership in the church as integral participation in the body of Christ. As one is baptized into the church, one becomes a member of Christ's body, which is formed by the biblical narrative and liturgical practice with a distinguishing character. Christianity entails participation in the corporate body of Christ by definition, not option. Furthermore, the church is inoculated against a negative identity by the character of Jesus Christ that it inhabits collectively. The four classical marks of the church provide a constructive agenda delineating what the church is "for" in its corporate life: peacemaking, social justice, creation care, and respect for human dignity. Each of these themes is developed based on the biblical narrative that authorizes the church's commitment to this distinctive ministry agenda.

The eight chapters of the book build the constructive argument that the church participates in God's mission both through the work of evangelizing and the work of social ministry. These two go hand-in-hand as the primary forms of the church's engagement with the world that God seeks to bring to wholeness.

The New Testament metaphor of the church as the body of Christ provides the basis for imagining how the character of Jesus Christ infuses its communal existence in the world. The four marks of the church, as classically formulated in the Nicene Creed, are not only theological descriptions of the church's essence but entail involvement in a powerful ministry agenda.

Chapters Four through Seven examine how the church, immersed in the biblical narrative, acquires particular character or virtues that lead to the engagement of the body of Christ in distinctive social ministry practices. These virtues are demonstrated by how they have been embodied in particular lives—Mahatma Gandhi, Martin Luther King Jr., A. J. Muste, Dorothy Day, Oscar Romero, Mother Teresa, Francis of Assisi, Chief Seattle, Wendell Berry, Bartolomé de Las Casas, Sojourner Truth, and Desmond Tutu—which embolden the church in its responsibility for peacemaking, justice, creation care, and respecting human dignity. These twelve figures were especially selected for how they have given leadership to movements for social change, not just for their inspirational value as individual witnesses. Each of these four chapters includes guidance for congregational ministry practice, as does the concluding chapter (which also addresses formidable contradictions based on the sinful history of the church). Together the interconnections among the four central themes constitute the fabric of what I am calling "shalom church." A shalom church embodies what it means for the church to be one, holy, catholic, and apostolic in ethical responsibility to God for the life of the world.

Recent ecumenical conversations have focused increasingly on the retrieval of the four classical marks of the church in the Nicene Creed for the faith and life of the global church in our times (for example, *The Nature and Mission of the Church: A Stage on the Way to a Common Statement,* Faith and Order Paper 198 of the World Council of Churches or *One Holy, Catholic and Apostolic Church: Some Lutheran and Ecumenical Perspectives,* edited by Hans-Peter Grosshans and produced by the Lutheran World Federation). These discussions have accomplished much for reclaiming the relevance of these four marks for the advancement of ecumenical understanding. However, this book seeks to make a further constructive contribution to this process by interpreting the intended unity, holiness, catholicity, and apostolicity of the church in ethical categories and connecting these to the church's social ministry efforts. In this way, characteristics of the church that have been traditionally considered matters of "Faith and Order" in the ecumenical movement become inextricably linked to the matters of "Life and Work." Even more, the Conclusion of this book proposes making these ethical considerations core to interreligious dialogue and cooperation.

Finally, it is God's purpose to mend the world. This concept is wonderfully expressed in the Hebrew notion of *tikkun olam*. Literally, *tikkun olam* refers to the "repairing" or "perfecting" of the world God has made. This phrase is included in the Jewish prayer, the *Aleinu*, which according to tradition is to be recited three times each day. The *Aleinu* praises God for allowing the Jewish people to serve God and expresses hope that one day the entire world will recognize God and abandon idolatry. When all people of the world abandon false gods and acknowledge God, the world will have been perfected. By following the commands of God, people of faith contribute to the mending of God's creation. It belongs to the work of the shalom church to participate in God's purposes of mending and perfecting the world. The idea of *shalom* is itself a reflection of a world perfected—where peace, justice, care for creation, and respect for human dignity are grounded in the love of God and neighbor, a restored creation.

Shalom Church: The Body of Christ as Ministering Community is a book designed both for personal study and group discussion. The Study Guide provides guidance for personal reflection and questions for group discussion. The bibliography provides suggestions for further reading, and the appendix summarizes key themes from Part II. In addition to use in academic settings it is my hope that the book will prove useful to all of those engaged in congregational ministry, including pastors and lay leaders. Social ministry committees and organizations should find particular value in the biographical sketches for exploring how social ministry has been embodied by leaders of social movements and in the twenty core practices for the purposes of concrete implementation. For convenient reference, the appendix summarizes the twenty virtues, twelve representatives, and twenty core practices of the shalom church in a concise list.

I am grateful to the Board of Directors—Chair Rita Dudley—and Administration—President Duane Larson—of Wartburg Theological Seminary for granting me a sabbatical in 2008–2009, during which time I had the opportunity to complete this book. Sabbaticals are a particularly important gift for those engaged in the vocation of teaching and scholarship, providing the stimulus for fresh insights to enrich future work. I also thank my student assistant, Andrew Dietzel, for help with the text and indexing. This book is dedicated to the faculty of Wartburg Theological Seminary. In particular I want to express deep gratitude to Ann Fritschel for her service as Acting Dean during my sabbatical in what proved to be a challenging year. Moreover, I thank God for the gifts of Paul Baglyos, Norma Cook Everist, Fritz Lampe, Elizabeth Leeper, Kristine Stache, and all my other colleagues on the faculty during the 2008–2009 academic year, whose dedication to their callings amazes me over and over again. I am profoundly grateful for their partnership in the stewardship of the gospel!

Easter 2010
Dubuque, Iowa

Part I

The Shape
of the Shalom Church

For the Mending of Creation

The Place of Social Ministry in the Mission of God

The place God calls you to is the place where your deep gladness and the world's deep hunger meet."[1] This book explores the nature of the world's deep hunger and God's mission to feed that hunger through the ministry of the church.[2] God is calling the church as the body of Christ to act as a servant for the mending of creation (*tikkun olam*). By giving itself away to nourish a world in need, the church discovers its vocation as a ministering community. Jesus told his disciples: "If any want to become my followers, let them deny themselves and take up their cross daily and follow me. For those who want to save their life will lose it, and those who lose their life for my sake will save it. What does it profit them if they gain the whole world, but lose or forfeit themselves?" (Luke 9:23-25). The church's engagement in social ministry is one of the most controversial of its callings. As we will discover, however, social ministry belongs to the very heart of the church of Jesus Christ. When the church follows its calling to address the world's deep hunger as a ministering community, thereby it discovers deep gladness—in the company of the Crucified One.

Taking up the cross of Jesus Christ is risky business. It involves getting our hands dirty in the messiness of the world's disease. For those who assume the business of religion is to appease my troubled conscience and assuage my inner soul in order that I may function effectively and succeed in my individualized pursuits (for example, the "prosperity" gospel), the cross challenges me to think again. Instead, it is more aligned with the way of Jesus to understand the cross as God's provocative act "to comfort the afflicted and afflict the comfortable" (Finley Peter Dunne). Jesus became so immersed in the ambiguity of this world that the good religious people accused him of becoming compromised: "Look, a glutton and a drunkard, a friend of tax collectors and sinners!" (Luke 7:34). Jesus Christ became sin, indistinguishable from the world's ambiguity (cf. 1 Cor 5:21). As a consequence of his living for the sake of the world's most vulnerable, imperfect, oppressed, and rejected ones, is it any wonder this Jesus ended up hanging on his own cross?

The church of Jesus Christ finds its vocation in following Jesus to the places he chooses to frequent. It does so not in order to imitate the way of Jesus but because the church itself exists as the body of this selfsame Jesus Christ alive in the world today. The call to social ministry is not about what the church should be doing in this world in response to the call of Jesus. Rather, social ministry is an expression of the very character of the church as the body of Christ. Because the church participates in the incarnation of Jesus Christ in the world today, the body of Christ organically lives out its calling as a reflection of Jesus' own character. The church enters into the very places Jesus Christ chooses to be found:

> "[F]or I was hungry and you gave me food, I was thirsty and you gave me something to drink, I was a stranger and you welcomed me, I was naked and you gave me clothing, I was sick and you took care of me, I was in prison and you visited me." Then the righteous will answer him, "Lord, when was it that we saw you hungry and gave you food, or thirsty and gave you something to drink? And when was it that we saw you a stranger and welcomed you, or naked and gave you clothing? And when was it that we saw you sick or in prison and visited you?" And the king will answer them, "Truly I tell you, just as you did it to one of the least of these who are members of my family, you did it to me." (Matt 25:35-40)

In discovering Jesus in the faces and bodies of the world's lost and forsaken ones and by ministering to him there, the church discovers its deep gladness.

Social Ministry *and* Evangelism: Engaging the World's Deep Need

What is the world's deepest need? A troubling conflict commonly emerges among churches as they analyze the core of the human predicament. Is the central issue one of spiritual alienation and separation from God that requires a spiritual solution through salvation in Jesus Christ? Or is the central issue one of physical alienation and material deprivation that requires a material solution through the cause of peace and justice? Churches differ dramatically regarding the relative priority they think should be given to these two agendas. On the one side, evangelism emerges as the chief missionary aim of the church: to bring all people into life-giving relationship with God in Jesus Christ by their spiritual conversion. On the other side, social ministry emerges as the chief expression of the church's mission: to strive for justice and peace in all the earth through concern for physical welfare. We note how the ecumenical movement itself at the formation of the World Council of Churches sought to bring together these two impulses, with the joining of the Faith and Order movement on the one side and the Life and Work movement on the other. But the joining of these two agendas remains a delicate balancing act, much as discerning the proper relationship between faith and works remains a formidable theological conundrum.

Finally, as I shall explore in the next section, setting evangelism and social ministry in opposition to each other establishes a false dichotomy between them. It is imperative that we construe a theological paradigm that honors *the centrality of both evangelizing and social ministry as indispensable to the church's mission*, just as we must theologically imagine how to relate faith and works constructively—honoring both. When we operate within a theological framework that diminishes either evangelism or social ministry, we undermine the fullness of the church's ministry and mission. Fortunately, God is not limited in mission by the inability of theological systems to reconcile apparent contradictions.

Because this is a book emphasizing social ministry, it is important thereby not to give a false impression about the crucial place of evangelism (or, more accurately, the "evangelizing church")[3] in the church's mission. The church of Jesus Christ is by definition an "evangelizing church" or it is no church at all. Proclamation of the gospel belongs to the foundational concerns of Jesus and the church that follows him in discipleship. To treat "evangelism" as one matter among many others—compartmentalizing it as just another program—distorts the centrality of the preaching of the Christian *kerygma* for the very existence of the church. Any attempt to interpret the social ministry of the church that fails to reckon with the vital importance of evangelizing is doomed to inadequacy from the outset. At the same time, those theologies of evangelism that take no account of the centrality of social ministry in the witness of Jesus and the life of his church also must be deemed lacking. Both evangelizing and social ministry belong to the original vision of Jesus and the kingdom he proclaimed and enacted. What God has joined together, let no one tear asunder!

At the same time as it is imperative to claim that the church of Jesus Christ is an evangelizing church or no church at all, this book argues that *the church of Jesus Christ is simultaneously a shalom church or no church at all*. By "shalom church" I am primarily talking about God's mission through the church to mend the torn fabric of creation (*tikkun olam*)—God's mission to reestablish created goodness in relation to human beings, the created world, and all creatures. The Hebrew word *shalom* has often been translated simply by the English word *peace*. However, the idea of peace, especially when it is understood merely as the absence of conflict, does not convey the magnitude of shalom.

Shalom involves all members of God's creation living in harmonious and life-giving relationship one with another.[4] Shalom begins with the prayerful and wor-shipful relationship of the human being with God. God is the ultimate source of shalom as God chooses to live in generous relationship with us. God desires to bless us with a sense of belonging and to provide for every need, spiritual and physical. Human beings respond to God's goodness with lives of thankfulness, praise, and worship. Shalom at the same time entails human beings living together in har-mony with each other, both sharing what is needed for the physical well-being of all and nurturing one another emotionally and spiritually. Living in shalom with one another, human beings pay particular attention to the needs of the most fragile and vulnerable. Furthermore—and this dimension has become acutely important in the twenty-first century—shalom involves human beings living in balance with and respect for the whole of creation.[5] Ecology is teaching us many lessons about the costs of having neglected our solidarity with creation. Shalom leads human beings to foster the flourishing of God's creation for God's sake.

The concept of shalom resonates with vision of an ideal society in other cul-tures as well, notably in Asia and Africa. In Asia, *sangsaeng* is an ancient concept "of sharing community and economy together."[6] In Africa, the concepts of *ubuntu* and *ujamaa* describe respectively the wholeness of life and life in community. *Ubuntu* involves the sharing of life as a gift from God: "The individual's identity is inseparable from identity within the wider community, which includes past, pres-ent, and future generations, as well as flora and fauna, the physical environment and the spiritual realm."[7] *Ujamaa* extends this idea by emphasizing the values of family and relatedness. In each of these concepts the focus is on "life-giving civilization which affirms relationships, co-existence, harmony with creation, and solidarity with those who struggle for justice."[8]

The Hebrew concept of shalom is closely akin to the central motif of Jesus' own proclamation—the in-breaking of the kingdom of God. Jesus taught and enacted the coming of God's peaceable and just kingdom in his parables, teach-ings, and ministry. The arrival of this kingdom would be the fulfillment of Israel through the participation of all nations as inheritors of God's ancient promises. The coming of the kingdom meant spiritual reunion between God and human-kind through the forgiveness of sins and reconciling love. At the same time the emergence of God's kingdom entailed the healing of disease, the exorcism of demons, miraculous feeding of the hungry, restoration of broken relationships, and the promise of a bounteous creation. In enacting God's new covenant Jesus left his followers a meal, the Lord's Supper, which characterizes life in the kingdom: *at this meal all are welcome and there is enough for all*. At this meal we discover the essence of shalom. The crucifixion of Jesus reveals the extent to which God chooses to suffer in order that the kingdom prevails. God's raising Jesus from the dead verifies the authenticity of the kingdom Jesus came to inaugurate. Even more, the resurrection of Jesus Christ from the dead is the first fruits of the reality of God's eschatological shalom arriving in time. Together, the Hebrew concept of shalom, the Asian term *sangsaeng*, the African words *ubuntu* and *ujamaa*, and the New Testament idea of the kingdom combine to offer us a glimpse of what God is seeking to accomplish—both now and forever.

The Word of God discloses God's purpose to mend the creation distorted by sin (*tikkun olam*). Israel became God's chosen people to serve in this mission of recreating the broken creation. The God of Israel has been revealed to us throughout the Bible as the God of justice and righteousness. Throughout the testimony of Scripture, God is disclosed consistently as a God who defends the poor, protects the weak, does justice for the oppressed, and insists on righteousness on the part of those who rule. There runs through the Bible an enormous collection of texts that witness to God's way of justice and peace.[9] This "justice trajectory" begins with God's selection of Israel to be the chosen people when God hears the cries of the slaves in Egypt and comes to their deliverance. In the laws of Israel we discover God's partiality in protecting from harm the poor, the widows, the orphans, and the strangers.

When Israel turned to the rule of a king, God sent prophets to remind the royal house of its responsibility to do justice to the poor and to care for the least. These prophets arose in defiance at the abuses of the upper classes and declared God's judgment. When the Messiah would come, God would usher in the kingdom of perfect shalom, including reconciliation between humans and all God's creatures, "the calf and the lion and the fatling together, and a little child shall lead them" (Isa 11:6). Jesus as the Christ came to fulfill all these hopes as he blessed the poor, reconciled enemies, fed the hungry, healed the sick, forgave sinners, and brought the kingdom. On the cross Jesus suffered the consequences from those who resisted the implications of God's shalom by defending their own interests, winning victory over the principalities and powers. By the miracle of the resurrection, God vindicated the cause of Jesus and guaranteed the ultimate arrival of the kingdom, launching the mission of the shalom church in the mean time. To this day, the church of Jesus Christ follows his way of discipleship in caring for human reconciliation and the wholeness of creation.

Social ministry can be defined as the work of the church to serve God in alleviating human suffering and the degradation of creation. While the ministry of evangelizing focuses the church's attention on the proclamation and sharing of the good news so that all may believe in the saving power of the gospel of Jesus Christ, social ministry concentrates on the inexorable implications of the gospel for the mending of creation (*tikkun olam*). Social ministry involves attending to the physical needs of all people for food, water, health, shelter, clothing, and fulfilling work, while at the same time mindful of the spiritual need of humankind for trusting the gospel of Jesus Christ. Furthermore, and especially at this moment in history, social ministry entails intentional care for the well-being of all creation—wisdom about the symbiotic relationship between human beings and all other members of creation in a single web of life. In the ecology of the divine Trinity, all creatures exist in life-giving relationship one with another. Given their status as those created in God's image, human beings are called to accountability before God as they steward the balance and well-being of the whole.

The world's need for the church's social ministry is evident each new day in multiple arenas. The reality of extreme poverty continues to plague tens of millions of human beings on a daily basis, leaving them suffering from malnutrition, inadequate water supplies, homelessness, and lack of basic health care. Diseases, many of them curable through basic preventive measures and treatments taken for granted in the circles of affluence, leave many populations of the world decimated. Political unrest, economic disparity, war, and natural disasters contribute to the migration of massive numbers of people, raising issues of relief, the legal status of refugees, and human rights. Nations and factions within nations turn to violence in order to attempt to rectify what they perceive to be injustices, leaving countless victims dead, injured, and in anguish. Torture, sex trafficking, and slavery emerge as threats to fundamental human dignity, unimaginable in their horror. Moreover, environmental degradation through depletion of the earth's resources, ecological imbalances, and toxic wastes threaten the very infrastructure of life upon which all depend for their existence. Finally, increasing numbers of people find themselves made idle through the lack of meaningful, adequate employment through which they might contribute to the common good.

This book develops a theologically grounded ecclesiology as the basis for the church's social ministry in response to the deep need for the mending of creation (*tikkun olam*). For this project I draw on many resources from the biblical and theological tradition—Paul, Luther, and Bonhoeffer chief among them. I will also draw on the expertise of those who are engaged with a range of social issues, such as those described in the previous paragraph. In the next section I draw constructively upon Luther's concept of the two kingdoms for understanding the nature of the church's ministry as indispensable to God's overall mission to the world.

God's Two Strategies for the Mending of Creation (*Tikkun Olam*)

How do we imagine God's mission to the world through the church? Many conceptualizations have been offered over the centuries. Although misinterpretations have given it a checkered history (leaving many to despair at the possibility of its constructive retrieval), Luther's two-kingdoms teaching, properly understood, continues to offer creative insight for imagining what it is God seeks to accomplish in the world through the church. While I have elsewhere developed the historical grounding of Luther's thought, here I will draw constructively from Luther's thinking for the life and mission of the church today.[10]

One of the central misunderstandings of Luther's two-kingdoms teaching has been the assumption that the "first" kingdom refers to the world and the "second" kingdom to the church. This has led to the false assumption that what Luther was talking about was, in essence, the separation of church and state (that is, the church has to do with religion and the state with everything else). To construe Luther's thought according to the separation of church and state has led the church into quietism, whose disastrous effects have been evident not only in Nazi Germany but also in our own North American context. According to this misunderstanding, the church needs to stay out of politics. However, the church cannot begin to engage in social ministry without engaging matters that are by nature political.

We do well at this point to recall how Jesus himself got involved in political matters pertaining to the arrival of the kingdom of God: feeding the hungry, healing the sick, advocating forgiveness and nonviolence, welcoming strangers. This kingdom agenda involved Jesus in heated controversy with the religious and political establishment of his time, provocatively leading to his eventual execution by the government. For those who would prefer political quietism, we discover little comfort or support in the witness of Jesus. Nor do we gain much support from the life of Luther, whose religious message contained political dynamite. Excommunicated by the pope and outlawed by the emperor, Luther engaged throughout his career in trenchant critique not only of the religious but also of the economic and political affairs of his time. His letters and treatises disclose how fully Luther was engaged in the arts of political persuasion and advocacy, albeit (like Jesus) within the societal order of his time, which is not the same as our own.

To begin to grasp the meaning of Luther's two-kingdoms paradigm, we have to acknowledge how Luther, according to his worldview, envisioned life as an avid

contest between God and Satan with the fate of humanity very much hanging
in the balance. God struggles against a very real and very well-equipped foe. In
his diabolical purposes, Satan appeals to all that make perverse and distort God's
benevolent intention for creation: egoism, selfishness, self-diminishment, greed,
envy, lust, lies, slander, violence, and hatred. We could list all of the seven deadly
sins and much more. In Luther's worldview Satan makes use of all the powers of
evil in order to win over humankind to his agenda of ultimate destruction and
death. God opposes Satan in this battle, employing the forces of life to defeat
the devil's wiles: concern for neighbor, altruism, spiritual wholeness, generosity,
honor, truthfulness, charitable speech, peaceful relations, love, and seeking the
other's welfare. Above all, God sends the beloved Son, Jesus Christ, to deliver
humanity from the clutches of Satan. Ultimately, God wills to usher into existence
the realm of life-giving relationships among all creatures in a restored creation,
the reality we call the kingdom of God, shalom.

While some might find Luther's late medieval worldview antiquated or even
off-putting in its vivid depiction of God's cosmic battle with Satan, existentially
there is much to commend it. Those engaged in the ethical life so often experience
themselves caught between competing forces as they seek to live with integrity.
We know the discrepancy between "what is" and the way things ought to be.[11]
Moreover, those who become involved in political advocacy know what it is like
to contend with the principalities and powers. Walter Wink has written a remark-
able trilogy (later condensed into one volume) that recovers for our time the significance of the biblical concept of God's engagement with the powers, which
was so vivid also for Luther.[12] We might go so far as to imagine the task of social
ministry in the church as aligning our efforts with the things of God in contest
with the demonic distortions perpetrated by God's arch enemy. In this battle we
might brace ourselves also for the difficulty of the struggle.[13]

The genius of Luther's contribution to our thinking involves the way he articulates God's two distinct *strategies* (or kingdoms) in this combat. Following Luther's
imagery, God employs both a right-hand and a left-hand strategy in the mission
of defeating Satan and ushering in the kingdom of God, shalom. The right-hand
strategy entails God's mission of bringing the gospel of Jesus Christ to the world
through the church. The primary instruments for carrying out this strategy are
the proclamation of the gospel and the sharing of the means of grace, baptism
and the Eucharist. Word and sacrament ministry are central to the church in its
worship life and are stewarded by those called to ordained ministry. God seeks to
encounter us in Word and sacrament in order to forgive sin, deliver us from the
powers of the evil one, and bring us to eternal life (following Luther's summary in
his Small Catechism). By his cross and resurrection Jesus Christ has done all that

was necessary to disarm the principalities and powers, ensuring their ultimate demise. The reality of Christ's victory is mediated to us through the proclamation of the gospel and through Christ's real presence in the sacraments of baptism and Holy Communion. Furthermore, the church carries the gospel to the world by its engagement in evangelizing.

Examining in more detail how the Holy Spirit works in the right-hand strategy, there are several aspects that deserve our special attention. First, according to Luther, the law of God functions in the right-hand strategy to convince human beings of their sinfulness and need for God's grace. This is a peculiar theological understanding of the law of God. When the law is proclaimed in this way, the hearers become acutely aware of having failed to live up to the expectations God has for our lives and also to the obligations we know we owe to others. The theological use of the law brings us to the conviction that we sin "in thought, word, and deed, by what we have done and by what we have left undone."[14] Within the right-hand strategy the law functions to prepare us for hearing the gospel by convicting us of our sins. The Holy Spirit works in this way the death of sinners, in order that the gospel can resurrect the new human being in Christ. The death and resurrection of Jesus Christ, by the power of the theological use of the law and the reality of the gospel mediated by Word and sacrament, become enacted again in the lives of those baptized into Christ.

A second consideration involves the place of reason, works, and righteousness in the right-hand strategy. It is commonly (but wrongly!) believed that Luther had an exclusively negative view of human reason, good works, and works-righteousness in his theology. In fact, Luther had a very complex and carefully differentiated view of these key concepts. We would do well not only to speak of the first and second use of the law in Luther's theology, but also of a first and second use of reason, works, and righteousness. Without elaborating in detail, the "second use" of reason, works, and righteousness as part of the right-hand strategy is rejected by Luther as human presumption, while the "first use" of reason, works, and righteousness within the created order are affirmed as good and necessary. According to God's right-hand strategy Luther indeed claimed that as human effort these three are to be rejected. However, when we next develop the contours of God's left-hand strategy, all of these three—reason, works, and righteousness—are to be considered as indispensable gifts to be received with gratitude from God's hand.

Luther saw all too well that as part of the right-hand strategy each of these gifts becomes distorted and misused when employed as human attempts to contribute to God's salvation. Reason cannot contribute anything but presumption to the enactment of God's plan of salvation in Jesus Christ. Human reason sees the cross only as foolishness (1 Cor 1:18-25). Works too are out of place as attempts to please or satisfy God and win God's pleasure in the scheme of salvation. Our purported good works in the right-hand strategy only deceive us into thinking we have a constructive role to play (if even a tiny one) in accomplishing salvation. They lead us to think we can cooperate with God's purposes. In a parallel way, human righteousness is nothing in the presence of the holy God. Before God we have no human righteousness to offer that is God-pleasing. We are totally dependent on the alien righteousness of Christ that makes us holy. Note well that this is not all Luther has to say about reason, works, and righteousness. However, the proper arena for each of these human capacities is not the right-hand but rather the left-hand strategy of God.

Through the power of the proclaimed gospel, God sets the sinner free. This is the genuine meaning of Christian freedom. God in Jesus Christ grants us true freedom to become again what God created us to be. In his treatise *The Freedom of a Christian*, Luther elaborated brilliantly the dual thrust of the liberty God gives us.[15] Freedom is both freedom *from* something and freedom *for* something. Typically in the church we have concentrated on what God has freed us *from*. We are grateful that in Christ, God has set us free from the power of sin, death, and the devil. The forgiveness of sins, the gift of eternal life, and deliverance from bondage have thereby all been secured as gifts of God's love and grace. Yet, while these are illimitable gifts for which we rejoice and give profound thanks, Christian freedom does not end there. The freedom of the Christian also means freedom *for*! Freedom for loving my neighbor! Freedom for living out my baptismal vocation in the world on behalf of those in need! Freedom for serving all those in need, including the wounded creation! We need to recognize how the Christian life in service to the world, including our involvement in social ministry, flows directly out of what God has done for us in Christ through the gospel.

Through the right-hand strategy, mediated by the proclamation of the gospel and the sacramental means of grace, the Holy Spirit sets us free *from* all that holds us in bondage—guilt, painful memories, past failures, addictions, fear of death—and sets us free *for* engaging the world on behalf of the needs of others. The centrifugal force of the gospel propels us outward in Christian freedom to care for a world in need. The church has been freed by Christ to participate in God's right-hand strategy of spreading the gospel to all people—through inviting them to meet Jesus Christ at worship as the assembly gathers for Word and sacrament and through active involvement of the baptized in the work of evangelizing. Worship and evangelizing are core activities for the implementation of God's right-hand strategy for the life of the world. At the same time, the people of God are also freed by the gospel for participating in God's left-hand strategy of bringing the kingdom of shalom. To the elaboration of this left-hand strategy I now turn.

The second, left-hand strategy of God for defeating Satan and ruling this world involves what Luther called the "temporal order." God does not only operate within the confines of the church. God is also God of this world, indeed of the entire universe. In engaging the "rest" of the world, God employs a particular and different strategy that has its own peculiar means toward the end of bringing the kingdom, shalom. This left-hand strategy involves the establishment of a just, equitable, peaceful social order that entails distinct attention to four arenas: family, work, church, and state. It is crucial to notice how Luther does not abandon the world to its own devices by relegating the activity of God only to what happens in the church building. Rather, Luther sees all of life, organized according to these four arenas, engaged by God through the left-hand strategy.

As a distinctive strategy, God uses distinctive means to accomplish the just, equitable, and peaceful ordering of the world. Above all, God employs the law to bring order to a world distorted by sin and to approximate justice in a fallen creation. Luther called this the *first* (or political) use of the law. Throughout the Bible we read how God sought to foster life by establishing the laws by which people can live in peace with equity. Wherever just laws are implemented to structure families, the workplace, the institutional church, or the government, these should be seen in principle as expressions of God's left-hand strategy. God seeks to accomplish divine purposes through the establishment of a rule of law that protects the weak and fosters the common good. Because just laws are of concern to God, Christian engagement in the process of adopting and refining those laws is not only authorized but indispensable. While human society will never achieve perfection through the implementation of a flawless set of laws, God's left-hand strategy always strives toward approximations of legal justice.

In the left-hand strategy, human reason, works, and righteousness find their good and proper place. In understanding the world, reason is one of the best gifts God has bestowed on humankind. We are to use our minds to analyze, reflect, and comprehend the ways of the world in order to come to the most intelligent ethical conclusions. Quality education is, accordingly, an extremely important enterprise for the well-being of human society and the foundation for the participation of all people in the process of ordering life justly. Science has contributed much to the advancement of human knowledge by refining the methods by which we investigate and solve perplexing problems. At the same time, the liberal arts contribute their own rich methods, traditions, and insights for appreciating and understanding the mysteries of life. Human reason is one of the chief gifts God has given us for negotiating the world and participating in God's left-hand strategy.

Within the left-hand strategy, it is crucial to emphasize how Christians are called upon to reason and cooperate with those of other religious faiths or no faith at all. We live in an increasingly pluralistic world in which all people must be respected according to the laws of society. The goal is not the enactment of "Christian" laws or policies; the goal is the enactment of laws and policies that are equitable and just to all. For this reason, according to the left-hand strategy, Christians seek to build coalitions with those who share their reasoning about the benefits of particular legislation or policies. Christians can welcome cooperation with and support from those who do not share their religious commitments, yet who do share their political reasoning and agenda. Moreover, Christians are free to join in supporting the agendas and projects initiated by others, insofar as they accord with sound reasoning. Christians are to view themselves as part of a diverse population in which they do not have all the answers. Instead, as part of the reasoning process, Christians can listen humbly to the viewpoints of others, evaluate carefully the persuasiveness of the arguments, and choose to join common cause (or not). This approach guards Christian political engagement against parochialism or even triumphalism, opening the church to the larger give-and-take of the political process.

If Luther decried the attempt to justify ourselves before God on the basis of our good works and righteousness, he was just as insistent that good works and righteousness have their necessary place in relationship to the good of the neighbor. The neighbor in need—whether a family member, colleague at work, church member, or someone across the globe—is in need of our good works. The gospel in fact frees us from self-preoccupation about our own salvation and eternal destiny so that we may devote our undivided attention to meeting our neighbors' genuine needs. Good works are those works of mercy and justice that our neighbors need to survive and thrive in their own lives. We perform such good works not to secure our relationship with God but purely because this is what serves the neighbor's well-being. Under the theology of the cross, Christians seek not their own self-preservation but life for others. This is a radically other-oriented and ethical understanding of good works that has nothing to do with works as a way of appeasing God.

Similarly, righteousness (correctly understood)—what Luther called "proper" righteousness—is that righteousness we demonstrate in care for the needs of others. While in the right-hand strategy of God, the only appropriate form of righteousness is the "alien" righteousness that we receive from Christ as a gift, in the left-hand strategy we are free to express human righteousness in relationship to what is needed by others—whether that be the need for food, water, clothing, shelter, meaningful work, or any other actual need. In this way, it is profoundly accurate to say that human beings were created exactly for good works and righteousness for the sake of the neighbor.

God's two strategies for mending the world (*tikkun olam*), the right-hand strategy of the sharing of the gospel and the left-hand strategy of bringing justice, belong together as the core dimensions of God's mission in the world. God is ambidextrous! God invites Christians to participate in the right-hand strategy through the ministry of a worshiping, evangelizing church and the left-hand strategy through the embodiment of shalom church. God's entire mission to the world and creation can be encompassed by means of this paradigm, which we find best articulated by Luther and as clarified by his later interpreters.[16] While this book concentrates on the involvement of the church according to God's left-hand strategy, we must remain ever vigilant never to lose sight of the intrinsic importance of the right-hand strategy. Within the life of the church the left-hand strategy unfolds in two distinct ways: through the lives of the baptized engaged in their various arenas of daily life and through the corporate vocation of a public church. To the discussion of these matters I now turn.

The Vocation of the Baptized in the World and the Vocation of the Public Church

Social ministry is carried out by the church in faithfulness to God's left-hand strategy for the life of the world in manifold ways. In one sense, every act of service in the world by every baptized person, every organized act of charity by every congregation, and every collective effort to meet human need by denominations, organizations, or agencies are expressions of social ministry. This broad view provides a starting point as we next begin to reflect more systematically about the various forms of social ministry, distinguishing among them through the elaboration of constructive categories.

An initial distinction is between social service and social advocacy. By "social service" I refer to those forms of social ministry that provide direct assistance to relieve human need. One might think immediately of disaster relief, hunger programs, medical assistance, or housing projects. Also falling into this category are many of the common ministries by denominational social-service agencies: adoption programs, counseling services, refugee resettlement, job training, homeless shelters, sheltered workshops for those with disabilities, assistance to people who are blind or deaf, support for single parents, programs for the elderly, and a host of other charitable works. While there is great consensus among members of the church about the importance of social service, when we turn to social advocacy, we enter an arena that can be highly contested.

By "social advocacy" I mean efforts on the part of the church to change societal structures, promote economic policies, or enact legislation that is consistent with its understanding of God's kingdom, shalom. The charters of organizations like Bread for the World and Amnesty International provide a reference point for this distinctive type of social ministry. Denominational advocacy efforts with regard to racism, sexism, heterosexism, poverty, hunger, homelessness, violence, war, arms proliferation, prisons, capital punishment, environmental concern, and others fall into this category. Likewise congregations, or members thereof, may wish to raise their voices on behalf of a particular cause that entails changing societal structures.

The controversy over the place of social advocacy in the church's outreach has come about for many reasons. Fundamental to the debate are conflicting views about the proper relationship of church and state, in particular the role of the church in society. According to a very popular view, the primary role of the church is to minister to the spiritual needs of people through worship and pastoral care with the secondary role of offering charitable assistance to people in need. The ministry of the church belongs to the private realm of individuals and families who choose to participate in it. The mediation of the church's ministry is highly personal, based on concern for the spiritual welfare of persons and helping with individual needs. In this view the ministry of the church is relegated to the private sphere. It remains properly separated from matters debated in the public square, except when those debates threaten the rights of the church's functioning in the realm belonging to it. Beginning with the nineteenth century, the church has been subject increasingly to the privatization of religion, with its relegation to a separate sphere, leading to the quietism of the church in public affairs.

A second and dramatically contrasting approach for relating church and state has been taken, for example, by the so-called Christian right.[17] In this approach, the church is called to be vigilant in ordering society according to Christian principles. In the Bible God has revealed the truth about key social issues (for example, regarding abortion, marriage, homosexuality, or the teaching of evolution) and it is a Christian's responsibility to become involved in the political process to ensure that the "Christian" position on each of these issues prevails. Churches operating with this mindset often issue directives to their membership about how to vote, not only on particular issues but also for particular political parties and candidates who they reckon will offer the best support for their agenda. These churches also actively advocate with legislators according to their established agenda.

In U.S. society there are many Christians who understand the relationship of church and state according to this paradigm. This approach has had significant influence on the outcome of key elections. This has led many politicians to calculate how they can best appeal to the power of this voting block. At the same time the assertiveness of the Christian right has led to a significant backlash by those who reason differently and have come to different conclusions on the issues, including many Christians. Many secular citizens and those from other faith traditions often wrongly assume that all Christians share this approach to politics. This complicates all the more the challenge facing Christians who operate out of other paradigms for relating church and state, such as God's two strategies developed in this chapter.

Social advocacy belongs to the responsibility of the baptized, according to the left-hand strategy of God, both through their personal initiative as citizens and through the collective efforts of the institutional church in its functioning as a public church. There is a major difference, however, between the political approach of the Christian right and the nature of advocacy according to God's left-hand strategy. I have already emphasized the constructive use of reason as God's gift in analyzing and understanding the world. When it comes to political involvement by Christians, rather than basing their judgments on explicitly biblical warrants or religious arguments, effective Christian participation in politics requires that Christians employ reasonable arguments that are intelligible and coherent to all citizens, not just to those who share their Christian theological commitments. Christians are to use a language and reasoning that is accessible to all. They are to direct their attention primarily to the well-being of the neighbor in their advocacy, reasoning according to what contributes most to the common good of society, with particular concern for those who are suffering under the current policies and programs.

This approach differs dramatically from the politics of the Christian right, which is heavy laden with biblical and religious arguments and whose goal is to impose its particular viewpoint on the whole society. By contrast, based on Christian motivation—freed by the gospel of Jesus Christ for neighbor love—Christians participate in God's left-hand strategy by speaking out and engaging in the political process as citizens who advocate for the well-being of the neighbor, using reasonable arguments that appeal to the consciences and common sense of others, building coalitions wherever possible with those who have a common vision, and avoiding special pleading based on a narrowly "Christian" agenda. While Christians certainly base their political involvements on their faith—also contemplating the significance of Scripture for their convictions—when they move into the public arena, they favor reasoning and explanations that are accessible to all. This allows the left-hand strategy to be informed by Christian motives and values as these are translated into political reasoning that appeals to Christians and non-Christians alike, people of faith and people who claim no faith at all. It is an approach that honors the authentic spirit of the separation of church and state as the studied avoidance of allowing the state to impose any religious view upon its citizenry. Again, this is dramatically different from the approach of the Christian right, which on almost every issue has as its agenda the legal imposition of its religious conclusions on society.

In participating in God's left-hand strategy for ruling the world, Luther and the reformers stressed four arenas in which the baptized exercise responsibility for the sake of the common good and God's just ordering of human affairs. The *first arena* is the family. God sustains the well-being of creation by placing us in families and giving us obligations to fulfill for the nurture and flourishing of those to whom we are related by blood or by adoption. Parents have responsibility to care for the health and maturation of their children. Children are to honor their parents in mutual love, especially demonstrating concern for aging parents who find themselves in need of physical and emotional care. Siblings have responsibility to encourage one another to grow in maturity and responsibility for others. All members of the extended family—grandparents, aunts, uncles, cousins, and others—are to live in relationships of mutual care, especially tending those who have special needs of any kind. Moreover, families are responsible to instill the fundamental posture of learning to look beyond the bonds of kinship to care for the world and all people in need. [18]

The *second arena* in which the baptized are to express their responsibility according to God's left-hand strategy is the workplace. As God blesses each of us with particular gifts that can be employed in the service of others, so God desires that each person have productive and meaningful work where these gifts can be channeled into the care of others. In his time, Luther celebrated the value of all kinds of honest labor. The world needs able and honest shoemakers, farmers, and shopkeepers to keep the creation running smoothly. [19] The Reformation sought to overcome the notion that explicitly religious vocations (clergy, monks) were superior by nature to service in non-religious vocations (for example, accountants or nurses). Instead, every useful occupation contributes to God's purposes of ordering the world for the good of all. Each worker is to contribute to God's care for the world through her or his daily work.

This concept is severely tested, however, in the modern world, where the financial benefits and status of some vocations is vastly disproportionate to those of others. [20] Whereas some discrepancies in pay and status are inevitable, the degrees of separation demand redress, if we are to approximate a more just society. Moreover, this concept is also radically tested where people either cannot find employment at all, or they languish in jobs that do not give expression to their creativity and talent. [21] One of the important matters for Christian advocacy must involve full employment and fair labor practices, if we are to create a system in which people have access to viable jobs with adequate pay and a sense of meaningful work—in the spirit of Luther's imagination for the workplace as an arena for serving God and neighbor.

The *third arena* for the involvement of the baptized in the life of the world involves the ministry of the institutional churches and other faith communities; today we might refer more generally to nonprofit organizations. Here we are depicting churches, faith communities, and nonprofit organizations as institutions serving the good of society, through acts of charity and benevolence on behalf of others. According to God's left-hand strategy of caring for the world, there is an urgent need for non-governmental agencies that offer service to others, especially to those in most acute need. As part of God's left-hand strategy, we are not referring in this place to the explicit ministry of the church in the area of worship, spiritual care, and evangelizing. Rather, churches, faith communities, and nonprofit organizations can contribute to human welfare and the care of creation apart from their peculiar efforts to propagate their religious beliefs. The baptized render valuable and needed service to the upkeep of God's created order, whenever they become involved in volunteer activities through faith communities and nonprofit organizations designed to assist the neighbor. Likewise the public church renders service to society through all forms of social ministry, the subject matter of this book.

The *fourth arena* for the participation of the baptized in service to the world is as citizens of a particular nation, state, and local community. Already I have sought to distinguish the particular character of this participation by those seeking to cooperate with God's left-hand strategy for ruling the world (in contrast to the approach of the Christian right). But here it is important to stress that political involvement truly belongs to the responsibility of the baptized as they care for God's world. It does make a difference which candidates are elected, which laws are enacted, and which governmental policies are implemented. These things make a difference regarding how the resources of government are distributed on behalf of the common good or not. Christians employ their best reasoning as they get involved in the political process. It is all too evident that different Christians can and do reason differently about how to accomplish what they perceive to be the most urgent political goals. While we may sometimes fear the fallout from political arguments, these differences among us can be a good thing for the whole democratic process, if we genuinely believe that the collective reasoning process will be better than that of any private individual.

There are a variety of ways for Christian citizens to get actively involved in the political arena. The first involves becoming educated on issues in general and especially on legislation currently under deliberation by legislators and other elected officials. Second, Christian citizens have an obligation to exercise their right to vote and also to seek to influence the votes of others by the art of persuasion. A strict boundary must be maintained, however, between the active involvement of Christians as citizens in the electoral process and partisan politics in the church. Because we come to worship as those baptized in the name of the same Savior, matters of party affiliation are suspended there due to our shared belief in Jesus Christ. We gather at worship as brothers and sisters in Christ, not as members of political parties. At the same time, in its Christian education activities, it is most appropriate to engage in deliberation of *moral and political issues*, provided that we can set aside our partisanship for the sake of the mutual pursuit of better knowledge and deeper commitment.

Third, Christian citizens can participate in active advocacy for particular causes and political agendas. Christians do so not because any particular issues are "Christian" but because the reasoning is sound and the cause compelling. To this end the advocacy offices of church bodies and the efforts of various lobbying organizations can help church members to become better educated on the issues and to insert themselves into the debate in the most constructive way—through letters, emails, petitions, and phone calls to our elected representatives. Fourth, Christians may choose a political vocation by running for elected office or working for a governmental agency. While the ethical dilemmas faced by politicians and elected officials are stunningly complex, God also needs responsible officials who care for the common good in order to accomplish the divine purposes in the left-hand strategy.

Not only do individual Christians get involved in the political process as a way of living out their baptismal vocations in the world, but Christians also engage corporately in the political process through advocacy efforts by church representatives who work on behalf of regional judicatories and denominations. Such involvement belongs to the most controversial activities on the part of the public church in its responsibility for the ordering of the world according to God's left-hand strategy.[22] The church, in its exercise of responsibility for the common good, goes public with its best reasoning, analysis, and conclusions on specific issues affecting the well-being of society.

There are several methods by which the public church may voice its concerns about matters of public policy. In some cases the public church adopts social statements on major and perennial issues, delineating a framework for the deliberation of urgent ethical questions. At other times, the public church weighs in on specific pieces of legislation before the legislature, especially through its designated office of governmental affairs. On occasion, the leaders of judicatories or denominations may issue commentary on current events from the perspective of the Christian faith. In every instance, however, it is the responsibility of the public church to pay particular attention to the needs of the weakest members of society in its deliberations, not merely to pursue its own self-interest.

There are several salutary consequences deriving from the public church's development of social statements. First, the moral deliberation of the church can serve as a very constructive teaching role for congregations and individual Christians. As church members face social issues in their personal and corporate lives, the social teaching of the church is a vital educational resource for learning about the issues and examining different points of view. Second, the process by which the church engages in moral deliberation provides a salutary example of how congregations and Christians can themselves participate in the discernment process. In a world of highly polarized political discourse, often we lack constructive models of how to engage issues without acrimony and in a spirit of goodwill. Third, the public church's moral deliberation provides specific guidance to Christians facing ethical dilemmas in their own experience (for example, regarding abortion, the death penalty, genetic engineering, and human sexuality). Those who are confronted with acute moral crisis can greatly benefit from the public church's balanced reasoning that seeks to consider issues holistically. Lastly, the church's adoption of social statements can guide the denomination in its own institutional decision making and in its advocacy of particular political legislation. Because of the thorough and highly participatory process undertaken by denominations in developing social statements prior to their adoption, these documents convey wisdom to the church as it engages in social advocacy regarding current legislative bills and policy decisions. Such statements offer sound reasoning for the positions that the public church takes on the issues of the day.

This opening chapter has oriented the reader to several key issues regarding the calling of the church to live in service of God's shalom through social ministry. I have (1) explored the inextricable relationship between social ministry and evangelizing as core to the church's mission, (2) articulated how the mission of God comes to expression in the world through two distinct strategies, and (3) offered concrete guidance for how the church can engage in social ministry both through the lives of the baptized and through the corporate engagement of the public church. In the next two chapters I will develop the biblical (chapter 2) and theological (chapter 3) foundations that ground social ministry in the very character of the church, exploring what it means to be the body of Christ in the world. Thereby I will construct an ecclesiology for the shalom church.

Constructing Ecclesiology
for Social Ministry
Body of Christ in the New Testament

Is social ministry just one activity of the church among many other activities? This is how we often think about social ministry, as one discrete ministry alongside others, such as stewardship, evangelism, or education. The authors of *The Evangelizing Church* have argued that the church by definition engages in evangelizing or it is no church at all;[1] this book makes a parallel claim: The church of Jesus Christ is a shalom church or it is no church at all! Social ministry belongs to the core mission of what the church by nature is and always has been. The ministry of Jesus Christ himself would be unimaginable without the acts of mercy Jesus demonstrated among the people whom he encountered—healing the sick, feeding the hungry, reconciling the estranged. So too the church has always been involved in sharing love, mercy, and compassion with those in need, all in the name of the same Jesus Christ. Rodney Stark goes so far as to claim that the growth of the earliest church was directly related to the way those early Christians engaged in acts of mercy to the most miserable and abandoned people of their time.[2]

In order to advance the argument that the church of Jesus Christ is by nature a shalom church, we need to build the case by paying strict attention to ecclesiological foundations. Ecclesiology involves the fundamental concept of the church—what it is and what it does. Where in the New Testament and in the theological tradition do we discover the warrants for the bold claim that the character of the church necessitates social ministry, the existence of shalom church? The next two chapters build these ecclesiological foundations by examining what it means to consider the church as the body of Christ. In this chapter I will examine the New Testament references to the body of Christ in order to construct an ecclesiology that resounds with sacramental realism: the church *is* the body of Christ. Furthermore, in the next chapter, I will build theologically upon these biblical foundations with special reference to the insights of Dietrich Bonhoeffer, who formulated the seminal idea that the church *is* Jesus Christ existing as church-community, the collective person Jesus Christ alive in the world. As a constructive proposal, I will then explore the "ethical character" of this collective person Jesus Christ in relationship to the needs of the world. This will establish the theological basis for the claims to be made about shalom church.

The New Testament abounds in diverse images for the church. In his comprehensive survey, Paul Minear identified ninety-six different metaphors appearing in the New Testament.[3] Among the most prominent images are "people of God," "the new Israel," "community of the Holy Spirit," "new creation," "servants," and "salt of the earth."

As one analyzes these various images, it becomes clear that each of them reveals some important facets of ecclesial reality, even as each one by itself conceals other aspects of what it means to be church. For example, the metaphor "people of God" discloses the continuity of the church with the Old Testament people of God, Israel. The people of God have existed corporately from the call of Abraham through the entire witness of Scripture. At the same time this image conceals much of the christological content that is peculiar to the church of Jesus Christ by its lack of reference to him. Because the different images vary in frequency in the New Testament and convey distinctive meanings, many interpreters argue for an approach that stresses how the multiple images are complementary with one another. No one image says it all. The contrasting images must shed mutual light one on another, if the description of the church is to be adequate and fulsome.

Granting the need for complementarity among the various images of the church, I will investigate in particular the metaphor of the church as the body of Christ. This image is given preference for providing depth and fullness to an organic sense of the church's life in the world and evoking a profound sense of the church's mission. This book explores the significance of the body of Christ image for the identity and mission of the church as it lives out its calling in social ministry. I will proceed by examining the New Testament texts that employ body of Christ imagery for the church and systematically develop the themes that derive from these texts. This leads in the final section to the articulation of the explicitly ethical themes related to the church as the body of Christ. In the next chapter I then relate the body of Christ metaphor to ethical claims based on the four classical marks of the church—one, holy, catholic, apostolic—drawing significant implications for our present mission context.

Examining the New Testament Texts

Jesus' words at the Last Supper provide essential background for understanding the meaning of *body of Christ* in the New Testament. According to Mark 14:22-25:

> While they were eating, he took a loaf of bread, and after blessing it he broke it, gave it to them, and said, "Take; this is my body." Then he took a cup, and after giving thanks he gave it to them, and all of them drank from it. He said to them, "This is my blood of the covenant, which is poured out for many. Truly I tell you, I will never again drink of the fruit of the vine until that day when I drink it new in the kingdom of God."

The most obvious link between Jesus' words at the Last Supper and the Pauline body of Christ image is the explicit saying: "This is my body." It is especially in the Eucharist that the church is constituted as the body of Christ by participation in the meal. The Christian sacramental reenactment of the Lord's Supper is a concrete instance of entering into the realm of Christ's living activity, what Paul refers to as being "in Christ." The body of Christ in bread nourishes the community called the body of Christ.

Yet, there is another dimension to Jesus' words that deserves reflection. When Jesus addressed the twelve at table, declaring, "Take; this is my body," was he referring only to the loaf of bread? Do his words not contain a double entendre, referring simultaneously to the gathered assembly itself? In this case, a communal interpretation of "body of Christ" may be derived from a dominical saying of Jesus.

This text is crucial not only for connecting the body of Christ image with the Lord's Supper but even more for joining it with Christ's passion and death. Jesus sacrifices his own body on the cross, laying down his life as a ransom for many (Mark 10:45). The body of Christ metaphor inextricably connects the church as body of Christ with the saving work of Jesus accomplished by his death and resurrection. Jesus proclaims his death as the sealing of a new covenant: "This is my blood of the covenant, which is poured out for many" (Mark 14:24). To be the body of Christ is to be grounded in Christ's redemptive and reconciling atonement. The body of Christ is dependent upon Christ's salvific work for its very identity. This dimension of the metaphor becomes explicit wherever Christ is named as the "head" of the body, the church.

Body of Christ as an explicit metaphor for the church appears exclusively in the Pauline corpus (1 Corinthians, Romans, Ephesians, Colossians). Particularly in 1 Corinthians, Paul employs this image in creative ways to counteract beliefs and practices introduced by charismatic individuals who were influenced by what we might describe as a form of Gnosticism. Paul addresses several controversial issues within the congregation at Corinth, challenging them to consider what it means to be members of one body in Christ. At issue were the questions of participating in cultic prostitution, eating meat that had been sacrificed to idols, discriminating against poor members of the congregation in conjunction with the sharing of the Lord's Supper, and properly evaluating spiritual gifts.

In 1 Corinthians 6:15-19, Paul asserted that the bodies of individual Christians are collectively "members of Christ." Paul argued against the libertine attitude that prostitution was permitted as a matter of Christian freedom. He developed the idea that individual bodies have been joined to Christ, which precluded joining them to a prostitute. Just as those who are united to a prostitute become one body with her, those baptized into Christ have become one body with him. "Do you not know that your bodies are members of Christ?" (6:15). Implicit in this text is the body of Christ image, which will be developed more fully in 1 Corinthians 12.

In 1 Corinthians 10:14-22, Paul addressed the issue of eating meat sacrificed to idols. In doing so, he made a powerful analogy that linked participation in the Lord's Supper with becoming the body of Christ: "The cup of blessing that we bless, is it not a sharing in the blood of Christ? The bread that we break, is it not a sharing in the body of Christ? Because there is one bread, we who are many are one body, for we all partake of the one bread" (1 Cor 10:16-17). The body of Christ eaten in the meal makes those who receive it members of the one body of Christ. This is the most profound Pauline text stating the relationship between Eucharist and church as the body of Christ. Many members become one body by sharing the one cup and one loaf.

In 1 Corinthians 11:17-34 Paul criticized the Corinthians for scandalous behavior at the Lord's Supper. Divisions had arisen in the community. These came to expression when certain members joined together for a common meal prior to sharing the Lord's Supper, while they excluded other members of the church: "For when the time comes to eat, each of you goes ahead with your own supper, and one goes hungry and another becomes drunk" (1 Cor 11:21). Paul rehearsed for the Corinthians the tradition he received from the Lord regarding his supper: "This is my body that is for you. Do this in remembrance of me" (1 Cor 11:24). Paul makes a direct connection between eating the body of Christ at the Supper and being the body of Christ in community: "Whoever, therefore, eats the bread or drinks the cup of the Lord in an unworthy manner will be answerable for the body and blood of the Lord" (1 Cor 11:27).

Paul chastised them for their divisive behavior: "For all who eat and drink without discerning the body, eat and drink judgment against themselves" (1 Cor 11:29). Within the context of Paul's entire argument, "discerning the body" refers to the corporate body of the congregation in which the discriminatory eating practices had taken place. It has nothing to do with *believing properly* about how Christ is present in the elements. Furthermore, this is very different from the moralistic and individualistic interpretation of the text that prohibited those with guilty consciences from coming to the Lord's Table because they were "unworthy." The Lord's Supper is the body of Christ, which has definite implications for how the church lives out its corporate existence as the body of Christ.

1 Corinthians 12 contains the most extensive exposition of the body of Christ image in the New Testament. As in chapter 6, emphasis on the one body parallels emphasis on the one Spirit. In fact, Paul operated according to a triadic formula— one God, one Lord, one Spirit.[4] The immediate occasion for this chapter was the need to address divisions in the charismatic Corinthian congregation over the proper evaluation and exercise of spiritual gifts. Paul resisted beliefs and practices that purported that the believer already has fully entered eschatological reality by the power of the Spirit.

Verses 4-11, under the rubric of the one Spirit, elaborate many of the same themes that verses 12-31 develop according to the image of the one body. Paul acknowledged the variety of spiritual gifts but insisted that they derive from the one Spirit. These gifts have been given for a purpose: as acts of service. The gifts are to be exercised for the common good (not for the spiritual satisfaction of the individual). When Paul listed specific gifts, he placed the gift of tongues last. This indicates that, of all God's gifts, this one has the least significance. Apparently at Corinth there were some who claimed the very opposite.

In 1 Corinthians 12:12-31 Paul took up the body of Christ metaphor in detail. Unlike the Stoics, who employed the body as an image for the cosmos itself, Paul clearly referred to the body as the body of Christ, that is, the church. The body metaphor is organic—implying growth and dynamic activity. One becomes a member of the body by baptism. Because the body and Spirit are one, all physical and social distinctions are abrogated ("Jews or Greeks, slaves or free"). Paul elaborated these consequences of baptism also in Galatians 3:27-28.

Dale Martin in his detailed book on the body metaphor in the Corinthian correspondence, *The Corinthian Body*, stresses that Paul sought to overcome the hierarchical understanding of the members of the body common in Greco-Roman literature:

In 1 Corinthians 12–14, as elsewhere in the letter, Paul argues for a version of Christ's body in which status indicators are reversed, with greater honor given to those normally regarded as having lower status and less prestige accorded to those normally accorded badges of honor. Throughout these chapters, supposedly "given" status indicators are rendered problematic.[5]

Paul hereby subverts one of the chief markers of conventional society, hierarchy of the strong over the weak.

The members are many, yet one body. Paul directed this chapter especially against those who were as individuals dissociating themselves from the church. Without all its members, the body would be deficient. God arranged the body according to its various parts. Just as it is absurd to imagine an argument among the different members of your physical body, even so absurd is it for members of Christ's body to denigrate one another. Dale Martin comments: "In his uses of the body analogy and the mind/spirit dichotomy, Paul pursues the same rhetorical strategy: identifying himself with the position of the Strong and then calling on them to give up their own interests for the sake of the Weak."[6] Paul asserted that the weak and unseemly parts are especially necessary and deserve special concern. By lending "greater honor to the inferior member," dissension in the body is overcome.

In a glorious extension of the organic image of the body, Paul wrote: "If one member suffers, all suffer together with it; if one member is honored, all rejoice together with it" (v. 26). So closely knit together are the many members! Driving home the impact of the body metaphor, next Paul declared: "Now you are the body of Christ and individually members of it" (v. 27). This address functions as performative language not only to name but create the reality of the church as one body in Christ. As Paul referred to specific forms of service—apostles, prophets, teachers, deeds of power, gifts of healing, forms of assistance, forms of leadership, and, finally, various kinds of tongues—he submitted them all to a higher norm, "a still more excellent way," namely, love.

According to Martin, Paul's central argument in 1 Corinthians involves a revision of the conventional hierarchical ordering of the body common in the surrounding society:

Throughout 1 Corinthians Paul attempts to undermine the hierarchical ideology of the body prevalent in Greco-Roman culture. He attempts to make the strong weak and the weak strong. He calls on Christians of higher status to please those of lower status. He insists that those who see themselves as spiritual ones modify their behavior, such as speaking tongues in the assembly, to accommodate those they consider spiritual inferiors. Paul even implies that higher-status Christians should follow his example and lower themselves socially in order to identify themselves with those of lower status.[7]

This background of the body metaphor within Greco-Roman culture only magnifies the radicalism of what Paul is proposing about the nature of the church.

A much briefer but comparable usage of the body of Christ metaphor occurs in Romans 12:4-8. The reference in Romans appears more formal and is not associated with addressing a particular controversy. Paul balanced evenly the two components of the body image, that the body consists of many members and that they are all one. The various members of the one body have differing gifts whose origin is God's grace. The listing of gifts varies from 1 Corinthians 12: prophecy, ministry, teacher, exhorter, giver, leader, and the compassionate. The gift of tongues is not mentioned at all. Still, the varied gifts are only of value when they are exercised on behalf of others. As with 1 Corinthians 12–13, this passage is followed by the exhortation to love (Rom 12:9-10).

In the deutero-Pauline epistles of Ephesians and Colossians, new dimensions of the body of Christ image come to expression. Ephesians 1:22-23 introduces two new themes that are more fully elaborated in chapters 4 and 5: "And he has put all things under his feet and has made him the head over all things for the church, which is his body, the fullness of him who fills all in all." First, Christ is depicted as the head of the body. This addition to the body of Christ metaphor makes explicit both how the body is dependent on Christ and that it is connected to Christ's entire saving work. Second, the expanse of Christ's influence through the church attains cosmic proportions, "the fullness of him who fills all in all."

Other themes introduced in 1 Corinthians abide, for example, the joining of Jews and Gentiles in the one body by the power of the cross (Eph 2:16 and 3:6) and the linking of the emphasis on one body with that on one Spirit (Eph 4:4).

The passages employing body of Christ imagery in Ephesians demonstrate a later stage of reflection and development. In Ephesians 4:11-16, for example, the listing of gifts is provided not primarily to emphasize the unity of the body, as earlier with Paul, but equally to stress that these gifts are given "to equip the saints for the work of ministry, for building up the body of Christ" (4:12). Unity becomes more an eschatological goal to be reached than an already in-breaking reality.

The body develops through an organic process of growth, that is, the body reaches "maturity," "full stature" (v. 13), and comes to "grow up in every way into him who is the head, into Christ" (v. 15). Christ is the one "from whom the whole body, joined and knit together by every ligament with which it is equipped, as each part is working properly, promotes the body's growth in building itself up in love" (v. 16). Notice how Ephesians elaborates on certain anatomical details. The references to "love" in verse 16 and earlier in 15 ("speaking the truth in love") continue the pattern of defining the higher purpose of the body according to love.

Because the reference to the subordination of wives to their husbands in Ephesians 5:21-33 now appears antiquated, the beautiful imagery regarding the church as the body of Christ in this passage threatens to be lost. What does this text contribute to a greater understanding of the nature of the church? "Christ is the head of the church, the body of which he is the Savior" (v. 23). For Christ to be the head means that Christ's saving work is efficacious for the body. Verses 25-27 detail the nature of Christ's saving work, although they depart from the body of Christ imagery. Verses 29 and 30, however, return to the primary metaphor, highlighting how Christ nourishes and cares for his own body, the church. This is the most explicit text in the New Testament for describing how the body benefits from Christ's salvation. Without its head, the body would be lost. For this reason the body must be subject to its head.

The final references to the church as the body of Christ occur in Colossians. Even more so than in Ephesians, the sphere of Christ's influence is cosmic: "He is the head of the body, the church; he is the beginning, the firstborn from the dead, so that he might come to have first place in everything" (1:18). Christ's reconciling and peacemaking work on the cross has universal significance. The author of the epistle wrote that his suffering for the sake of the Colossians completes "what is lacking in Christ's afflictions for the sake of his body, that is, the church" (1:24).

As in Ephesians, it is necessary to adhere to true teaching, "holding fast to the head, from whom the whole body, nourished and held together by its ligaments and sinews, grows with a growth that is from God" (2:19). The organic integrity of the body would be destroyed, were the body severed from the head. One consequence of maintaining the body's wholeness is the capacity to dwell in peace (cf. 3:15).

Systematic Gleanings from the Texts

The body of Christ metaphor provides a rich fountain of insights for systematic reflection on the nature of the church. Foundational for understanding the particularity of this body is its relationship to Christ. On the night of his betrayal unto death, Jesus broke bread, saying, "This is my body." By means of the body image, Jesus inextricably connected the sacrifice of his own body on the cross (1) to the meal shared in his remembrance and (2) to the community that continues to gather in his name. Both the meal and the church by very definition partake of the identity and mission of Christ. Anamnesis, the remembering and re-invoking of Christ's saving deeds, remains the perennial task of the church both at worship and in its common life.

The church owes its existence to the self-giving death of Jesus on the cross. All of the metaphors employed to articulate the significance of Jesus' atonement—redemption, sacrifice, reconciliation, etc.—describe the work that Christ has accomplished on behalf of the church. The church lives from the nourishment of Christ's offering up his body on its behalf. This is what is entailed in naming Christ as the head of the body, the church. The church is a creature dependent on Christ as the source of its life. While the church may constantly undergo the threat of amnesia, it cannot succumb without losing its head. And a body without its head simply ceases to exist.

The church receives its identity as the body of Christ through participation in the sacraments of baptism and Holy Communion. In baptism, the individual members are joined to the body of Christ. By so doing, they leave behind previous identities and commitments that contradict existence "in Christ." The old sinful self is drowned by baptism into the death of Christ, and a new Christ-like person emerges by the power of Christ's resurrection. Differences which determined one's status in the world—Jew/Gentile, slave/free, male/female—are no longer applicable within the body of Christ. By means of baptism, one becomes a member in concert with all the other baptized within the one body of Christ.

The Eucharist sustains and nourishes the identity of the members of Christ's body. Partaking of the bread and wine (that is, the body and blood of Christ) feeds the church with all the gifts deriving from Christ's death on the cross. The church receives from Christ forgiveness, love, deliverance from evil, and the gift of eternal life. The church receives the body of Christ in order to become the body of Christ in the world. The Eucharist thus has consequences for communal life. As the body of Christ, the church shuns idols. As the body of Christ, the church shares its bread with the hungry.

The metaphor of the church as the body of Christ succeeds in combining an emphasis both on its oneness and its diversity. As every body has a unified integrity, so Christ's body is one. This image succeeds like no other in concretely depicting the unity of the church. Although the members vary, they live in mutual interdependence. Without all its parts working as one, the body would die. Paul parallels his stress on the oneness of the body with an accompanying reference to the one Spirit. The body of Christ image counteracts all forces that would justify its division into competing factions. A body at war with itself is an absurdity. Without all of its parts joined as one, the body is maimed.

At the same time, there is an honoring of the many members who constitute the one body. The gifts of each member are valuable and to be treasured. No particular gifts are worth more than the others. Each member is a vital part of the body, whose absence would entail a diminishment of the whole. In order to preserve the wholeness of the body, a special measure of concern and attention is due to those members appearing to be weak or unseemly. This is an admonishment for the church to remain vigilant in caring for those members who, according to worldly standards of importance, would be easy to disregard.

The body of Christ metaphor is dynamic. The image invites analogies based on anatomy and organic growth. If Christ as the head of the body grounds the church in justification by grace through faith, the notion of the body's organic development undergirds an evangelical understanding of sanctification in Christ. Bodies grow and mature; they attain full stature. The various parts work together to promote life. All parts are necessary. Putting on the mind of Christ, the body lives in Christ-like humility and service (cf. Phil 2:5-11).

There is a unity of purpose to the entire body. Bodies sustain life. This is no less true for the body of Christ. The body exists to promote the common good. The gifts belonging to the various members are for Christ-like service. Those in leadership of the church have as their charge "to equip the saints for the work of ministry, for building up the body of Christ" (Eph 4:12). The body functions in mutual care and concern. When one member of the body suffers, the entire body suffers. When one member rejoices, the entire body celebrates. All of the gifts that the various members bring to the body have their highest purpose in selfless love.

The mission of the body of Christ is not confined to its own internal health and maintenance, however. Connected to Christ, the firstborn from the dead, the mission of the church takes on cosmic proportions. As Christ accomplishes God's mission of universal reconciliation, so the body of Christ serves as agent of Christ's reconciling and peacemaking work. The salvation Christ has accomplished on the cross is for the re-creation of the entire cosmos. The church exists to the penultimate moment of time when Christ subjects even himself to God, "so that God may be all in all" (1 Cor 15:27). Until that moment, the church as the body of Christ lives as an eschatological sign of God's reign in the world.

The Ethical Significance of the Church as Body of Christ

Having examined the New Testament texts that articulate the church as the body of Christ and having explored several themes systematically, I next highlight the ethical character of the body of Christ metaphor. Of primary importance is the relationship between the body of Christ and the person of Jesus Christ. The body of Christ participates in the fullness of Jesus Christ—who he is and what he does.

The incarnate Jesus Christ conveys his own self to the church as the body of Christ through the sacramental meal, which is itself the body of Christ. The identification of the incarnate body of Christ with the meal and with the church associates the church with everything Jesus Christ said, did, and represents. In particular, this means the church participates in the death and resurrection of Jesus Christ for the life of the world. By being the body of Christ, the church manifests the character of Jesus Christ's love for the world. As Jesus Christ died for the sake of others, so the church gives itself away for the sake of others. As Jesus Christ was raised by God from the dead, so the church participates in Christ's resurrection, offering hope to the nations. As Jesus Christ fed the hungry and thereby sustained life, so the church feeds the world through its sacramental meal, at which all are welcome and where there is enough for all. Consider the vast ethical implications of a meal at which all are welcome and there is enough for all!

The body of Christ is one. Just as there is only one Spirit, there is only one body of Christ. This means there is *fundamental unity* among all who belong to Jesus Christ.[8] All alienation and animosity are overcome by virtue of the oneness afforded to the members of Christ's body. Because of the oneness of the body, all things that would sever the body must be repaired. Conflict and division in the body are distortions of its fundamental unity. Those who set up criteria of exclusion within the body of Christ, as in the distortions manifest in the Corinthian congregation's practice of eating and drinking the meal, direct damnation at themselves. Not only is the body of Christ to live together as one, but the church bears responsibility for extending Christ's ministry of healing and reconciliation to others. There is a clear ethical imperative for reconciliation and peacemaking which belongs inherently to the ministry of the one body of Christ (Col 1:20). If the body of Christ is to be one, the power of Christ's forgiveness, reconciliation, and peacemaking must be at work in the face of real obstacles to this unity.

In the body of Christ there are *many gifts*. We celebrate in the church the abundance of gifts God bestows. There is no scarcity to God's benevolence. Paul names many of the gifts belonging to the body of Christ in 1 Corinthians and Romans: apostles, prophets, teachers, deeds of power, healing, forms of assistance, leadership, tongues, ministry, exhortation, generosity, diligence, compassion, cheerfulness, etc. In no way are these listings to be understood as exhaustive. The number and variety of gifts that God grants to the body of Christ are plentiful and ever expanding. Moreover, each of these gifts is necessary to the functioning of the whole body. God gives no superfluous gifts. Each one contributes something essential to the well-being of the whole. What this means ethically for the church is, first of all, a celebration of the diversity of those who are its members. We are not all the same, yet each one is precious and belongs to the whole. We view the body of Christ through the lens of appreciative inquiry, counting our blessings one by one. Moreover, each one has a place of significance for the sake of the whole body. All are called; each has a meaningful vocation.

The further implication of the reconciled diversity in the body of Christ involves God's work of uniting those who have been separated or estranged. The primary instance of this *principle of inclusion* involves the joining of Jews and Gentiles into the one church. This measure was revolutionary for the ancient world. The death and resurrection of Jesus Christ subordinated even ethnic differences in favor of a transcending unity. We see in the ministry of Jesus and the letters of Paul further implications of this impulse toward inclusion. Jesus challenged the divisions between religious and sinner, clean and unclean, rich and poor. Paul claimed that in Christ there is no longer male or female, neither slave nor free. The church is a new manifestation of the restored goodness of creation, toward the eschatological fulfillment when God will be all in all (1 Cor 15:28). In the body of Christ there is no room for a hierarchy of the few over the others. With Christ as the head, each member welcomes and values all the others for each one's giftedness.

In this gifted body of Christ, *special honor is ascribed to the least*.[9] In this respect, the world's order is turned upside down. Those who are held in positions of particular status in this world—according to the standards of wealth, fame, beauty, or power—find themselves in the strange position of having been rendered equal in relationship to the gifts of others. In the body of Christ, while each one does have a special gift to contribute to the whole, particular value is placed on those with humble gifts. This is a kind of preferential option for the weak. In order for all to be included and valued, those neglected according to the standards of worldly esteem are given exceptional honor. In this way, the body of Christ—consistent with Jesus Christ's own ministry—pays extraordinary attention to the sick, the child, the poor, the hungry, the thirsty, the homeless, the imprisoned, the naked, the aged, the handicapped, the discarded, the excluded. The body of Christ here embodies a theology of the cross by honoring the gifts of those who are in need or suffering. Thereby the church also engages in an ethics of the cross, giving ethical priority to those who are suffering.[10]

The orientation of the many gifts God has given to the church is *toward service*. The gifts God bestows on the body of Christ are not for personal gain or self-aggrandizement. Rather, they are gifts that find their proper expression and fulfillment in care for the other, the neighbor. Just as the gospel of Jesus Christ sets the church *free for* the needs of the world, so the body of Christ is blessed with its many gifts for the sake of caring for the neighbor. In the language of Ephesians 4, the gifts God gives are "to equip the saints for the work of ministry, for building up the body of Christ" (v. 12). Gifts of grace are not ends in themselves; rather they are a means toward the end of service. The church of Jesus Christ employs its gifts in relationship to the needs of the world. Whether the world's need comes to expression through intractable conflict, deprivation of basic needs, environmental degradation, or the violation of human dignity, the body of Christ draws upon the gifts that God has provided in order to serve in God's restorative healing work. Not only does the church of Jesus Christ serve the needs of its own members, but the needs of all those who are afflicted. This is the very purpose of the church: to participate in God's own service of ministering to the needs of the world.

In offering acts of service, the body of Christ lives together in *mutual solidarity*. "If one member suffers, all suffer together with it; if one member is honored, all rejoice together with it" (1 Cor 12:26). The members of the body do not exist in isolation. They are not left to fend for themselves. They are not forced to rely on their own limited resources. Rather, the community provides sustaining energy, courage, and hope. Whereas alone we are unable to face the overwhelming needs and challenges of the world, together in community we are empowered to draw from a deep well, the mystery and creative power of the living God manifest in our life together. This communal life is grounded both in shared moments of lament and times of feasting. The church raises a soulful lament wherever it encounters the face of suffering. And the church celebrates a holy feast wherever God's redemptive purposes come to pass in our midst. Solidarity with one another provides food for the journey on the way to shalom.

In this world the body of Christ engages in a process of development and transformation. Paul draws upon the organic language of *growth and maturation* to describe the church's struggle to be faithful: "For now we see in a mirror, dimly, but then we will see face to face. Now I know in part; then I will know fully, even as I have been fully known" (1 Cor 13:12). Although the church really is the body of Christ in the world, at the same time sin clings to all its efforts at service and solidarity. Only by the power of the Spirit does the church cast off its hypocrisies and fallibilities to draw nearer in proximity to the ecclesial life God intends. The church as the body of Christ aspires to incarnate the very personhood of Jesus Christ in its life and ministry. Toward this end, the body of Christ must continue to submit to the will and way of Christ through worship and spiritual practices. The church must repeatedly undergo the way of the cross and resurrection as the crucible that makes its common life cruciform. This is the cost of discipleship.[11]

God's final goal for the mission of the body of Christ is *love*: "But speaking the truth in love, we must grow up in every way into him who is the head, into Christ, from whom the whole body, joined and knit together by every ligament with which it is equipped, as each part is working properly, promotes the body's growth in building itself up in love" (Eph 4:15-16). The organic functioning of the church as the body of Christ, in accord with its maturation, finds its fullest expression in acts of love. This is likewise the momentum of 1 Corinthians 12—with its detailed exploration of the body of Christ metaphor—as the discussion culminates in 1 Corinthians 13 with the glorious conclusion that "the greatest of these [gifts] is love" (1 Cor 13:13). We underscore how the body of Christ participates in the purposes of God revealed in the person of Jesus Christ, which are concisely summarized as the manifestation of God's love (cf. John 3:16). The love of God comes to expression in the works of love shared with others by the members of the body of Christ.

We discover in this discussion the ethical significance of the New Testament metaphor of the church as the body of Christ. The several layers may be capitulated as follows: Jesus Christ is manifest in the world today in the form of the church as the body of Christ. Although consisting of many diverse members, this body coheres in a fundamental unity. Where divisions threaten the church's oneness, the Spirit works reconciliation to repair the fracture and restore harmony. Each and every member of the church, Christ's body, has been given particular gifts. All of these gifts are valuable and needed for the proper functioning of the body. The church is an inclusive body in which the divisions of the world are overcome in Christ. In order for this principle of inclusivity to become manifest, special honor accrues to those members of the body who are considered inferior by worldly standards. Taken together, all of the gifts which God has bestowed on the church have as their purpose the service of others: service of the neighbor in need. This service is exercised through the functioning of the church as a community of mutual solidarity, solidarity one with another and solidarity on behalf of the needs of the world. Along the way, the church continues to be perfected as it matures and is transformed to approximate its full stature as the body of Christ in the world. Finally, the church discovers its calling as the body of Christ as it lives out God's own love for the world in Jesus Christ.

The Church as the Collective Person Jesus Christ

Grounding the Ethical Character of the Body of Christ

The metaphor of the church as the body of Christ is deeply grounded in New Testament theology. This provides one of its greatest strengths as we seek to articulate ecclesiology for the sake of social ministry. Now, on the one hand, the image of the church as the body of Christ may appear to some as being overly familiar. The term *body of Christ* is frequently employed as a synonym when talking about the church. We make routine reference to the gifts that the Spirit bestows on each member of the body when we attempt to recruit people for various tasks in the congregation. On the other hand, when referring to the church as the body of Christ we seldom plumb the theological depths that this metaphor subsumes. Systematic and ethical reflection on the meaning of the church as the body of Christ, as we have seen in the previous chapter, unleashes an energy that bursts forth in power for mission.

A key resource for exploring the richness of the body of Christ metaphor is found in the theology of Dietrich Bonhoeffer, particularly in his early work, *Sanctorum Communio: A Theological Study of the Sociology of the Church.*[1] This book was written when Bonhoeffer was only twenty-one years old and was submitted as his doctoral dissertation. It is difficult to fathom the genius that produced this masterpiece at such a precocious age. Note the subtitle of this book. In an unprecedented move, the young Bonhoeffer sought to place sociology and social philosophy in the service of a fully theological elaboration of the church as the body of

Christ. From the very beginning of his theological career, Bonhoeffer understood the importance of stressing the social dimension of Christianity and the church.

In this seminal work Bonhoeffer introduced two concepts that are crucial for interpreting the church's life and mission in the area of social ministry. First, he explains how human groups take on a persona that transcends who they are as separate individuals. This is what he means by the idea of a "collective person." In this case Bonhoeffer claims that the church exists as a particular collective person, Jesus Christ. Second, Bonhoeffer refers to the church as "Christ existing as church-community." The living Jesus Christ continues to exist in the world in the form of the body of Christ. By the power of the Word and sacraments, Jesus Christ comes alive through the functioning of the church as a social reality.

This chapter begins with a rehearsal of Bonhoeffer's creative exploration of the church as the *sanctorum communio* the communion of saints. I pay special attention to what Bonhoeffer meant when he described the church as a collective person and as Christ existing as church-community. Next I employ these concepts to examine how the church as the collective person, Jesus Christ, is born and nurtured in Word and sacraments. It is through the power of the Spirit at work through the Word and the means of grace that the church puts on the mind of Christ. Finally, I ask about the marks of character that define this collective person. I claim that there are distinctive character marks that inhere to the church as the collective person of Jesus Christ. The character of Christ existing as church-community is known by these marks: one, holy, catholic, and apostolic. These classical marks of the church do not merely offer a classical description of the church but also establish a dynamic agenda for the church as it lives out its mission as the body of Christ in the world. Not only do these marks help provide a theological definition of the church through the ages, even more they ground an ethical program for the church in its social ministry.

Christ Existing as Church-Community

Rampant individualism is a curse on the life of the church. In American society, the individual has become the measure of all things. As a matter of course, congregational life has come to be shaped decisively by attempts to cater to and meet the needs of individuals. In fact, the most common way of conceiving the nature of salvation involves exclusive concern for the individual's relationship with God: "Have you made your individual decision for Christ?"

Bonhoeffer's theology provides an antidote to the solipsistic poison of excessive individualism. Yes, Bonhoeffer does begin by acknowledging the mystery of the individual person. Bonhoeffer agrees with the assertion that each of us is an undeniably individual person standing in the presence of God. Yet simultaneously he insists that this individual, this I, only becomes known in relationship with a concrete "You." Our personhood is essentially social. We belong in relationship with one another.

A distinction must be made between a metaphysical concept of the individual defined without the mediation of others and an ethical concept of the person, based on ethical-social interaction.[2] Bonhoeffer defends the ethical concept of the person, one who receives identity in relationship with the person of God. In Bonhoeffer's formulation, the person is both unique and distinct from all other persons and at the same time created for social relations with others. One does not need to assert the sacredness of the individual at the expense of affirming that each of us exists only in relationship first with God and second with other persons: "The individual becomes a person ever and again through the other, in the 'moment.'"[3]

The fundamental activities of a person—thinking, willing, feeling—are all oriented toward human sociality. We think, will, and feel in relationship to other people and ultimately in relationship to God. Language, by its very character, serves a social function. Bonhoeffer goes so far as to claim "there would be no self-consciousness without community—or better, that self-consciousness arises concurrently with the consciousness of existing in community."[4] I come to know myself finally only in relationship to a "You." Bonhoeffer asserts that from the perspective of God, we are not isolated individuals "but in a natural state of communication with other human beings."[5] Bonhoeffer is keen to construct the social dimensions of theological anthropology.

Referring to the disciplines of sociology and social philosophy, Bonhoeffer next argues that human community does not consist merely of the conglomeration of what is thought and done by individuals. In true community there emerges a consensus of wills around some commonly held convictions. Various individuals form community by assenting to certain purposes held in common. Bonhoeffer calls this the "reciprocal will."[6] This does not mean the wills of the individuals are fused into one. Rather, community is always a living, dynamic organism where the reciprocal will is continually forged anew in the interplay of the separate and even competing wills of the different participants. Tension, competition, and strife are therefore a given condition in every community. This is an important insight that reminds us to remain realistic about the existence of conflict in every human community. Cooperation occurs where the conflicting wills of individuals yield to a common purpose. Bonhoeffer offers this compact definition:

> Community is a community of wills, built upon the separateness and difference of persons, constituted by reciprocal acts of will, finding its unity in what is willed, and counting among its basic laws the inner conflict of individual wills.[7]

Bonhoeffer names the entity that emerges from the free exchange of separate wills into the reciprocal will as the "collective person."

Bonhoeffer here employs a fundamental sociological concept, the assertion that each human group assumes an "objective spirit" that is different from and greater than the sum of the individual wills that constitute it. This objective spirit encompasses the members of a group as something that is not only a product of their collective willing but as something "other" than any of them as individuals.[8] Within a community this objective spirit can be ascribed personal character. It assumes the traits of a distinct personality. It can be comprehended and encountered as a "collective person."[9] "The collective person is metaphysically autonomous in relation to the individuals, though at the same time genetically dependent."[10]

In order for Bonhoeffer to apply this sociological concept to the church, he must locate it within a theological framework. As a first qualification he therefore interprets the doctrine of original sin not only with reference to fallen individuals but especially with regard to the brokenness of human community. The church must not be idealized but rather named for what it really is, sinful community. This means the church cannot be equated with the kingdom of God. The kingdom of God is the future destiny of the creation, toward the arrival of which the church plays an important role as an agent of God's mission. But the church remains an imperfect vessel in service of God's eschatological realization of the kingdom. What makes the church unique as a particular community is that, unlike any other human community, it has been created by the revelation of God.

Bonhoeffer insists on the divine origin of the church. This distinguishes it from other human groups. It does not suffice to say that the church, like other religious communities, is based on the religious interests of its constituents. No, the church originates from God's revelation in Jesus Christ: "Only the concept of revelation can lead to the Christian concept of the church."[11] This is a conviction that finally can be accepted only by faith.

The New Testament image of the church as the body of Christ decisively shapes Bonhoeffer's understanding of ecclesial existence.[12] It is particularly important to stress how Jesus Christ is present in the life of the church. Taken together, the affirmations that the members of the church *are* the body of Christ and the assertion that Christ *is* the head of the body establish a virtually sacramental identification of Jesus Christ with the church. While Bonhoeffer gives expression to a highly realistic concept of the church as actually *being* the body of Christ, he resists making a complete identification based on the proviso of Christ's ascension into heaven. Nevertheless, Bonhoeffer forcefully argues that because of God's revelation and the power of the Holy Spirit, Jesus Christ is alive in the church:

Paul repeatedly identifies Christ and the church-community (1 Cor. 12:12, 6:15, 1:13). Where the body of Christ is, there Christ truly is. Christ is in the church-community, as the church-community is in Christ (1 Cor. 1:30, 3:16, 2 Cor. 6:16; Col. 2:17, 3:11). "To be in Christ" is synonymous with "to be in the church-community."[13]

The image of the church as Christ's body gives rise to the thought that the church has a collective personality. The church *is* "Christ existing as church-community."[14] This reality comes into existence by the power of the Holy Spirit.

Bonhoeffer continued to develop new implications from these basic insights into the nature of the church as the body of Christ—Jesus Christ as a collective person and Christ existing as church-community—in the development of his later theology. In his *Ethics*, for example, Bonhoeffer composed an important section on the topic, "Ethics as Formation." In this passage (and others) in his *Ethics*, Bonhoeffer insists on the reality of Jesus Christ forming the Christian person and the church in the image of Jesus Christ:

> Formation occurs only by being drawn into the form of Jesus Christ, by *being con-formed to the unique form of the one who became human, was crucified, and is risen.* This does not happen as we strive "to become like Jesus," as we customarily say, but as the form of Jesus Christ himself so works on us that it molds us, conforming our form to Christ's own (Gal 4:9). Christ remains the only one who forms. Christian people do not form the world with their ideas. Rather, Christ forms human beings to a form the same as Christ's own.[15]

Notice Bonhoeffer's christological realism about the participation of the church in the reality of Jesus Christ. Ethics derives from the formation of the person and church by the very person and way of Jesus Christ. Jesus Christ is alive and present to effect this formation.

What would it mean for the church to take seriously the theological conviction that Jesus Christ is present in the world today as a collective person in the form of the church? How would we need to revise our individualistic notions of the Christian faith? Instead of focusing on what Christ has done and can do for *me*, I would instead see myself as a member whose functioning contributes to the well-being of the whole body. Rather than expecting Christ to take care of my individual needs, I begin to search for how Christ encounters *us* as members of the body of Christ. I begin to think corporately about how *we* together give expression to Christ's presence in the world.

> The church-community . . . is conceived of as a single life to such an extent that none of its members could be imagined apart from it. But in the church-community every member is moved by the Holy Spirit; all have their divinely appointed place

and their wills moved by the Spirit. Whoever lives in love is Christ in relation to the neighbor—but, of course, always only in this respect. "We are God through the love that makes us charitable toward our neighbor."[16]

This is a dramatically alternative vision for what it means to be a member of the church. To become captured by such a vision leads to a total revision of how we go about our business as the church. The church is reborn as the image of Jesus Christ in the world today—with each of us as members of the whole.

Word and Sacraments: Putting on the Mind of Christ

The clashing of individual wills that is inevitable to the existence of every human group finds a reason for unity as the members of the church receive their common identity in Jesus Christ. Bonhoeffer writes extensively in the middle sections of *Sanctorum Communio* about the nature of Christian community as grounded in love for God and neighbor. These are themes that he would take up again in his primer on Christ-centered community, *Life Together*, and they serve as a guiding theme for his *Ethics*. Bonhoeffer underscores that this particular group *is* Christ existing as church-community. The church-community really exists as the body of Christ: "The body of Christ is a real presence in history, and at the same time the norm for its own history."[17] The wills of these members are forged into the unity of the collective person, Jesus Christ.

Bonhoeffer's sacramental realism about the church as the body of Christ is qualified by the recognition that sin permeates the life of the *sanctorum communio* in the world. The church, like the individual sinner, has the character of *simul justus et peccator*, simultaneously existing as the collective person Jesus Christ present in the world and at the same time fallen and imperfect. It is the Holy Spirit that sanctifies the church to make it into the body of Christ. However, the reality of sin makes a total identification of the church with the body of Christ impossible. This causes the *sanctorum communio* and the *peccatorum communio* to exist in dramatic tension with each other. God's gracious will for the church by the power of the Holy Spirit is contested by the empirical distortions and faithlessness of the church. We await the eschatological resolution of this tension when the Holy Spirit's power will prevail. In the meantime, "the Holy Spirit uses the objective spirit as a vehicle for its gathering and sustaining social activity in spite of all the sinfulness and imperfection of the individuals and of the whole."[18] This realism about the contradictions that mar the body of Christ informs the systematic treatment of the church to be developed in the following chapters and will be confronted directly in chapter 8.

How does the church become the body of Christ? This happens only by the power of God in Christ through the work of the Holy Spirit! Whether we are dealing with the church on a global scale, as a local congregation, or where only two or three are gathered together in the name of Christ, it is God's activity that gives birth to the body of Christ. And what divine activity gives birth to the collective person of Jesus Christ in the form of the church? Jesus Christ comes alive in the body of Christ by means of Word and sacraments. The Holy Spirit breathes life into the church body through the means of grace! The church puts on the mind of Christ (cf. Phil 2:5-10) as it assembles for worship, hears God's Word preached, receives Christ in the sacraments, and ministers through pastoral care.

Jesus Christ constitutes his body through the assembling of the community for worship. At the center of the assembly is the Word of God, through which the Holy Spirit works to bring into existence the collective person, Jesus Christ. It is through the preached Word that the Spirit activates the *charismata* (gifts) of the members of the body. In order to continually reclaim its identity as Christ's collective body, the church regularly assembles to hear God's proclaimed Word and receive the holy sacraments: "In the assembly the church-community pledges itself to God, according to God's will; and here God pledges to be present within the church-community."[19]

Stanley Hauerwas and Samuel Wells have elaborated constructively the significance of worship for Christian ethics in an approach fully resonant with Bonhoeffer's seminal insights. Interestingly, they build their argument with explicit reference to the body of Christ metaphor:

> God has given his people everything they need. What he wants is for them to worship him, be his friends, and eat with him. Through employing what he has given them to these ends, they will become the people he wants them to be. So to understand Christian ethics, it is necessary to explore the gifts God gives to his people. We shall explore how God gives his people one gift, Jesus, in three forms. . . . Each of these three meanings is conveyed by the term "the body of Christ."[20]

"In the first place, the body of Christ means Jesus, born of Mary, who suffered under Pontius Pilate, was crucified, dead, and buried, and who rose again."[21] "A second understanding of the body of Christ is as God's gift of the Church."[22] "The third understanding therefore concerns what it means to eat with him. This is the body of Christ as the Eucharist—or more particularly, the living bread, broken for the life of the world."[23] This third meaning of body of Christ links the ethical formation of the church to the practices of worship as the locus where it receives its fundamental character.

Regarding formation for the Christian life, Hauerwas and Wells grant normative status to what takes place at worship, reversing our conventional assumptions about the relationship of worship to "real" life: ". . . life is in fact a rehearsal
for worship—that, within an eschatological perspective, it is worship for which
humanity and the creation were made, and it is worship that will make up the
greater part of eternity, within which what is called 'life' and 'the real' will appear
to be a tiny blip."[24] As the church engages in the practices of worship, it becomes
conformed to the person and way of Jesus Christ:

> Worship is about words and actions. Worship is an ordered series of activities that
> Christians carry out regularly together in obedience to Jesus' command, as a way of
> becoming more like him, and as a witness to God's world.[25]

It is vital to understand how the church becomes the body of Christ at worship:

> Worship is where people are conformed to Christ, join in his work, are accepted
> back into fellowship, and dance to the beat of his drum. Worship anticipates heaven,
> where all these things are gloriously fulfilled. But worship is also a training for dis-
> cipleship on earth. . . . That is why worship is the key to Christian ethics. Through
> worship God trains his people to take the right things for granted.[26]

Through the distinctive elements of the liturgy, the church becomes the collective
person Jesus Christ—confessing its sin and receiving absolution, praising God,
attending to God's Word above all things, praying for the things of God, sharing
the peace of God, and partaking of Christ's own body and blood—all in the process of becoming conformed to Christ. And the church is sent at the conclusion
of worship with the divine blessing to live and serve as the body of Christ in the
world through word and deed.

Note how this construal of the ethical formation of the body of Christ at worship resonates with Bonhoeffer's ecclesiology. Bonhoeffer asserted that from the
sinful individuals who comprise this assembly, God forges a new creation based on
the reciprocal will that belongs to the collective person Jesus Christ. This entity
has an objective spirit: Christ existing in the form of church-community, the very
body of Christ. By means of the office of preaching, the Holy Spirit enlivens the
Word of God and forms the members into the body of Christ. By means of baptism, God incorporates new members into the church-community. By means of
the Lord's Supper, Christ imparts himself to the community.

> Christ gives community with himself, i.e., his vicariously suffering unto death is for
> my benefit; and Christ gives the church-community, i.e., he renews it, thus giving
> it to itself. . . . That Christ is present, and that the church-community is the body
> of Christ, already imply that Christian love is established as well. . . . In substance

Christ's presence means community with God through Christ and realization of the church-community as bearer of the individuals.[27]

As the church-community lives together, Christ ministers in their midst as the members of the body of Christ extend care for each other.

Bonhoeffer maintains his doctrine of the church as God's holy creation in close connection with the empirical reality of the church in its historical manifestation. To believe in the church does not entail confusing the empirical church with either some invisible church or the eschatological kingdom of God.[28]

> Instead we believe that God has made the concrete, empirical church in which the word is preached and the sacraments are celebrated to be God's own church-community. We believe that it is the body of Christ, Christ's presence in the world, and that according to the promise God's Spirit is at work in it.[29]

Faith embraces the empirical church as that church in which Christ comes alive. Within history the empirical church and the church as the collective person, Jesus Christ, coexist. Only with the arrival of the eschatological kingdom will the tension between these two be resolved. Only with the consummation of God's eternal kingdom will it be revealed unambiguously that the church *is* Christ existing as church-community.[30]

In the closing sections of *Sanctorum Communio*, Bonhoeffer makes several creative, enticing, and suggestive comments that are decisive for the ecclesiology that is developed in the remainder of this book. As we have seen, Bonhoeffer appeals to faith as the way we apprehend that the empirical church, with all its ambiguities, truly *is* the body of Christ. The means of grace are effective to accomplish God's purposes of creating this body of Christ, the communion of saints, by the power of the Holy Spirit. Toward the end of his argument, Bonhoeffer makes this compelling and insightful reference to the significance of the classical marks of the church:

> Thus we believe the means of grace to be effective within the empirical church and hence have faith in the holy church-community created by these means of grace. We believe in the church as *una* [one], since it is "Christ existing as church-community," and *Christ is the one Lord* over those who are all one in him; as *sancta* [holy], since the Holy Spirit is at work in it; as *catholica* [catholic], since as *God's church* its call is to the entire world, and wherever in the world God's word is preached, there is the church.[31]

In addition, we believe in the church as *apostolica* [apostolic], since it is sent at the command of Christ with the power of the Holy Spirit to proclaim the Gospel and make disciples to the ends of the earth.

Drawing impetus from Bonhoeffer's ecclesiology, I will construct a model of the church based on the New Testament image of the church as the body of Christ. If the church *is* the body of Christ with Christ as the head of the body, this casts in new light Paul's powerful exhortation in Philippians 2:5-8:

> Let the same mind be in you that was in Christ Jesus,
>   who, though he was in the form of God,
>   did not regard equality with God
>   as something to be exploited,
>   but emptied himself,
>   taking the form of a slave,
>   being born in human likeness,
>   and being found in human form,
>   he humbled himself
>   and became obedient to the point of death—
>   even death on a cross.

The church is the body of Christ; Christ is its head. In light of the ambiguities that plague the empirical church, Paul summoned the church to put on the mind of Christ. If the church is to truly live according to its Spirit-endowed identity as Christ's body, then its existence must be permeated by the mind of the humble Christ. The body of Christ puts on the mind of Christ. The church becomes saturated with Christ's way of service to others that made him obedient to the point of death, even death on the cross.

Extending this metaphor, we note that every person has certain distinguishing marks of character. Jane is bold, forthright, and compassionate, a woman of integrity. Robert is kind, gentle, and quiet, a man who listens intently to others. Each of us is defined by certain traits of character that are known to others. Thus we may sometimes comment, "He was not himself today." Or we may remark, "She was acting just like herself." A person's character is a way of being in the world and in relationship to others that persists over time. Character is forged from the personality traits with which each of us is born, shaped by social formation processes, and tested by the defining experiences of life, especially in times of crisis.

Character is known through a pattern of behavior that consistently discloses the core commitments of a given person. The original root meaning of the Greek word *character* is "engraving tool." Character refers to those marks that are indelibly etched on the very constitution of a person; character is distinguished by certain deeply embedded traits that persevere in the face of challenges. "Character is the name given to the moral being of a person or group as that is forged into a distinctive constellation."[32]

The significance of character and virtues for Christian ethics is in the process of being recovered in recent philosophy and theology.[33] The formation of character originates in relationship to a significant story or narrative, according to which one orders one's life and toward which one's life becomes oriented. This narrative serves as the *telos* (goal) toward which the entirety of life becomes directed. For this reason the choice of the core narrative is decisive for the shape of the ethical life. Character is formed as one is immersed in a particular narrative to the degree that the person begins to think and act according to the values of that narrative.

> Our character is not merely the result of our choices, but rather the form our agency takes through our beliefs and intentions. So understood, the idea of agency helps us see that our character is not a surface manifestation of some deeper reality called the "self." We are our character.[34]

Lives ordered according to a particular narrative acquire certain virtues as a matter of habit. The virtues function in the ethical life to direct human desire toward God-pleasing ends. While desire belongs naturally to human existence, our desiring must become focused on those things that make for meaningful life. In the Christian tradition we refer to the four cardinal virtues (prudence, justice, temperance, and fortitude/courage) and the three theological virtues (faith, hope, and love/charity) that derive from the Christian narrative. These virtues, instilled by the biblical narrative and grounded in one's character, come to expression in the Christian life as practices.[35] A rich literature has emerged in recent years devoted to the articulation of Christianity according to certain core practices.[36]

In this book I have emphasized shalom, or the kingdom of God, as the *telos* (goal) toward which the church is oriented in the Christian narrative. Character is formed as we are immersed in the reality of Jesus Christ—his teachings, life, death, and resurrection. The body of Christ is that community whose character has been shaped by the narrative of Christian worship to the degree that it lives according to the virtues that belong to Jesus Christ. "Likewise, Christian ethics must serve and be formed by the Christian community, a community whose interest lies in the formation of character and whose perduring history provides the continuity we need to act in conformity with that character."[37] Through our immersion in the biblical story and participation in the Christian liturgy, we become shalom church. This identity leads the body of Christ to engage in particular practices that are coherent with its character as the collective person Jesus Christ.

What are the defining marks of character for the collective person Jesus Christ (Christ existing as church-community, the body of Christ)? While the four cardinal and three theological virtues have great significance for articulating Christian

character, I turn instead to the four classical marks of the church, as noted in the
Nicene Creed, as my guide for reflecting on the church's character in its engagement as ministering community. I propose that the church as the collective person Jesus Christ, having put on the mind of Christ, has four distinctive marks of
character that correspond to the four classical marks of the church (*notae ecclesiae*):
one, holy, catholic, and apostolic. These marks of character adhere to the church
over time. We know the church as the collective person Jesus Christ by these four
marks of character. The four classical marks of the church are not merely ancient
wisdom about the nature of the church but rather characterize how the church
is summoned to live out its ethical commitments in the world. They define the
church's identity and its central practices. These four marks of character give rise
to a bold agenda for the church in mission and social ministry.

The Character of the Body of Christ: One, Holy, Catholic, Apostolic

The four classical marks of the church are rooted in the body of Christ metaphor
within the New Testament. Although the Nicene Creed originated as a doctrinal
confession in the context of the fourth century, it provides a concise summary of
central theological insights derived from the Scripture and the Christian tradition.
This section links the New Testament image of the church as the body of Christ
(as developed in this and the previous chapter) with the comprehensive presentation of the character of the body of Christ in social ministry that follows in the
next four chapters. As I discuss each of the four marks of the church, I build upon
what was discovered in the examination of the relevant New Testament passages.
I proceed by exploring the implications of this study for the social ministry of the
church in our time.

One. By baptism each individual person becomes a member of the one body
of Christ. The distinctions that separate us from one another according to human
opinion and the divisions that characterize the world are rendered relative to our
fundamental unity as members of Christ's body. Neither gender, nor status, nor
wealth, nor age, nor ethnicity, nor geography, nor power should be considered
categories for dividing the body of Christ. The importance of unity is fore-fronted
by Paul's very selection of the body of Christ metaphor. In the face of factions in
the church at Corinth and the idiosyncratic expression of individual spiritual gifts,
Paul emphasized the oneness of the body in Christ. In baptism the members of
the church are knitted together in a unity that connects them with one another
organically. One spirit and one body are the constant refrain in these passages. The
unity of the body is further accented with reference to the members' participation

in the one loaf and one cup of the Lord's Supper. With Christ as its single head, the body must be one, lest it be divided against itself.

What does this mean for the social ministry of the church? The body of Christ is one. The body has integrity. It is not a dismembered body. The Spirit is at work to create unity among those who belong to Christ, who is the head. In terms of its mission, this means, first of all, that the church engages faithfully in the work of ecumenism to repair the divisions that threaten its oneness. The church aims at reconciling the diversity among all those who claim the name of Christ. Thereby, the church aims to remove a scandal that undermines the integrity of its message. Furthermore, the church promotes unity among all people in efforts at nonviolent conflict resolution and serving as an agent of peacemaking wherever conflict threatens. Violence is rampant in this world as the favored method of dealing with conflict, whether we think of domestic violence, child abuse, gang activity, crime, or war. The roots of violence are within us and come to expression in a multitude of ways. In a world where vicious circles of violence threaten destruction on every side, the mission of the church is to serve as an agent of reconciliation and unity through engagement in peacemaking. The church is called to be skilled in nonviolent conflict resolution in the name of Jesus Christ.

Holy. The members of the body have been rendered holy by the sacrifice of Jesus' own body on the cross. Through Christ's saving work, the church has received forgiveness, redemption, and reconciliation. Holiness comes to the church as a gift from Christ. Holiness is mediated to the body of Christ through baptism and the Eucharist. That Christ is the origin of the body's holiness is made most explicit when Christ is called the head of the body. Because the church is dependent on Christ, it reflects his holiness by conforming to his way through holy living, shunning idols, and demonstrating mutual care. Such behaviors are never the church's own achievement but always an expression of thanksgiving for how Christ's own holiness is becoming manifest in the body. The holiness of Christ becomes particularly evident as the church pays special attention to the weak and suffering, both by caring for the members of the body who are experiencing distress and by ministering to "the least of these" who are suffering in the world (cf. Matt 25:40, 45). The church's holiness entails attending to the basic spiritual and physical needs of all people.

What does this mean for the social ministry of the church? The body of Christ is holy. Jesus Christ's death and resurrection are God's means of sanctifying the church and making it holy. The church is justified by grace through faith in Christ's saving death and resurrection. The Spirit is at work to make and keep the church holy. In terms of social ministry, this means the church holds fast to the centrality of the doctrine of justification. This conviction guarantees that the church remains centered on Christ, its head. By the power of Christ's justifying activity, the body of Christ is made just. Justification and justice belong together. The body of Christ, justified by Christ's saving work, responds to what Christ has done for us by engaging in acts of justice. The church engages both in acts of mercy and courageous advocacy on behalf of those in physical need. In a world where tens of millions are hungry and homeless, persecuted and powerless, social ministry by the body of Christ serves those who lack the basics necessary for human survival.

Catholic. The catholicity of the church situates the local congregation within a universal horizon. In 1 Corinthians, Paul testifies to this particular congregation, "Now you are the body of Christ and individually members of it" (12:27). Every local assembly of the baptized is a manifestation of Christ's body, a concrete expression of the church catholic. At the same time the body of Christ can be envisioned in cosmic terms. Both Ephesians and Colossians depict the expanse of the church in universal proportions. God "has put all things under his feet and has made him the head over all things for the church, which is his body, the fullness of him who fills all in all" (Eph 1:22-23; cf. Col 1:18). The church as the body of Christ is catholic, reaching from the local congregation to the breadth of the entire creation. Following this direction, it is imperative at this moment in history to think even more radically about the catholicity of the church. Catholicity involves the solidarity of the church with the entire creation insofar as we are all composed of the same matter. The church of Jesus Christ as a cosmic reality is constituted of the same elements as the stars, the earth, the sea, and other living creatures. We are created in solidarity with all God has made, composed of the same stuff, the same catholic matter: hydrogen, oxygen, carbon. Such vision lends new meaning to the claim that "Christ is all and in all!" (Col 3:11).

What does this mean for the social ministry of the church? The body of Christ is catholic. The body of Christ extends throughout time and space. The universal church includes all those saints who have gone before us in the faith and anticipates the arrival of future generations. It is by baptism that all these have been made one and are incorporated into the catholic body. The Spirit is at work to connect the various members of the body through bonds of interdependence. Furthermore, in our age of ecological degradation, the catholicity of the church in its concern for the integrity of the body must extend to concern for the integrity of the entire creation. Because human beings are completely intertwined with and dependent upon the health of the created world, we are summoned to ethical responsibility for the well-being of creation in an unprecedented way. Being created in the image of God entails stewardship of the good creation God has made. Our human future is inextricably dependent upon the sustenance of the natural world. Thereby, attending to the catholicity of the body of Christ entails the defense of the ecosystem that God created as the foundation of all life.

Apostolic. The apostolic mission of the congregation begins with the mutual ministry of the baptized. God blesses the church with a rich variety of spiritual gifts. Many of these are named explicitly in the epistles (for example, *charismata* for evangelism, teaching, or generosity); others are left unmentioned. These gifts of the Spirit are given for the common good, for the building up of the body of Christ. God has equipped the saints for the work of ministry. Not only are these gifts to be directed inwardly for the flourishing of the Christian community, but they are also to be directed outwardly toward the whole society. The church acknowledges that every human being has been created in the image of God. This affords every human being an inherent sacred dignity that deserves utmost respect. The Spirit empowers members of the community both for the work of evangelizing and for the defense of human rights. The body of Christ is to be bold in its proclamation of God's apostolic message both by word and by deed. Paul is insistent that those who bear the name of Christ live a life worthy of their calling. This encompasses both sharing the gospel with others and defending the fundamental human dignity of each one created in God's own image.

What does this mean for the social ministry of the church? The body of Christ is apostolic, a people sent into the world with God's truth. Jesus Christ sends the members of the body forth with a message and a mission. This means the church is characterized by its evangelical proclamation. Evangelizing belongs to the core of Christian missionary activity. The church is faithful to its apostolic commission when it speaks the gospel authentically, so that those who hear it will believe in Christ and, receiving baptism, become members of the body. At the same time, the apostolic church is sent to respect the human dignity of each person who has been created in God's own image. Wherever human rights are threatened, the church speaks out prophetically in faithfulness to its apostolic mission. The church witnesses to Christ's universal gospel that overcomes the barriers of nationalism, sexism, ethnocentrism, and classism that threaten to tear the body apart. The testimony of the body of Christ takes place both through its words and through its actions. The church makes witness through the very lives of those who bear the name of Christ. In the early church this witness unto death was known as martyrdom, on occasion even costing members their lives. Yet, by God's power, the blood of the martyrs becomes the seed of the church. In faithfulness to its apostolic character, the body of Christ must be ready to lay down its life for the cause of Christ.

By their character you will know them. The church of Jesus Christ, the church that *is* Christ existing as church-community, has peculiar marks of character.

These connections between the New Testament image of the church as the body of Christ and the four classical marks of the church in the Nicene Creed inform the ecclesiology for social ministry developed in the following chapters. I propose that the identity of the church, Christ's body, can be recognized by exactly these four characteristics: one, holy, catholic, apostolic. Each of these four marks of character has urgent implications for social ministry, given the global context in which the body of Christ serves at this moment in history.

The next four chapters will elaborate the significance of the four classical marks of the church for the church's social ministry. I claim that these four marks describe the character of the church as the collective person Jesus Christ in the world. Each of the four marks encompasses a crucial dimension of the church's social ministry. I proceed in each of these chapters according to a common formula. First, by way of introduction, I explore the historical meaning of each particular mark of the church and articulate its ethical significance. Next I rehearse and develop the biblical narrative that undergirds each of these marks of the church by retelling significant Old Testament and New Testament stories. Immersion in the biblical narrative instills in the church each distinctive character mark and the according virtues that distinguish the body of Christ in the world. The virtues instilled by the narrative of Scripture serve to instill God-directed desire into the human soul, which forms the human person for the ethical life. These virtues are then illustrated with reference to the biographies of saints who embodied them in practice as leaders of social ministry movements. Finally, I articulate those core practices that can assist congregations to participate in God's mission of mending creation (*tikkun olam*) through social ministry.

Part II

Marks of the Shalom Church

The Body of Christ Is One

The Practice of Reconciliation and Peacemaking

The Niceno-Constantinopolitan Creed has made this confession a fundamental affirmation about the church by Christians throughout the world: "We believe in one holy catholic and apostolic Church."[1] This description of the church provides a classical statement about its character. The whole ecumenical church is united around these four characteristics (*notae ecclesiae*) that define the church's reality. Forged into the creed at a particular moment in church history, these marks are recited week by week in assemblies of the faithful in dramatically different contexts from that of their origin. In their original context, these marks of the church sought to bring conformity to a church threatened by dissidence and division.[2]

What is particularly surprising, given their historical importance and widespread usage in Christian liturgy, is how little systematic reflection has been offered on the four classical marks of the church by contemporary theologians. Even in the most rigorously orthodox of theological treatments, the four marks of the church are discussed in rather summary fashion, almost taking them for granted as definitive and in little need of elaborate commentary.[3] In some major works dealing with the nature of the church, the four classical marks are scarcely given systematic attention at all.[4]

When the four classical marks of the church have been called upon theologically, it has almost always been because of the church's need to be corrected or reformed according to some deficiency or flaw in the church's life. This was already likely the case in their original context of the fourth century. That century was rife with theological conflicts over the teachings of the Arians and Donatists.[5] These controversies posed a threat to the unity of the church greatly desired by the emperor. Therefore, first the Council of Nicea (325) and later the Council of Constantinople (381) were summoned to meet in order to resolve the divisions and promote the church's oneness. The various marks of the church embedded in the Niceno-Constantinopolitan Creed also have functioned in other contexts to address perceived defects in the church's life. For example, the Protestant reformers stressed the holiness of the church by emphasizing that holiness was a gift won by Jesus Christ on the cross that justified us with respect to our sinfulness apart from works of law. The church's holiness depended entirely on Christ's alien righteousness; this was to criticize the works righteousness of the late medieval church and its theology. By way of another example, in reaction to the splintering of the church, Roman Catholic theology has especially emphasized the unity of the church as it comes to expression through communion with the bishop of Rome and the ordering of bishops according to the historic episcopacy.

This discovery and insight is very important for the treatment of the four marks of the church in the following chapters. The marks of the church have distinguished their relevance for the life of the church primarily as correctives to the church's brokenness and sinfulness as it has manifested itself in history. The four classical marks of the church have been employed to mitigate distortions and address discrepancies between the church as it is and the church as it is called to be. This makes particularly relevant the comment by Michael Fahey:

> Just as in other parts of the Christian credo, the assertion of the church as one holy catholic and apostolic is meant to be understood eschatologically. By that is meant that these characteristics are associated with the church not to describe purely what visibly exists to the beholder; rather they are part of a prayer of longing and hope that the church may in fact become what it is called to be by reason of its lofty vocation.[6]

The recognition of their eschatological character becomes especially important for the ethical rendering of the marks of the church for social ministry in the next chapters.

Typically, the marks of the church have been used as criteria for measuring the inner life of the church, serving in particular as a means of critique and correction.[7] For example, insistence on the oneness of the church has served as rationale for the entire ecumenical movement. Jesus' "high priestly prayer" in John 17 has summoned the church to ecumenical conversations and agreements in the twentieth and twenty-first centuries that are unprecedented in all previous church history.

Similarly, the remembrance of the church's apostolicity has summoned the church to renew its life by inspiring the mission of sharing the gospel to the ends of the earth. This has been a keen motivation for the church in its outreach through global mission from the eighteenth and nineteenth centuries to the present. It is important to recognize through these examples how the classical marks of the church have functioned to address and correct acknowledged flaws, limitations, or deficiencies in the church's life and mission.

I intend to take a dramatic constructive step in this work. Not only can the four classical marks of the church serve as correctives to the disposition of the church in its inner constitution as the church of Jesus Christ; even more, each of the four marks contains a fundamental ethical impulse that transcends its relevance for the inner life and identity of the church. *I will uncover and develop the core logic of each of the four classical marks of the church and claim them for a mission by the church that has universal ethical implications.* For example, the insistence on the church as "one" not only has significance for the church in seeking to reconcile the many expressions of diversity through the ecumenical movement, as vital as that agenda may be for the church's life and mission;[8] the reality of the church of Jesus Christ as *one* also unleashes energy for reconciliation and peacemaking that extends beyond the precincts of the baptized to the entire world, wherever alienation divides and violence threatens. It is the call of Jesus Christ not only to manifest the church as one through ecumenical rapprochement but even more to foster relationships among all people in the spirit of *shalom*. The reality of its oneness beckons the church to the ministry of reconciliation and the work of peacemaking.

We see how the teachers of the church have witnessed to this drive toward reconciliation and peacemaking over the ages. Tertullian (c. 155–220), around the end of the second century, pointed to this impulse with reference to the church's struggle against heresy:

> Therefore the churches, although they are so many and so great, comprise but the one primitive church, [founded] by the apostles, from which they all [spring]. In this way all are primitive, and all are apostolic, whilst they are all proved to be one, in [unbroken] unity, by their peaceful communion, and title of brotherhood, and bond of hospitality—privileges which no other rule directs than the one tradition of the selfsame mystery.[9]

Tertullian underscores the church's "peaceful communion, and title of brotherhood, and bond of hospitality" as qualities known not just to other Christians but as a witness to the entire world. At Vatican II, the Dogmatic Constitution on the Church (*Lumen Gentium*) described the church as "a kind of sacrament or sign of intimate union with God, and of the unity of all humanity."[10] Reflecting on the church as the people of God over the ages, Michael Schmaus refers to Vatican II's affirmation of the unity of the church as "a harbinger of the universal peace it promotes."[11] Expanding this view, Conrad Bergendoff comments on the universal significance of the church's oneness:

> Ultimately we are not concerned only with the unity of the church. Christ is the unity of the world. Not only the middle wall of partition separating Jew and Gentile must be moved if Christ is to realize the unity of the Church, but all the walls of partition dividing peoples, classes, generations, from each other. The New Israel is the people made one with God in the atonement of Christ, and one with each other through the ministry of reconciliation. . . . Here is a unity without which the world falls apart into meaningless and antagonistic segments. It is a breath-taking vision, too daring for the faltering reason of [humans] to follow or comprehend. But it is the apostolic message of unity for which the Church is founded. . . ."[12]

It is this expansive vision of the unifying energy of the church in its mission to the world that directs the logic of this chapter.

In the next four constructive chapters, I follow a consistent procedure. After an opening introduction, linking each particular mark of the body of Christ to the social ministry agenda of the shalom church, I devote a section of the chapter to the recounting of the biblical narrative which undergirds the particular focus. For example, in this chapter I rehearse the biblical story about God's work of reconciling and peacemaking. This will be followed by a section, building on the respective narrative, that articulates how the biblical story instills distinctive virtues in the church as the body of Christ. This section will also include biographical sketches of significant figures in the history of the church, who have embodied these virtues and given exemplary leadership to the church in its mission to the world. Finally, each of these four chapters will conclude by elaborating a set of five concrete practices to inform the life and mission of the congregation in its social ministry. In each case, I move from the biblical narrative to the virtues of the church as the collective person Jesus Christ to the social ministry practices that derive consequently from that character.

The Biblical Narrative: God's Work of Reconciling and Peacemaking

Humankind was created by God as good (Gen 1:26-31). All peoples were created from the dust of the earth as those into whom God breathed the spirit of life (Gen 2:7). The original harmony and peace of God's creation was, however, soon tragically rent asunder by the power of sin. One immediate and devastating consequence of human waywardness was the eruption of violence into the human sphere. Cain murders his brother Abel (Gen 4:8) and immediately fears retribution in kind (4:10). The vicious cycle of violence and retribution here emerges for the first time, a pattern that has become paradigmatic for all of human existence.

Violence rapidly spreads across the face of the earth: "The Lord saw that the wickedness of humankind was great in the earth, and that every inclination of the thoughts of their hearts was only evil continually. And the Lord was sorry that he had made humankind on the earth, and it grieved him to his heart" (Gen 6:5-6). As judgment against human wickedness and violence, God wrought the great flood as God's own act of violence to end all violence. The theme of God's vengeance and (later in the narrative) God's authorization of human acts of violence serves as a troubling counterpoint to the story of reconciling and peacemaking we seek to tell. It poses a radical question about whether God's own character is one of reconciliation and peacemaking, or destruction and violence. Noteworthy is God's own resolve to transcend violence at the end of the flood story: "[T]he Lord said in his heart, 'I will never again curse the ground because of humankind, for the inclination of the human heart is evil from youth; nor will I ever again destroy every living creature as I have done'" (Gen 8:21b). God repents of the violence of the flood and pledges to divine a different response to human wickedness. The rainbow is appointed as a sign of the covenant of God with Noah never again to destroy the earth by flooding (Gen 9:12-17).

The people of the earth, nevertheless, perpetrate by their pride deep divisions, culminating in the confusion of languages and the scattering of the nations after Babel (Gen 11:1-9). In response to this thwarting of God's intent, God's work of reconciling and peacemaking is initiated anew through the promise made to Abraham: "Go from your country and your kindred and your father's house to the land that I will show you. I will make of you a great nation, and I will bless you, and make your name great, so that you will be a blessing. I will bless those who bless you, and the one who curses you I will curse; in you all the families of the earth shall be blessed" (Gen 12:1-3). *In you all the families of the earth shall be blessed!* With this promise, God's deliberate and patient strategy for the restoration of peace and reconciliation among all peoples is launched. As the narrative continues to unfold, the question arises whether or not God will (be able to?) fulfill this promise in the face of all the hatred and violence that threatens to undo it (cf. Gen 19:1-29, Sodom and Gomorrah).

A first and major crisis in the fulfillment of God's promise involves the childlessness of Abraham and Sarah. With no child to inherit it, already the promise would be thwarted after the first generation. Miraculously, a child is born to Abraham and Sarah, at ages 100 and 90, respectively! The promise lives on!

The joy and laughter did not last long, however. God commands Abraham to sacrifice Isaac on an altar (Gen 22:1-19). While some speculate whether this soul-shattering story was told to bring to an end the dreadful practice of child sacrifice, it plays another critical role in the whole narrative. Again it poses the radical question about whether God intends to keep the promise to bless all the families of the earth through Abraham. Instead of the sacrifice of Isaac, however, and the end of the promise, God provides a ram, even as the knife is poised by Abraham to kill the precious child of the promise (22:10-14).

The patriarchal traditions continue to explore the theme of how the promise falls into repeated peril: the contest between Esau and Jacob (Gen 27), and the sale of Joseph by his brothers into slavery in Egypt (Gen 37:12-50). For all the trials and tribulations of humankind graphically depicted in Genesis, the book culminates with the grand story of Joseph forgiving his once-hateful brothers at their request: "Even though you intended to do harm to me, God intended it for good, in order to preserve a numerous people, as he is doing today. So have no fear; I myself will provide for you and your little ones" (Gen 50:20-21). God's reconciling power, as testified by Joseph, preserves the promise from all the foibles and depravity of human waywardness.

How are we to read the Old Testament stories about human atrocities perpetrated by Israel against, for example, the Canaanites and God's authorization of sacred violence against Israel's enemies (cf. the Gideon narrative in Judg 6:11—8:35 or the Samson narrative in Judg 13–16)? These many stories from Exodus to 2 Kings depict a constant theme of war and violence carried out in God's name. In later generations these narratives have legitimated acts of violence and counter-violence in a seemingly endless spiral. Every power which desires to legitimate violence for its cause can appeal to the Bible for warrants: "If any harm follows, then you shall give life for life, eye for eye, tooth for tooth, hand for hand, foot for foot, burn for burn, wound for wound, stripe for stripe" (Exod 21:23-25). We are faced with a first-order hermeneutical decision. Is the central message of Scripture one of endorsing violence? Certainly this is an arguable conclusion, because in many passages one can see how the turn to violence is commanded by God. Were one to arrive at that conclusion, then the Bible as a document only feeds all the cycles of violence that are spinning out of control in our world. There is another alternative, however. While the Bible depicts the horrors of violence with graphic clarity and while God appears to authorize human violence in many passages, this is not the core and normative message of Scripture. Instead, the promise of God—culminating in the passion of Jesus Christ—is finally a narrative about the overcoming of violence by God. It is this alternative narrative that we will claim as the authoritative reading of the Bible regarding violence.

God reestablishes the promise to Israel in relationship to the house of David: "Your house and your kingdom shall be made sure forever before me; your throne shall be established forever" (1 Sam 7:16). The covenant with Abraham is renewed and redirected through the promise to David. With this promise to the house of David, there emerged clear expectations that the rule of the perfect Davidic king would usher in a reign of enduring peace: ". . . but to David, and to his descendents, and to his house, and to his throne, there shall be peace [shalom] from the Lord forevermore" (1 Kings 2:33). This expectation took deep root in the traditions of Israel. We find it reflected repeatedly in the Psalms, the songbook of Israel: "Pray for the peace [shalom] of Jerusalem: 'May they prosper who love you. Peace [shalom] be within your walls, and security within your towers'" (Ps 122:6-7). Whenever the royal house failed to contribute to the cause of peace, the prophets railed out in dramatic protest: "They have treated the wound of my people carelessly; saying 'Peace, peace,' when there is no peace. They acted shamefully, they committed abomination; yet they were not ashamed, they did not know how to blush" (Isa 6:14-15). Only on the foundation of justice and righteousness can peace be attained: "Steadfast love and faithfulness will meet; righteousness and peace [shalom] will kiss each other" (Ps 85:10).

The promises to Abraham and David led in the history of Israel to the expectation of a messianic age in which all the peoples of the earth would be led into unity and live together in peace:

> In the days to come the mountain of the Lord's house shall be established as the highest of the mountains, and shall be raised up above the hills. Peoples shall stream to it, and many nations shall come and say: "Come, let us go up to the mountain of the Lord, to the house of the God of Jacob; that he may teach us his ways and that we may walk in his paths." For out of Zion shall go forth instruction and the word of the Lord from Jerusalem. He shall judge between many peoples, and shall arbitrate between strong nations far away; they shall beat their swords into plowshares, and their spears into pruning hooks; nation shall not lift sword against nation, neither shall they learn war any more. (Mic 3:1-3)

The narrative yearns for the dawning of this age, to be ushered in by the messianic king, a descendent of the house of David: "For a child has been born for us, a son given to us; authority rests upon his shoulders; and he is named Wonderful Counselor, Mighty God, Everlasting Father; Prince of Peace [shalom]. His authority shall grow continually, and there shall be endless peace [shalom] for the throne of David and his kingdom" (Isa 9:6-7). This reign of peace will extend to the entire creation: "The wolf shall live with the lamb, the leopard shall lie down with the kid, the calf and the lion and the fatling together, and a little child shall lead them" (Isa 11:6).

Jesus' Davidic genealogy points to him as the fulfiller of all these messianic promises (Matt 1:6). Jesus was born into a world where violence continued to rage (Matt 2:16-18, the massacre of the innocents). His birth, however, was hailed by the angels as the genesis of a new age of peace: "Glory to God in the highest heaven, and on earth peace among those whom he favors!" (Luke 2:14). At the center of Jesus' proclamation was the message of the coming kingdom of God which resonates with expectation at the inauguration of the age of God's reconciliation and peace: "Blessed are the peacemakers, for they will be called the children of God" (Matt 5:9). Jesus radicalized in many ways the meaning of peacemaking for his followers: "You have heard that it was said, 'An eye for an eye and a tooth for a tooth.' But I say to you, do not resist an evildoer. But if anyone strikes you on the right cheek, turn the other also. . . ." (Matt 5:38-39). Jesus further radicalizes for his disciples the extent of reconciliation: "You have heard that it was said, 'You shall love your neighbor and hate your enemy.' But I say to you, Love your enemies and pray for those who persecute you, so that you may be children of your Father in heaven. . . ." (Matt 5:43-45). Jesus understood God in heaven to be the lover of enemies and bringer of peace to this world. The disciples are summoned to follow in this way.

One of the most provocative claims of Jesus relates to the authority to forgive sins, particularly the sins of those considered to be the wrong kinds of people, for example, a paralytic or the woman who anointed him (Matt 9:1-8; Luke 7:36-50). What was especially controversial about this activity was Jesus' bold claim already now to be anticipating the eschatological kingdom of peace when God's forgiveness would prevail. Jesus here claims authority for himself to enact the reconciliation belonging to the messianic age.[13] "The point about Jesus' welcome to 'sinners' was that he was declaring, on his own authority, that anyone who trusted in him and his kingdom-announcement was within the kingdom."[14] The audacity of this claim was one of the major causes for opposition to his message. Nevertheless, God's reign is characterized by reconciliation and peace; it was only by the forgiveness of sins that this kingdom could be dawning.

The passion narratives are crucial for revealing God's drama to restore humankind's lost unity through the in-breaking of universal reconciliation and peace. The tension that had mounted between Jesus and his opponents culminated in the events marking his arrest, trial, and death. Weeping over Jerusalem, Jesus prayed: "If you, even you, had only recognized on this day the things that make for peace!" (Luke 19:42). Jesus' provocation of the authorities by cleansing the temple of unrighteous mammon should be interpreted as a prophetic act, like unto the prophets of old, not as an act of violence. Nonviolence does not mean passivity; nonviolence is active in confronting and exposing wrong. Nonetheless, the timing of Jesus' arrest appears to be closely linked to his symbolic entrance into Jerusalem on Palm Sunday and his prophetic act at the temple. In response to his arrest, some of the disciples were prepared to engage in violent confrontation with Jesus' antagonists, yet Jesus was clear about his commitment to nonviolence: "Put your sword back into its place; for all who take the sword will perish by the sword" (Matt 26:52). Whereas the crowds on Palm Sunday may have hoped for a violent confrontation between Jesus and the Roman and temple officials, Jesus engaged in nonviolent resistance to their violence (Matt 27:11-14, Jesus' silence before Pilate).

On the cross Jesus witnessed to God's way of restoring unity by forgiving his enemies: "Father, forgive them; for they do not know what they are doing" (Luke 23:34). Jesus sought to end the spiral of violence directed against him through longsuffering and forgiveness.[15] Whereas the cross of Jesus might be viewed as the victory of violence over the man of peace, in fact God was working reconciliation and peace on a far greater, even cosmic, scale through the power of Christ's suffering love. We will see in the next section how Jesus' death on the cross functions to resist and put to an end all scapegoating violence.[16] Among the many metaphors employed to interpret the significance of Jesus' cross in the New Testament is the cross as peacemaking:

> But now in Christ Jesus you who once were far off have been brought near by the blood of Christ. For he is our peace; in his flesh he has made both groups into one and has broken down the dividing wall, that is, the hostility between us. He has abolished the law with its commandments and ordinances, that he might create in himself one new humanity in place of the two, thus making peace, and might reconcile both groups to God in one body through the cross, thus putting to death the hostility through it. So he came and proclaimed peace to you who were far off and peace to those who were near; for through him both of us have access in one Spirit to the Father. (Eph 2:13-18)

On the cross God was reconciling all peoples to each another and to Godself, recreating humanity as a community of Jews and Gentiles, in accord with the promise first made to Abraham. As Jesus prophesied about his death on the cross, so it came to pass: "'And I, when I am lifted up from the earth, will draw all people to myself.' He said this to indicate the kind of death he was to die" (John 12:32-33). God's promise of old to reconcile all peoples into one was coming to fulfillment by the cross of Jesus.

After the resurrection, the risen Jesus Christ initiates his disciples into the way of reconciling peace: "Peace be with you. As the Father has sent me, so I send you" (John 20:21). The preaching of the early church proclaims the gospel message to all, breaking down all human barriers (Acts 2:1-12, the day of Pentecost).

Peter declares, "I understand that God shows no partiality, but in every nation anyone who fears him and does what is right is acceptable to him. You know the message he sent to the people of Israel, preaching peace by Jesus Christ—he is Lord of all" (Acts 10:34-35). The sharing of Christ's peace becomes a core characteristic of early Christian greeting and worship: "The God of peace be with all of you. Amen" (Rom 15:33). Among the fruits of the Spirit bestowed on the church is the gift of peace (Gal 5:22).

In continuity with the promise of God to Abraham and David, the reconciling power of God in Jesus Christ reunites all people as one. The decision of the Council of Jerusalem to open the church of Jesus Christ to the Gentiles is a decisive sign that the promise of God through Isaiah 2:2-4 and Micah 3:1-3 (the uniting of the nations at Jerusalem) is coming to fulfillment (Acts 15:1-29). "I will rebuild the dwelling of David, which has fallen; from its ruins I will rebuild it, and I will set it up, so that all peoples may seek the Lord—even all Gentiles over whom my name has been called. Thus says the Lord, who has been making these things known from long ago" (Acts 15:16-17, with reference to Amos 9:11-12).

This new age of unity was being inaugurated in the world through the church by the power of Christ's death and resurrection: "He is the head of the body, the church; he is the beginning, the firstborn from the dead, so that he might come to have the first place in everything. For in him all the fullness of God was pleased to dwell, and through him God was pleased to reconcile to himself all things, whether on earth or in heaven, by making peace through the blood of the cross" (Col 1:18-20). Through the work of Jesus Christ, God was inaugurating the eschatological hope for the oneness of the nations through the people of Israel: "After this I looked, and there was a great multitude that no one could count, from every nation, from all tribes, and peoples and languages, standing before the throne and before the Lamb, robed in white, with palm branches in their hands. They cried out in a loud voice, saying, 'Salvation belongs to our God who is seated on the throne, and to the Lamb'" (Rev 7:9-10). In the heavenly Jerusalem, all peoples will be joined in the eternal worship of God (Rev 21:9—22:5). The chaotic sea will be no more; all peoples are united in God's peace (Rev 21:1). The promise of old, uttered by Isaiah, shall be fulfilled: ". . . for my house shall be called a house of prayer for all peoples" (Isa 56:7).

Character and Virtues in the Body of Christ: Reconciling and Peacemaking

As the biblical narrative demonstrates, God's hope for the world is that all people live together in peace, culminating in the reconciling power of Jesus Christ and his cross. This was the promise of God to Abraham and David, renewed by the prophets in their visions for a coming messianic age, and inaugurated through the coming of Jesus Christ. The church as the collective person Jesus Christ consists of those called to represent the reconciling and peacemaking activity of God in Christ in the world today. The members of the body of Christ are formed by the biblical narrative to be the people of peace: "If it is possible, so far as it depends on you, live peaceably with all" (Rom 12:18). The character of the people who dwell in this narrative are molded according to "the things that make for peace."[17]

Five Virtues

How do we articulate the virtues that belong to the church, as Christ existing as community, on the basis of this narrative? The biblical story discloses five discrete virtues that I will first summarize before illustrating them through the lives of three exemplary peacemakers who show us the way: Mohandas Gandhi, Martin Luther King Jr., and A. J. Muste.

The first virtue entails the *commitment to inclusivity*. Inclusivity is a contemporary term that aims to capture the breadth of God's promise to reconcile all people with one another in the coming kingdom. God's promise to Abraham and Sarah was that through them all the peoples of the earth will be blessed. The church's commitment to inclusivity entails trusting God's promise that no human distinctions be allowed to serve as the basis for exclusion from this communion—neither nationality, nor ethnicity, nor color, nor gender, nor age, nor physical form, nor mental condition, nor sexual orientation, nor any other quality. God in Christ intends to establish life-giving relationships among all peoples as an expression of the shalom God desires. The body of Christ has this vision of God's inclusive future instilled in its fiber as its guiding hope.

The second virtue that reflects the reconciling and peacemaking constitution of the body of Christ in the world is *love for enemies*. This acknowledges the reality of our having enemies in this world. Jesus himself had real enemies who sought his demise. Yet enemies cannot remain hated for that reason. Jesus challenged his disciples to adopt a radically different orientation toward those who have offended us: "Father, forgive them." Neither by our own resources nor because there is something likable about them but for Jesus' sake we are summoned to enemy love. This calls for a dramatic process of communal transformation. Only by total immersion in God's alternative reality of peace and by prayer is the church able to begin to reflect the command and example of Jesus to love our enemies. This requires understanding others as human beings, however flawed, and not allowing their humanity to be erased from awareness. Only through mutual encouragement and collective engagement can the church hope to approximate Jesus' love for the enemy. Particularly in a society that cultivates hatred of enemies as part of our civil religion, the radical nature of following Jesus becomes apparent in his command to love our enemies. The church is called to become dramatically countercultural by seeking to love and be reconciled with enemies.

A third virtue is the *readiness to forgive.* Core to the prayer Jesus taught his disciples was this petition: "Forgive us our sins as we forgive those who sin against us." The capacity to forgive the sins of others is predicated on the reality of the forgiveness God has already extended to us through the cross and resurrection of Jesus Christ. The church receives the gift of forgiveness as often as it rehearses the public confession and absolution of sins. The gift of forgiveness from God is efficacious. The sins of the church are actually forgiven by God, setting the church free to be a community of forgiveness for others. While the ability to forgive the sins of others is clearly facilitated when offenders demonstrate genuine remorse and repentance, finally the church is called to forgive others not because of any condition that the others have fulfilled but entirely for Christ's sake.[18] Both the command to love enemies and the injunction to forgive offenders press the church beyond the limit of what is natural for human beings. Only when innate human aggressiveness is held in check and transformed by the message of God's unconditional love and forgiveness in Jesus Christ can the body of Christ begin to follow these radical commandments.

A fourth virtue, closely related to the previous, involves *repenting of violence.* Human beings evolved as creatures for whom natural aggressiveness was an adaptive behavior to enhance survival.[19] However, given the evolutionary development of self-reflective consciousness by human beings and the technological development of weapons of mass destruction, the trait of aggressiveness is no longer adaptive; indeed it must be overcome by cultural symbols that mediate nonviolent conflict resolution (more capably than the human impulse toward aggression), if we are to survive in our new evolutionary situation. The Christian symbol that can most make a dramatic contribution to the overcoming of violence, perhaps ironically, is the cross. The cross of Jesus needs to be understood as having put an end to human violence, particularly insofar as violence is a consequence of accusing and blaming others.

With revolutionary insight, René Girard has interpreted the crucifixion of Jesus as the end of scapegoating violence. Girard has examined in depth the literature, mythologies, and defining stories of diverse cultures from ancient times to the present.[20] From this research he has identified a single mechanism by which people of every era and place have dealt with social fear and anxiety: the identification of a sacrificial victim, the scapegoat. The way human beings cope with their collective angst is by selecting an individual or identifiable group as the cause of their problems. As fears mount in a society, a particular victim is identified and targeted as the source of its troubles. This victim functions as scapegoat as the society directs its animosity and anger against it, culminating in physical violence against and the killing of the scapegoat. By this mechanism, peace is restored—at least for a while—until another scapegoat is required to allay new anxieties.

In Girard's research into the reality of scapegoating, he noticed how consistently the given society remains blind to what it is doing—identifying and acting out against a scapegoat. In virtually every tradition, the society remains deeply persuaded that the victim is only receiving its due and deserves its punishment. This has only one exception: the crucifixion of Jesus.[21] For the first time in human history, Girard argues, through the Christian passion narrative, the age-old pattern is unveiled for what it really is: scapegoating violence.[22] The death of Jesus on the cross thereby discloses to Christians the mechanism by which scapegoating unfolds. The theological significance of this discovery cannot be underestimated. Jesus, though innocent, died as a scapegoat amid the fears and anxieties of his cultural world. By disclosing the truth about how scapegoating works, the passion narrative of the Christian Gospels calls into question the legitimacy of every act of scapegoating violence. Jesus died to be the final scapegoat. Of all people on earth, Christians are called to be those who recognize and name scapegoating violence for what it is. Only by Jesus' way of innocent suffering can the endless spirals of scapegoating violence finally come to an end. At the heart of Christianity, in the cross of Jesus, violence is undone and nonviolence prevails as God's way of restoring oneness to divided humanity.[23] At the cross, human beings are summoned to repent of violence and learn to resolve conflict nonviolently.

The fifth virtue for the church in its reconciling and peacemaking is *nonviolent resistance.* When Jesus counseled love for enemies and turning the other cheek, he was not advising compliance or passivity in the face of violent oppression. Rather, Jesus was teaching the way of resistance through nonviolent means. Walter Wink makes the strong case that Jesus' instruction to turn the other cheek is not about submission but defiance:

> You are probably imagining a blow with the right fist. But such a blow would fall on the *left* cheek. To hit the right cheek with a fist would require the left hand. But the left hand could be used only for unclean tasks . . . the only feasible blow is a backhand.
>
> The backhand was not a blow to injure, but to insult, humiliate, degrade. . . . By turning the other cheek, the servant makes it impossible for the master to use the backhand again. . . . The left cheek now offers a perfect target for a blow with the right fist; but only equals fought with fists, as we know from Jewish sources, and the

last thing the master wishes to do is to establish this underling's equality. This act of defiance renders the master incapable of asserting dominance in this relationship.[24]

Turning the other cheek is thus not an act of compliance but one of resistance. The church is summoned by Jesus to imagine creative methods of countering violence through nonviolent means of resolving conflict and catalyzing social change. The witness of three exemplary peacemakers shows us the way toward nonviolent resistance.

Three Peacemakers

How have these virtues, rooted in the biblical story of reconciling and peacemaking, come to expression in the lives of paradigmatic peacemakers? I will examine three figures from diverse contexts, each of whom has been decisively shaped by the biblical narrative and given leadership to movements for peace and reconciliation. Each of these figures was not only personally engaged in working for reconciliation but a major leader in movements for peaceful change.

MOHANDAS K. GANDHI

First, I examine the commitments of Mohandas K. Gandhi (1869–1948), also known as Mahatma, meaning "great soul." Although not a Christian by profession, Gandhi was profoundly influenced by the biblical narrative and particularly by the teachings of Jesus in the Sermon on the Mount. Commenting on Jesus' command to also give one's cloak when only asked for one's coat (Matt 5:40-42), Gandhi said:

> Your non-cooperation with your opponent is violent when you give a blow for a blow, and is ineffective in the long run. Your non-cooperation is nonviolent when you give your opponent all in the place of just what he needs. You have disarmed him once and for all by your apparent cooperation, which in effect is complete non-cooperation.[25]

While Gandhi never embraced the dogmatic claims of Christianity about the divinity of Jesus Christ and remained loyal to the Hindu tradition, he discovered in the Christian Scripture universal truths about the way of peacemaking. Gandhi was especially impressed by the writings of Leo Tolstoy, who opened him to the "true message of Jesus" as epitomized in the Sermon on the Mount and its "law of love." "In Tolstoy Gandhi found a confirmation of his own inclination to distinguish between the message of Jesus and the teachings and practice of the Christian church. Thus, Jesus became for Gandhi an object of reverence and devotion, uncompromised by the failures and betrayals of his Christian followers."[26] In addition to his appreciation for the witness to nonviolence in the Sermon on the Mount, Gandhi was moved by the example of Jesus' self-sacrificing suffering and death for his cause.

Employing a philosophy of nonviolent direct action, forged in part from what he had learned from Jesus, Gandhi became a leader of the struggle for the independence of India from Great Britain in the 1920s to 1940s. Core to Gandhi's thought were the ideas of *satyagraha*, or the power of truth, and *ahimsa*, or nonviolence. In engaging in the movement for change, it was essential to align oneself and one's movement on the side of the truth. Gandhi was convinced that truth ultimately prevails and that this conviction needed to be deeply owned by those struggling for freedom against an empire. Those who labor for change must also employ strategies and methods that are consistent with the way of truth, which entails nonviolence. Already as a lawyer in South Africa earlier in his career, Gandhi had tested the philosophy and methods of nonviolent civil disobedience in the cause of advocating for civil rights for the Indian community there. Returning to India in 1915, Gandhi gave leadership to people's movements in combating unjust land tax laws and discrimination.

After becoming the leader of the Indian National Congress in 1921, Gandhi organized national campaigns, employing nonviolent strategies, to alleviate poverty, win rights for women, build multi-ethnic and interreligious cooperation, promote economic independence, put an end to the Hindu caste of the untouchables, and win national independence from British control. Gandhi led the Indian people in the Non-cooperation Movement in 1921 against unjust laws of search, seizure, arrest, and imprisonment and, most dramatically, in the Salt March of 1930. Gandhi galvanized the nation in resisting Britain's attempt to impose a salt tax, when he defied the law by making salt after a long and highly publicized march to the sea. Gandhi was arrested and imprisoned many times in acts of civil disobedience. He employed fasting both as a form of self-purification and as an expression of protest in advocating nonviolent change. Public opinion from Gandhi's acts of nonviolent direct action eventually pressured Great Britain to grant India independence in 1947, marking one of the greatest achievements of nonviolent methods in human history.

What is most significant about the witness of Gandhi was how seriously he took Jesus' teachings about nonviolence and employed them with integrity in promoting social change. While Gandhi gave leadership to mass movements for change, the church has only begun to imagine how commitment to Jesus' truth and the way of nonviolence can inform its own advocacy and efforts at conflict resolution. One of the innovative figures in the United States who incorporated the philosophy and nonviolent methods of Jesus, learning from the example of Gandhi, was Martin Luther King Jr.

MARTIN LUTHER KING JR.

Dr. Martin Luther King Jr. (1929–1968) was propelled into national prominence in the wake of the Montgomery bus boycott, which had been sparked by the nonviolent resistance of Rosa Parks against the discriminatory law that required blacks to ride in the back of the bus. At the time of her act of protest, King was newly ordained as a Baptist minister whose ensuing vision, brilliance at strategizing, and eloquence helped ignite the civil rights movement. During the time of his doctoral studies at Boston University, King was mentored by Howard Thurman and others who instilled in him a deep commitment to the teachings of Jesus about peace, the model of Gandhi, and the way of nonviolence. During a trip to India to meet Gandhi's family in 1959, King said:

> Since being in India, I am more convinced than ever before that the method of non-violent resistance is the most potent weapon available to oppressed people in their struggle for justice and human dignity. In a real sense, Mahatma Gandhi embodied in his life certain universal principles that are inherent in the moral structure of the universe, and these principles are as inescapable as the law of gravitation.[27]

In spite of the bombing of his house and other acts of violent intimidation, King became ever more profoundly committed to the truth of nonviolence. As a founder of the Southern Christian Leadership Conference in 1957 and as a civil rights leader, King organized a series of campaigns of nonviolent direct civil disobedience to attain equal rights for African-Americans.[28]

During the campaign at Birmingham in spring 1963, King wrote from jail, appealing to the biblical legacy in defense of nonviolent direct action:

> Was not Jesus an extremist for love—"Love your enemies, bless them that curse you, pray for them that despitefully use you." Was not Amos an extremist for justice—"Let justice roll down like waters and righteousness like a mighty stream." Was not Paul an extremist for the gospel of Jesus Christ—"I bear in my body the marks of the Lord Jesus."[29]

The apex of the civil rights struggle was the March on Washington in 1963, where King delivered his classic "I Have a Dream" speech: "I have a dream that one day on the red hills of Georgia, the sons of former slaves and sons of former slave-owners will be able to sit down together at the table of brotherhood."[30] This speech appeals to the biblical narrative in which God unites all people into one as members of the Beloved Community, who will eat together in the shalom of God.

The year of 1964 marked two tremendous achievements on the part of the civil rights movement lead by King. In July the U.S. Congress passed the sweeping Civil Rights Act which outlawed racial segregation in schools, public accommodations, and the workplace. This legislation also won new equality for women and other minorities. Then in December, King became the youngest person ever to be awarded the Nobel Peace Prize. Instead of resting on these accomplishments, however, in the final years of his life King entered into new advocacy to oppose the war in Vietnam and to address the issue of economic injustice. He linked these two issues inextricably together, citing the war as a major contributor to increasing poverty. While continuing to support nonviolent methods for change, King's insistence on fundamental systemic change provoked new opposition against his leadership—both within the African-American community and from the white political establishment. While traveling to Memphis to support a strike by sanitation workers, King was assassinated on April 4, 1968. In the last speech before his death, King again gave expression to the biblical vision of peace and freedom for all peoples:

> I just want to do God's will. And He's allowed me to go up to the mountain. And I've looked over. And I've seen the promised land. I may not get there with you. But I want you to know tonight, that we, as a people will get to the promised land. And I'm happy, tonight. I'm not worried about anything. I'm not fearing any man. Mine eyes have seen the glory of the coming of the Lord.[31]

Throughout his career, King remained centered on the biblical vision of reconciliation among all peoples and the way of peace.

The public witness of Dr. Martin Luther King Jr. as a Christian minister continues to provide guidance to the church and inspiration for designing nonviolent means of conflict resolution and social transformation. In the cases both of Gandhi and King, the strategy of nonviolence had the ultimate goal of respecting the enemy as a human being, even while insisting on one's own human dignity, and thereby establishing the basis for a new relationship based on mutual dignity rather than oppression. The use of violence always leads to retribution and retaliation, which feeds the spiral of violence. Nonviolence appeals to the fundamental humanity of the oppressors and allows for the possibility of creating community and life-giving relationship with them. This approach anticipates and fosters the arrival of shalom, the kingdom of God, or, as King called it, the Beloved Community.

A. J. MUSTE

A. J. Muste (1885–1967) is a lesser known, though highly influential, Christian peacemaker. Born in the Netherlands, Muste migrated with his family to the

U.S. at the age of six and later became a naturalized citizen. He lived throughout his life as a principled pacifist, opposing war as an acceptable means to resolve human conflict. This led Muste to challenge every war fought in his lifetime from World War I to the war in Vietnam. As a consequence of preaching against the First World War in 1918, he was summarily dismissed as the pastor of his first congregation and forced to move out of the parsonage on the very afternoon of that sermon!

Like Gandhi and King, Muste found Jesus' teaching about nonviolence in the Sermon on the Mount overwhelmingly compelling. This teaching was interpreted not as wishful thinking about the way things ought to be but as "the most truly radical program for social transformation."[32] This led Muste to become an activist in the cause of pacifism:

> Pacifism—life—is built upon a central truth and the experience of that truth, its apprehension not by the mind alone but by the entire being in an act of faith and surrender. That truth is: God is love; love is of God. Love is the central thing in the universe.[33]

These convictions led Muste into a variety of social justice causes: the American Civil Liberties Union, the labor movement, and socialist politics. His primary passion, however, was the work of Christian peacemaking. Muste was a key leader of the American pacifist organization, the Fellowship of Reconciliation, from the 1930s to the end of his life; he served as its Executive Director from 1940 to 1953, and during these years (among many other involvements) he served as an advisor to King. Muste also was engaged as a member of the national committee of the War Resisters League, receiving its Peace Prize in 1958. During the heart of the Cold War in the 1940s and 50s, together with Dorothy Day, he helped organize resistance to civil defense drills in New York City:

> To create the impression of at least outward unanimity, the impression that there is no "real" opposition, is something for which all dictators and military leaders strive. The more it seems that there is no opposition, the less worthwhile it seems to an ever larger number of people to cherish even the thought of opposition.[34]

After his formal retirement, Muste remained an advocate for peace to the end of his life. He was arrested many times for protests at nuclear weapons sites.

In the 1960s Muste was a key leader of the Vietnam antiwar movement. In 1966 he was arrested in Saigon, after attempting to hold a peace vigil in front of the U.S. embassy. When asked how he thought holding a candle in peaceful protest might actually change the involvement of his country in the war, Muste replied, "Oh, you've got it all wrong. I'm not doing this to change the country.

I do it so the country won't change me."[35] He died at the age of eighty-two, a few weeks after returning from North Vietnam on a peace mission to witness the effects of U.S. bombing attacks. While pacifism remains one of the most controversial expressions of Christian peacemaking, it is important for us to wrestle with the legacy of those, like Muste, who have interpreted the biblical narrative, and especially the teaching of Jesus about loving one's enemies, as a call to the radical discipleship of pacifism in the midst of the violent conflicts in their times.

These three representatives offer a glimpse of how the virtues of Christian reconciliation and peacemaking have been embodied in the life of the people of God. Gandhi, King, and Muste each witness to the concrete implications of the five virtues articulated: the commitment to inclusivity, love for enemies, readiness to forgive, repenting of violence, and nonviolent resistance. Each of these figures testifies to the compelling vision in the Scriptures of God's desire to unite all peoples as one, with the path to that destination as the way of reconciliation and nonviolent peacemaking.

Practicing Reconciliation and Peacemaking as Ministering Community

The biblical narrative of God's reconciling and peacemaking agenda forms the character of the body of Christ and shapes God's people in the corresponding virtues. These virtues come to expression in the lives of those who live already now according to God's promise of uniting all peoples in the reality of shalom. The character and virtues of the church as the body of Christ, Christ existing as church-community, are embodied in practices that reflect the Christian values of reconciling and peacemaking. Craig Dykstra and Dorothy Bass define such practices as the "things people do together over time to address fundamental human needs in response to and in the light of God's active presence for the life of the world."[36] What are the specific practices in which congregations may engage in order to participate in God's purposes of bringing oneness to all peoples?

First, congregations engage in the *practice of praying for peace*. This practice is deeply embedded in liturgies from ancient times to the present. The church prays for peace in its worship:

- "For the *peace from above*, and for our salvation, let us pray to the Lord."
- "For the *peace of the whole world*, for the well-being of the church of God, and *for the unity of all*, let us pray to the Lord."

And the assembly responds, "Lord, have mercy." Note the profound connection between the coming of God's peace and the unity of all people expressed in the

Kyrie, reflecting the way of peace as the path to oneness. The prayers for peace are extended through carefully crafted intercessions that articulate the needs of the church, the world, and the whole creation for the peace of God. In the prayers of the church, we implore God not only for peace in a general way, but we pray for peace specifically in those conflicted places where hatred and violence are currently raging. The prayers also provide an occasion to recollect great historical events (for example, the destruction of Hiroshima and Nagasaki by nuclear attack, or the genocide of the Holocaust), begging God: "Never again!" The importance of prayer in the life of the congregation should not be underestimated. There is a real sense in which we become what we pray. In the liturgical prayers we have the occasion to rehearse the things that make for peace, trusting God will indeed form and shape the body of Christ as a reconciling and peacemaking people. Moreover, the people of God can be encouraged by their leaders to make prayers for peace a regular part of their devotional lives.

Second, congregations are called to the *practice of interpreting the actions of others in the kindest way*. In explaining the meaning of the Eighth Commandment, "You are not to bear false witness against your neighbor," Martin Luther wrote that we are not only to avoid betraying or slandering our neighbors, destroying their reputations, but "we are to come to their defense, speak well of them, and interpret everything they do in the best possible light."[37] The seed of human violence begins with the use of language to demean and degrade others. It is very easy to describe others in terms that rob them of their humanity, especially in reacting to provocations that appear to threaten our own well-being. Once we begin to interpret the actions of others by using language that fails to acknowledge their fundamental personhood, however, it becomes much easier to rationalize our own vindictive response. The use of epithets or stereotypes to label others is the first step in the spiral of violence, as "they" are objectified and dehumanized. Acts of violence against vulnerable groups (usually minorities) always begin with hate speech that constructs a world in which others are, at the very least, devalued or even turned into monsters. Such language, either on the personal or societal scale, can soon degenerate into rationalizing acts of retribution in the name of "justice." Once others have been dehumanized by our speech, all things against them become possible. As the body of Christ, by contrast, we are summoned to speak charitably of others, interpreting their actions in the best possible way. The choice to do so counteracts the spiral of violence.

Third, congregations participate in the *practice of forgiving*. Again, this practice is ritualized in the church's orders of confession and absolution—public and private. In one familiar form, the absolution declares: "God, who is rich in mercy, loved us even when we were dead in sin, and made us alive together with Christ.

By grace you have been saved. In the name of Jesus Christ, your sins are forgiven."[38] The ritual of confession and absolution makes real one of the central features of the Christian Gospel: the forgiveness of sins. What is more, the congregation at worship models the practice of forgiving one another in the passing of the peace. The passing of the peace is an ancient Christian practice: "Greet one another with a kiss of love. Peace to all of you who are in Christ" (1 Pet 5:16). The passing of the peace embodies through the liturgy God's desire for the congregation that we live together with one another in shalom. The liturgy paves the way for a practice that God wills to become reality in all of life, beginning with the household of faith.

Members of congregations often find it notoriously difficult to live together in peace, forgiving one another as we have been forgiven. Only as the body of Christ grasps more fully the extent of Christ's forgiveness will it be able to live in patient endurance and longsuffering, genuinely forgiving those who (we believe) have offended us. The practice of forgiveness is not merely a ritual that we recite at the beginning of worship. Forgiveness is one of the most needful realities in all of human life. Dietrich Bonhoeffer's wisdom about marriage is truly wisdom for all of life:

> In a word, live together in the forgiveness of your sins, for without it no human fel-
> lowship . . . can survive. Don't insist on your rights, don't blame each other, don't
> judge or condemn each other, don't find fault with each other, but accept each other
> as you are, and forgive each other every day from the bottom of your hearts.[39]

In his classic book *Life Together*, Bonhoeffer further elaborates the practice of forgiveness, encouraging private confession and absolution as essential to the survival of Christian community.[40] Only as the body of Christ practices forgiveness among its own membership, trusting profoundly in the priority of Christ's having first forgiven us, will it be able to act authentically as an agent of reconciliation in the midst of the world's strife. For this reason, it is crucial for congregations to be diligent in practicing the rite of confession and forgiveness and very deliberate in working consequentially at the skills of conflict resolution.[41] Otherwise, the world will see reflected in the life of the church only more of the same animosity it already knows too well. The hypocrisy of the church in the failure to practice forgiveness limits its effectiveness as a force for reconciliation and peace in society.

Fourth, congregations learn *the practice of resisting violence.* As mentioned above, one of the primary expressions of human violence involves the scapegoating of others. Human beings have within themselves an aggressive impulse that is easily aroused in response to a perceived threat. This aggression can quickly run out of control, unless it is held in check by either internal or external regulation. One of the chief religious sanctions that functions to control outbreaks of violence is, as discussed above, the practice of forgiveness. We learn to resist the violent impulse within our own hearts by focusing on how much we have been forgiven by God in Christ, therefore redirecting our impulses to revenge and retaliation. But the reality of group violence is a challenge of another order. As anxiety builds up in a community or nation, the impulse to identify and exact violence against a scapegoat (either an individual or group) becomes virtually irresistible. Based on the insight of Girard into how the pattern of scapegoating has been unmasked in the Christian passion narratives (that is, we acknowledge that Jesus died on the cross as an innocent victim), of all human groups the church, as the body of Christ, is summoned to resist the repetition of scapegoating wherever it threatens to occur. Whereas in virtually all other instances those perpetrating the violence believe themselves to be righteous and justified in scapegoating their victim(s), Christians are called to unveil and name scapegoating for what it is, the displacement of collective anxiety against the innocent. This insight becomes the key to resisting and ending the violence of scapegoating.

The various forms of scapegoating violence in our society are almost too many to name, let alone detail. The impulse toward scapegoating violence finds its victims in child abuse, domestic abuse, sexual abuse, rape, gang violence, school shootings, criminal activities, police retaliation, violent behavior in prisons, capital punishment (especially of the innocent), state-sanctioned military initiatives, torture, genocide, and war, among many other types.[42] While not all violence is a consequence of scapegoating, much of it is, more than will ever be acknowledged. Moreover, media violence valorizes much scapegoating violence in television programs, movies, the Internet, and especially through interactive video games.[43] Because of the propensity for scapegoating violence in our society, it is imperative that the church as the body of Christ, bearing the marks of the Crucified, raise a clear and unambiguous protest against all forms of scapegoating violence, while posing critical questions about its validity for resolving human conflict.

There are many specific ministries in which congregations may engage to resist violence and promote peace. One of the most basic procedures that should become regular routine is the securing of background checks from all those who work for the church, in particular those with responsibilities for children and youth. This screening process is a fundamental way of halting the very opportunity for violence. Moreover, it should become normal, standard practice that those who work with children and youth always be paired with at least one other person who is physically present at all activities. Congregations also need to serve as proactive educators about domestic violence and child, spouse, and elder abuse through written materials and by providing instruction to members. Information about referral to shelters should be readily available. Congregations can also offer support through donations made to the operation of local shelters.

Another opportunity to resist violence involves prison ministry, either through the personal involvement of members or by providing support to those who themselves do such ministry. As part of the youth ministry of the congregation, sex education is imperative, both to frame human sexuality as a gift of God for which God makes us responsible and to prevent violent expressions such as sexual abuse or rape. Such education is most effective when parents and children come together for well-planned learning experiences, led by pastors working in conjunction with sex educators. Education among youth may also include the examination of such topics as peer pressure, the phenomena of gangs and gang violence, and media violence.

Fifth, members of congregations can engage in *the practice of advocating nonviolence.* For many people, this is a bold and risky venture, because it dramatically challenges the prevailing social conventions about the necessity and validity of violence. This social convention is supported by the widespread belief in the myth of redemptive violence. According to this myth, violence is indispensable for solving conflict: only violence can save us, only war brings peace, only "might makes right."[44] Because this myth is so deeply embedded in our society, those who advocate nonviolence are going to be viewed by the majority as social deviants, naïve, and dreamers. Yet, as the witness of Gandhi, King, and Muste shows us, nonviolent resistance can be an extremely effective means for accomplishing social change. The challenge lies in organizing and implementing the methods of nonviolence on a sufficient scale. For this reason, those who seek to advocate nonviolence do well to affiliate with an organization that can assist congregational members in the educational and organizing efforts necessary for the practice of nonviolence (for example, the Fellowship of Reconciliation).[45] The connection with such a network of peace advocates can support congregational members to be effective in responding nonviolently to issues such as capital punishment, torture, state-sanctioned military violence, genocide, or war. While only in exceptional circumstances is it likely that whole congregations will achieve consensus about advocacy for and involvement in particular acts of nonviolent resistance (other than in the historic peace churches), members who are persuaded by the power of nonviolence can join together with members of other churches in an ecumenical coalition to pursue this path of engagement. Much work remains to be accomplished before the church is ready as the body of Christ to truly embrace the practice of advocating nonviolence.

Congregations are well suited to lead forums dealing with a wide range of social-ministry issues that involve the advocacy of nonviolence in the face of violence. Many denominations have social statements on topics such as capital punishment, genocide, or war that deserve wider discussion through educational events. Congregations can also organize forums dealing with local issues, such as violence in the schools or neighborhood watches against criminal violence. Such forums can provide the channel for those concerned about taking the next step to meet together and organize local activism. Above all, congregations can be safe communities for investigating nonviolent alternatives in a world of spiraling violence.

This chapter has examined the creedal confession about the church's oneness as the foundation for the church's ministries of reconciliation and peacemaking. The structure of this chapter will be followed again in each of the next three chapters as I take up successively the social ministry implications of confessing the church as holy, catholic, and apostolic. In this chapter I have rehearsed the biblical narrative about God's reconciling and peacemaking activity to make all people one. I have explored how this narrative forms the character of the body of Christ and instills particular virtues, forming it as a community of reconciliation and peacemaking in the world. Furthermore, I have seen how those virtues have been embodied in three particular peacemakers. Lastly, I have considered how congregations can participate in social ministry that serves God's way of reconciliation and peace-making. In the next chapter I turn to the second classical mark of the church and investigate the inexorable link between holiness and social justice.

The Body of Christ Is Holy
The Practice of Justice

The second classical mark of the church according to the Nicene Creed is "holy." For those who know even a little about the history of the church, this assertion appears at the very least paradoxical, at the most preposterous. In many respects the history of the church is one long scandal of hypocrisy and contradiction to the holiness of God. The prevalence of bickering, cases of abuse, and timidity in the face of evil by the churches continues to this day. Not only have Christians exhibited division and animosity among their own ranks, but they also have failed to demonstrate basic love for the neighbor in need. More than any other mark of the church, the claim to holiness appears to the world as disingenuous and self-serving. For those looking for a reason to remain distant from the church of Christ, the church's failure to be holy provides a most credible argument. The challenge of these contradictions will be confronted again in chapter 8.

Only God is holy and deserves our worship (not the church!). The idea of the holy gives expression to the primal otherness and sacredness of God. The concept of holiness seeks to describe that quality which is most distinctive of God alone, the very "godness" of God. Rudolf Otto described the holy as the *mysterium tremendum*, an infinite and uncanny source of transcendent energy—yet a reality that human beings find ultimately fascinating.[1] In the Hebrew Bible the experience of the holy is especially related to encounters with nature and revelation in the realm of history.[2] The holiness of God gives rise to the human need to worship, especially honoring the phenomenon of theophany, the intense encounter of the human with the divine. At the same time the holiness of God requires human beings to display sanctified lives, in accordance with God's truth and divine will.

In ancient Israel God's holiness was made manifest in the likes of purifying fire, jealousy against false gods, wrath against sin, awe-inspiring fear, and the insistence on cleanliness. While these themes informed the writers of the New Testament, the holy became revealed in a new and unique way by the incarnation of God in Jesus Christ (Mark 1:24; John 6:69; Rev 3:7). In particular, the holiness of Jesus Christ is identified with the living presence of God in him, the Holy Spirit (Luke 1:35). The church may be described as holy therefore only in a derivative sense, insofar as the power of God, Jesus Christ, the Holy Spirit makes it holy. In ecumenical commentary on the Niceno-Constantinopolitan Creed, the holiness of the church is explicated this way:

> The Holy Spirit dwells in the *holy church*. This Church has been set apart by God who is holy and who sanctifies it by the word and sacraments. The holiness of the Church signifies the faithfulness of God towards his people: the gates of hell will not prevail against it. Even at the darkest times in the Church's history, Christ continues to justify and sanctify those who remain faithful so that the Church even in such times is able to render its service for the salvation of humankind. It is also holy because of the holy words it proclaims and the holy acts it performs. Though it is a community of sinners, aware that God's judgment begins with them (1 Pet 4:17), it is holy because it is sustained by the knowledge that they have been and are constantly being forgiven. In spite of the sin in the Church, when it celebrates the Eucharist and listens to the word of God it is seized by the Holy One and cleansed.[3]

The church's holiness is a gift of God through Jesus Christ by the power of the Holy Spirit. This and this alone allows the church to dare call itself holy (Eph 5:25-27).

As a consequence of being made holy by God, the members of the body of Christ are frequently referred to as saints in the New Testament (Rom 1:7; 1 Cor 1:2; Phil 1:1). Sainthood is attributed to the baptized by virtue of the sanctifying work of Christ Jesus by the Holy Spirit. Curiously, in the New Testament holiness is rarely attributed to sacred objects, not even to baptism or the Lord's Supper.[4] Rather, it is only the believers themselves who are designated as the communion of saints (*communion sanctorum*), set apart for sanctity and service in the midst of a sinful world.[5] "Instead, as he who called you is holy, be holy yourselves in all your conduct; for it is written, 'You shall be holy, for I am holy'" (1 Pet 1:15-16).

Sanctification is the theological concept that articulates the effect of God's holiness in the lives of the saints. In the Hebrew Bible, God's holiness entails a sanctified ethical life. Leviticus 19:1-35 details the implications of God's holiness (v. 2) for the ethical treatment of the neighbor: leaving the gleanings of the field for the poor and alien (vv. 9-10); prohibition against stealing, dealing falsely, and lying (vv. 11-12); prohibition against fraud and dishonest business practices, especially misusing the deaf or blind (vv. 13-14); prohibition against unjust judgments, slander, and unjust profit (vv. 15-16); prohibition against hate and vengeance (vv. 17-18). The connection between the Spirit's work of sanctifying and ethical behavior is further developed in the New Testament: "But now that you have been freed from sin and enslaved to God, the advantage you get is sanctification" (Rom 6:22). The Holy Spirit grows the fruit of the Spirit in the lives of the saints (Gal 5:22-26). The entire lives of Christian people are to reflect God's holiness: "I appeal to you therefore, brothers and sisters, by the mercies of God, to present your bodies as a living sacrifice, holy and acceptable to God, which is your spiritual worship" (Rom 12:1).

Over the course of Christian history, sanctification has frequently been understood in an individualistic fashion, emphasizing personal piety and holiness. This focus on the individual's behavior is especially accented in many modern holiness movements that tend to reduce sanctification to the elimination of personal vices (no drinking, smoking, card playing, etc.). The larger momentum of the biblical witness, however, is geared less to the private sphere and far more to the public performance of holiness in public acts of righteousness and justice (Isa 5; Jer 5–7; Ezek 18; Hos 11; Amos 4–5). God's sanctifying of human beings according to divine holiness requires the people of God to demonstrate holiness through social justice and righteousness. Justification in Jesus Christ leads to just relationships with the neighbor. In the memorable formula of Luther, the gospel of Jesus Christ not only sets us free *from* sin, death, and the devil, but the gospel sets us free *for* serving our neighbor, starting with the neighbors most in need.[6]

From its earliest history the body of Christ, at its most faithful, has reflected God's holiness through a ministry of care for the most destitute. Rodney Stark describes the significance of the outreach of the early church in the context of urban chaos and crisis:

> To cities filled with the homeless and impoverished, Christianity offered charity as well as hope. To cities filled with newcomers and strangers, Christianity offered an immediate basis for attachments. To cities filled with orphans and widows, Christianity provided a new and expanded sense of family. To cities torn by violent ethnic strife, Christianity offered a new basis for social solidarity. . . . And to cities faced with epidemics, fires, and earthquakes, Christianity offered effective nursing services.[7]

Stark's sociological investigation attributes the rapid expansion of Christianity in the Roman Empire primarily to its responsiveness to basic human need.[8]

As demonstration of this pattern, Cyprian in the third century admonished the church to follow in the way of Christ by caring for others:

> [T]here was nothing wonderful in our cherishing our own people only with the needed attentions of love, but that he might become perfect who would do something more than the publican or the heathen, who, overcoming evil with good, and practicing a clemency which was like the divine clemency, loved even his enemies, who would pray for the salvation of those that persecute him, as the Lord admonishes and exhorts. God continually makes [the] sun to rise, and from time to time gives showers to nourish the seed, exhibiting all these kindnesses not only to [God's] people, but to aliens also.[9]

After the Constantinian transformation of the church in the fourth century, it was especially monasticism and various renewal movements that perpetuated the church's witness to God's holiness in neighbor love and concern for justice.[10] At the end of the twelfth century, Peter Waldo (c. 1140–1215) gave leadership to the Waldensian reform movement that challenged the church to live in apostolic poverty.[11] Other prominent figures, such as Francis of Assisi (c. 1181–1226), reminded the church of its obligations to the poor in the face of institutional forgetfulness.[12] Within Protestantism, the pietist movements of the seventeenth and eighteenth centuries, led by Philipp Jakob Spener (1635–1705) and August Hermann Francke (1663–1727), modeled for the church concern for the poor, care for orphans, and outreach to distant lands.[13] In more recent times representatives of the Social Gospel movement and liberation theology have insisted that God's holiness be reflected in the church's "preferential option for the poor" and social justice.[14]

While the body of Christ always retains a *simul* character—at the same time sinful and sanctified—the confession of the church as holy has given energy in every generation to impulses for social justice. Hans Küng expresses confidence in God's preservation of the church in spite of all hypocrisy and failure:

> [The church] may lose the way, make detours, take wrong turnings, it may stumble and fall, it may fall among thieves and lie half-dead by the roadside. But God the Lord will not pass by on the other side; [God] will pour oil on its wounds, lift it up, give it lodging and provide for its healing even that which could not have been foreseen. The Church will always remain the holy Church. This we know in faith: *credo sanctum ecclesiam*.[15]

The evidence for this claim, as presented in this chapter, is demonstrated by how the body of Christ has witnessed to and embodied God's justice over the centuries.

I turn next to the biblical narrative that provides the warrant for the church's social justice ministry.

The Biblical Narrative: God's Holiness and Justice

"Indeed the whole earth is mine, but you shall be for me a priestly kingdom and a holy nation" (Exod 19:5-6). God called Israel out of bondage in Egypt to be a holy people, displaying righteousness in every relationship, justice in all her dealings with others, and giving privileged attention to those who are weak. The vocation to be a holy people who demonstrate justice to the poor and powerless begins with the very character of God who hears the cry of the poor:

> I have also heard the groaning of the Israelites whom the Egyptians are holding as slaves, and I have remembered my covenant [with Abraham]. Say therefore to the Israelites, 'I am the Lord, and I will free you from the burdens of the Egyptians and deliver you from slavery to them. I will redeem you with an outstretched arm and with mighty acts of judgment. You shall know that I am the Lord your God, who has freed you from the burdens of the Egyptians. (Exod 6:5-7)

God delivered Israel out of the injustice and humiliation of slavery to live as a covenant people who are always to remember their responsibility not to treat others as they were once treated. God's holiness tolerates no forgetfulness about their deliverance from bondage, which obligates Israel to serve as a protector and deliverer of others (Jer 2:3-9).

The terms of God's covenant were established at Sinai with the giving of the Ten Commandments: "I am the Lord your God, who brought you out of the land of Egypt, out of the house of slavery; you shall have no other gods before me" (Exod 20:2-3). The terms of covenant faithfulness included for Israel the commands to right worship and right ethical conduct. Right ethical conduct is further elaborated in the law code of Israel, which prescribes special consideration and protection not only of the needs of the weakest members among the covenant people but also for strangers and aliens: "You shall not wrong or oppress a resident alien, for you were aliens in the land of Egypt. You shall not abuse any widow or orphan. If you do abuse them, when they cry out to me, I will surely heed their cry. . ." (Exod 22:21-23). Codified in the laws of Israel are also special provisions to protect the poor against unjust business practices: "If you lend money to my people, to the poor among you, you shall not deal with them as a creditor; you shall not exact interest from them. If you take your neighbor's cloak in pawn, you shall restore it before the sun goes down; for it may be your neighbor's only clothing to use as cover; in what else shall that person sleep?" (Exod 22:25-27). Furthermore the law insists upon justice in the courts: "You shall not pervert the justice due to your poor in their lawsuits. Keep far from a false charge, and do not kill the innocent and those in the right, for I will not acquit the guilty" (Exod 23:6-7).

Of particular significance is how legal protections are extended to aliens and strangers in the midst of Israel: "You shall not oppress a resident alien; you know the heart of an alien, for you were aliens in the land of Egypt" (Exod 23:9). The formative experience of the Exodus shapes and conditions who Israel is to be in relationship to others. Leviticus prescribes in detail the laws that guide Israel to preserve ritual and moral holiness. The defining relationship between God and God's people comes to classical expression in what we have received as the Golden Rule: "You shall not take vengeance or bear a grudge against any of your people, *but you shall love your neighbor as yourself*; I am the Lord" (Lev 19:18).

The wide reach of neighbor love and divine restorative justice is articulated in the provisions for a sabbatical year to renew the land and its laborers every seventh year (Lev 25:1-7) and especially in the declaration of every fiftieth year as a jubilee:

> [Y]ou shall have the trumpet sounded throughout all the land. And you shall hallow the fiftieth year and you shall proclaim liberty throughout the land to all its inhabitants. It shall be a jubilee for you; you shall return, every one of you, to your family. . . . If any who are dependent on you become so impoverished that they sell themselves to you, you shall not make them as slaves. They shall remain with you as hired or bound laborers. They shall serve with you until the year of the jubilee. Then they and their children with them shall be free from your authority; they shall go back to their own family and return to their ancestral property. For they are my servants, whom I brought out of the land of Egypt; they shall not be sold as slaves are sold. (Lev 25:9-10, 39-42)

Whether or not the jubilee year was ever practiced according to all its liberating and radical legal provisions, it established for Israel the expectations of the Holy God for economic and social justice. The heartbeat of God's concern for holy justice is concisely summarized in Deuteronomy 10:17-18: "For the Lord your God is God of gods and Lord of lords, the great God, mighty and awesome, who is not partial and takes no bribe, who executes justice for the orphan and widow, and who loves the strangers, providing them food and clothing."

Accordingly, the leaders of Israel were expected to uphold a high standard of justice. The judges were expected to judge righteously and the king of Israel was expected to serve as the chief representative of God's justice: "So David reigned over all Israel; and David administered justice and equity to all his people" (2 Sam 8:15). Likewise with regard to Solomon: "Blessed be the Lord your God, who has delighted in you and set you on the throne of Israel! Because the Lord loved Israel forever, he has made you king to execute justice and righteousness" (1 Kings 10:9). The Psalms resound with songs imploring God to make just the king of Israel: "Give the king your justice, O God, and your righteousness to a king's son. May he judge your people with righteousness, and your poor with justice. . . . May he defend the cause of the poor of the people, give deliverance to the needy and crush the oppressor" (Ps 72:1-2, 4). The king is held to this standard because God is a God "who executes justice for the oppressed; who gives food to the hungry" (Ps 146:7). Jesus would draw directly from this royal tradition when he announced the coming of God's kingdom.

Concomitantly with the inauguration of the office of king in the history of Israel, another office also emerged to serve as a check and counterpoint to the real possibility of the abuse of power by the king and the privileged class that accompanied the king's reign. This was the office of prophet. From the very beginning, the prophets of Israel spoke the word of the Lord to critique royal power whenever it failed to honor God's holiness and do justice. The prophet Nathan, for example, convicted King David for the death of Uriah and adultery with Bathsheba, his wife: "You are the man! . . . Why have you despised the word of the Lord, to do what is evil in his sight? You have struck down Uriah the Hittite with the sword, and have taken his wife to be your wife, and have killed him with the sword of the Ammonites" (2 Sam 12:7, 9). This pattern of speaking truth to power reverberates in the legacy of the prophets from beginning to end.

Isaiah pronounced God's judgment against those who unjustly accumulated the property of others: "Ah, you who join house to house, who add field to field, until there is room for no one but you, and you are left to live alone in the midst of the land! The Lord of hosts has sworn in my hearing: Surely many houses shall be desolate, large and beautiful houses, without inhabitant" (Isa 5:8-9). Such offenses are a violation of God's very holiness: ". . . for they have rejected the instruction of the Lord of hosts, and have despised the word of the Holy One of Israel" (Isa 5:24b). Amos joins the chorus of prophetic warnings against the privileged class of Israel prior to the destruction of the Northern kingdom: "Hear this word, you cows of Bashan who are on Mount Samaria, who oppress the poor, who crush the needy, who say to their husbands, 'Bring something to drink!' The Lord God has sworn by his holiness: The time is surely coming upon you, when they shall take you away with hooks, even the last of you with fishhooks" (Amos 4:1-2).

Likewise echo the words of the prophet Hosea: "There is no faithfulness or loyalty, and no knowledge of God in the land. Swearing, lying, and murder, and stealing and adultery break out; bloodshed follows bloodshed" (Hos 4:1b-2). Moreover, Micah declared:

> Hear this, you rulers of the house of Jacob and chiefs of the house of Israel, who abhor justice and pervert all equity, who build Zion with blood and Jerusalem with wrong! Its rulers give judgment for a bribe, its priests teach for a price, its prophets give oracles for money; yet they lean upon the Lord and say, "Surely the Lord is with us! No harm shall come upon us." Therefore because of you Zion shall be plowed as a field; Jerusalem shall become a heap of ruins. . . . (3:9-12)

Perhaps nowhere in Scripture does God plead for social justice in conformity with God's holiness more compellingly than in these words: "He has told you, O mortal, what is good; and what does the Lord require of you but to do justice, and to love kindness, and to walk humbly with your God?" (Mic 6:8).

Prior to the Babylonian exile, Jeremiah denounced the greed and injustice of God's people, which led them inexorably to the judgment of exile: "For from the least to the greatest of them, everyone is greedy for unjust gain; and from prophet to priest everyone deals falsely" (Jer 6:13). Only repentance from social injustice could restore them to covenant holiness:

> For if you truly amend your ways and your doings, if you truly act justly one with another, if you do not oppress the alien, the orphan, and the widow, or shed innocent blood in this place, and if you do not go after other gods to your own hurt, then I will dwell with you in this place, in the land that I gave of old to your ancestors forever and ever. (Jer 7:5-7)

Similarly, the judgment of the exile is cast by Ezekiel in terms of covenant holiness, including social justice:

> If a man is righteous and does what is lawful and right—if he does not eat upon the mountains or lift up his eyes to the idols of the house of Israel, does not defile his neighbor's wife or approach a woman during her menstrual period, does not oppress anyone, but restores to the debtor his pledge, commits no robbery, gives his bread to the hungry and covers the naked with a garment, does not take advance or accrued interest, withholds his hand from iniquity, executes true justice between contending parties, follows my statutes, and is careful to observe my ordinances, acting faithfully—such a one is righteous; he shall surely live, says the Lord God. (Ezek 18:5-9)

Ezekiel is fascinating for holding together as inseparable ritual and ethical holiness.

When the Messiah would come, this one would finally rule as a just king, representing God's righteousness:

> A root shall come out from the stump of Jesse, and a branch shall grow out of his roots. The spirit of the Lord shall rest on him, the spirit of wisdom and understanding, the spirit of counsel and might, the spirit of knowledge and the fear of the Lord.

His delight shall be in the fear of the Lord. He shall not judge by what his eyes see, or decide by what his ears hear; but with righteousness he shall judge the poor, and decide with equity for the meek of the earth. . . ." (Isa 11:1-4)

The vocation of peacemaking and administering social justice cohere in the coming reign of the messianic king: "His authority shall grow continually, and there shall be endless peace for the throne of David and his kingdom. He will establish and uphold it with justice and with righteousness from this time onward and forevermore. The zeal of the Lord of hosts will do this" (Isa 9:7). Consistently throughout the Hebrew Bible, God is revealed as the one who executes justice and who requires those responsible for the exercise of political, social, and economic power to uphold God's standards of holiness.

When Messiah Jesus finally arrived, he claimed to fulfill the ancient hope for the inauguration of fundamental social justice concomitant with the coming of God's kingdom:

[Jesus] stood up to read, and the scroll of the prophet Isaiah was given to him. He unrolled the scroll and found the place where it was written: "The Spirit of the Lord is upon me, because he has anointed me to bring good news to the poor. He has sent me to proclaim release to the captives and recovery of sight to the blind, to let the oppressed go free, to proclaim the year of the Lord's favor." And he rolled up the scroll, gave it back to the attendant, and sat down. The eyes of all in the synagogue were fixed on him. Then he began to say to them, "Today this scripture has been fulfilled in your hearing." (Luke 4:16b-21)

Was Jesus here invoking the arrival of the jubilee year? The inaugural sermon of Jesus at his hometown of Nazareth coheres well with the prayer Jesus taught to his disciples: "And forgive us our debts, as we also have forgiven our debtors" (Matt 6:12). Has the church spiritualized what Jesus intended in economic terms? Also in the Lord's Prayer, Jesus taught his followers to pray: "Your kingdom come" (Matt 6:10). At the center of Jesus' message was the proclamation of the kingdom of God. "Kingdom" is a political term. It was no accident that Jesus selected this guiding metaphor for his ministry, a term that summons forth Israel's hope for a just and righteous king in the face of oppression.

The proclamation, enactment, and embodiment of the kingdom by Jesus stood in direct continuity with the expectations for social holiness in the Hebrew Scriptures. In Jesus' teachings about the nature of the kingdom, the poor, sick, hungry, and oppressed have a privileged place. Consider the beatitudes and maledictions from Luke's Gospel:

Blessed are you who are poor, for yours is the kingdom of God.
Blessed are you who are hungry now, for you will be filled. . . .

> But woe to you who are rich, for you have received your consolation.
> Woe to you who are full now, for you will be hungry. (Luke 6:20-21, 24-25)

With the arrival of the kingdom as anticipated in the activity of Jesus, the excluded receive a welcome and the hungry are fed. Moreover, there is an eschatological reversal: the rich find themselves in want. In response to the inquiry by the disciples of John about his ministry, Jesus answered, "Go and tell John what you have seen and heard: the blind receive their sight, the lame walk, the lepers are cleansed, the deaf hear, the dead are raised, the poor have good news brought to them" (Luke 7:22). Furthermore, Jesus taught others to break down social barriers by caring for those who have been victimized, for example, the parable of the Good Samaritan (Luke 10:25-37): "Go and do likewise" (v. 37).

Jesus engaged in healing and performed exorcisms throughout his ministry: "Jesus went throughout Galilee, teaching in their synagogues and proclaiming the good news of the kingdom and curing every disease and every sickness among the people" (Matt 4:23). There are numerous stories about Jesus' ministry of healing in the Gospels.[16] Healing served not only as an individual act of mercy to the person who was healed but also had social implications for restoration into life-giving relationship with the community (cf. Mark 1:43). Likewise, Jesus was known for his power to cast out evil spirits: "And he went throughout Galilee, proclaiming the message in their synagogues and casting out demons" (Mark 1:39). Again, the act of exorcism restored the person into the community (Mark 5:19-20). Those who had been marginalized by illness or possession regained wholeness; in context, this was an act of social ministry and divine justice.

Jesus also was renowned for feeding the hungry (Matt 15:32-39). Especially in the Gospel of Luke, Jesus demonstrates compassion for the hungry and challenges those who have plenty to share with those who do not have enough. In the parable of the rich fool, the rich man fails to see the folly of his ways and is unprepared for final judgment (Luke 12:16-21). In the parable of the rich man and poor Lazarus, Jesus warns about the consequences for those who have the poor lying at their doorstep but fail to demonstrate fundamental human compassion and charity (Luke 16:19-31). Jesus summons the rich ruler to "sell all that you own and distribute the money to the poor," a form of repentance he is unwilling to undergo (Luke 18:18-25): "How hard it is for those who have wealth to enter the kingdom of God! Indeed, it is easier for a camel to go through the eye of a needle than for someone who is rich to enter the kingdom of God" (vv. 24-25). Zacchaeus demonstrates, however, that with God all things are possible, even surrendering one's possessions for the sake of the poor (Luke 19:1-10).

Jesus' ministry practice was characterized by unconventional table fellowship: "Why does he eat with tax collectors and sinners?" (Mark 2:16). The meals Jesus shared with others were signs of the kingdom's in-breaking. He warned those who held banquets, "When you give a luncheon or a dinner, do not invite your friends or your brothers or your relatives or rich neighbors, in case they may invite you in return, and you would be repaid. But when you give a banquet, invite the poor, the crippled, the lame, and the blind" (Luke 14:12-13). Consistent with his concern for the revelation of the kingdom at table, Jesus left his disciples a simple meal by which to remember him: "While they were eating, Jesus took a loaf of bread, and after blessing it he broke it, gave it to the disciples, and said, 'Take, eat; this is my body'" (Matt 26:26). The eating of Jesus with tax collectors and sinners provides the framework for all eating at the Lord's Table: an invitation to all, beginning with the outcast and sinners, the least. All are welcome at the table of Jesus. And at this meal there is enough for all.

In continuity with the great tradition of Israel, Jesus summarized the law with reference to the fundamental relationships to God and neighbor: "'Teacher, which commandment in the law is the greatest?' He said to him, 'You shall love the Lord your God with all your heart, and with all your soul, and with all your mind.' This is the greatest and first commandment. And a second is like it: 'You shall love your neighbor as yourself.' On these two commandments hang all the law and the prophets" (Matt 22:36-40). The full extent of neighbor love is communicated by Jesus in the great judgment parable about separating the sheep and the goats:

> Come, you that are blessed by my Father,
> inherit the kingdom prepared for you from the foundation of the world;
> for I was hungry and you gave me food,
> I was thirsty and you gave me something to drink,
> I was a stranger and you welcomed me,
> I was naked and you gave me clothing,
> I was sick and you took care of me,
> I was in prison and you visited me. (Matt 25:34-36)

When the righteous ask about when they did these generous and compassionate things for Jesus, the Son of Man replies, "Truly I tell you, just as you did it to one of the least of these who are members of my family, you did it to me" (Matt 25:40). The conviction that the kingdom entails social justice stretches from Jesus' inaugural sermon at Nazareth to this parable told at the brink of his passion.

Not only did Jesus proclaim the kingdom in his teachings and demonstrate its arrival through mighty acts of healing, exorcisms (Matt 12:28), and by feeding the hungry, but at the end of his life he enacted a parable of judgment against the use of the holy temple for unjust religious and economic practices: "Then Jesus entered the temple and drove out all who were selling and buying in the temple, and he overturned the tables of the money changers and the seats of those who sold doves. He said to them, 'It is written, "My house shall be called a house of prayer"; but you are making it a den of robbers' " (Matt 21:12-13). An emerging consensus of scholarship connects this prophetic parable at the temple with Jesus' eventual arrest and crucifixion.[17] With Jesus' insistence on the coming of God's kingdom through acts of healing, a welcome to outsiders, and social justice, it is no wonder that the charge against him, posted on the cross, read: "This is Jesus, the King of the Jews" (Matt 27:37). Jesus had dared to envision, declare, and enact the arrival of God's messianic and just kingdom in their midst.

After his death, the risen Jesus appeared to the disciples in the breaking of bread, continuing his practice of unconventional table fellowship (Luke 24:30-31; cf. also John 21:12-13). The apostolic church of Acts is remembered for how the sharing of goods flowed from this table fellowship: "All who believed were together and had all things in common; they would sell their possessions and goods and distribute the proceeds to all, as any had need. Day by day, as they spent much time together in the temple, they broke bread at home and ate their food with glad and generous hearts. . . ." (Acts 2:44-46). It is important to notice how the church gathering in Jesus' name practiced a basic form of communal ownership: "Now the whole group of those who believed were of one heart and soul, and no one claimed private ownership of any possessions, but everything they owned was held in common. . . . There was not a needy person among them, for as many as owned lands or houses sold them and brought the proceeds of what was sold. They laid it at the apostles' feet, and it was distributed to each as any had need" (Acts 4:32, 34-35). In this regard, it is important to recall the original reason the church began to collect an offering: as a collection for the poor.[18] When Paul beseeches the churches to contribute to a collection, it is designated for the poor in Jerusalem (Rom 15:25-28).

At the church in Corinth, distortions in the distribution of the Lord's Supper led to divisions within the body of Christ. Paul calls the Corinthian congregation to accountability for allowing some to go hungry at the meal (1 Cor 11:21). Just eating practices are to define the body of Christ.[19] Following this theme, the letter of James holds the Christian assembly accountable for how it does or does not minister to the poor in its midst: "What good is it, my brothers and sisters, if you say you have faith but do not have works? Can faith save you? If a brother or sister is naked and lacks daily food, and one of you says to them, 'Go in peace; keep warm and eat your fill,' and yet you do not supply their bodily needs, what is the good of that? So faith by itself, if it has no works is dead" (Jas 2:14-17). Referring to Jesus' own teachings about the poor, James asks: "Has not God chosen the poor of the world to be rich in faith and to be heirs of the kingdom that he has promised to those who love him?" (1:5). The church conforms to the way of Christ in every relationship: "[C]lothe yourselves with the new self, created according to the likeness of God in true righteousness and holiness" (Eph 4:24). The final measure of God's holiness in us is measured by how we love: "And this is his commandment, that we should believe in the name of his Son Jesus Christ and love one another, just as he has commanded us" (1 John 3:23).

Character and Virtues in the Body of Christ: Justification Leads to Justice

God's holiness makes the people of God holy. This is the way of sanctification; God's sanctity cleanses and purifies the lives of God's people. This message is the core of the biblical narrative about God's holiness deriving from the Hebrew Scriptures. It is a theme carried forward in the New Testament through the imagery of Christ as the Lamb of God whose blood cleanses from sin (John 1:29). This imagery is particularly evident in the letter to the Hebrews (2:11; 10:10-14; 13:12). The work of Christ in the Holy Spirit has sanctifying efficacy: "But you were washed, you were sanctified, you were justified in the name of the Lord Jesus Christ and in the Spirit of God" (1 Cor 6:11). Only for Christ's sake may Christians be deemed the "saints" of God (Rom 1:7; 1 Cor 1:2).

The New Testament adds this further dimension: Christ's justification makes the body of Christ just. The justifying work of Jesus Christ on the cross has an actual effect on the lives of believers; they are made righteous and just (Rom 5–6). Justification is not merely forensic and formal; it is actual. The Holy Spirit makes real the presence of Christ in the life of the Christian, effecting union between Christ and the believer.[20] For this reason the Pauline epistles follow this pattern: because you are "in Christ," therefore live accordingly (2 Cor 5:17-21). Justification and justice belong together inseparably.

Five Virtues

What are the virtues that belong to the church as the body of Christ in accordance with God's holiness and justice? The biblical narrative discloses five distinctive virtues that characterize the church as Christ existing as community. I will articulate the contours of each of these virtues before illustrating them embodied through biographies of three exemplary leaders in justice ministry: Dorothy Day, Oscar Romero, and Mother Teresa.

The first virtue involves *solidarity with the oppressed.* Before we are able to act justly, our hearts must be turned to compassion for those who suffer. Solidarity begins with sympathy, "feeling with" those facing trials, especially those who suffer at the hands of others. In a world saturated with images and news reports about those who suffer, how can we prevent our hearts from turning to stone? Our compassion must not become merely voyeuristic but instead move us to action in seeking ways to relieve the suffering we encounter. Our complicity in the suffering of others must turn to repentance with the hope that our initiatives to overcome oppression are worthwhile.[21] Almost always the turn to action is best accomplished by living in community with others who hold one another accountable for "doing something" as an act of solidarity. Solidarity also entails the search for accurate information about the conditions leading to particular forms of oppression. In our consumer society, the commercial media may be very limited in providing the information necessary for making informed decisions about effective strategies. Those desiring to live in solidarity need to become proactive in seeking out alternative information, for example, from international news agencies close to the ground of emerging events or even from private sources from whom reliable information may be secured by correspondence with those knowledgeable about breaking events through instantaneous electronic communications. Accurate information allows the plan of action to reflect the actual circumstances facing those who are suffering.

A second virtue for the body of Christ that serves justice is *hospitality to strangers.* Research has confirmed that suspicion and fear of those who are different from ourselves is a deeply grounded human reaction.[22] When the biblical narrative commands God's people to be hospitable to strangers, this expectation runs counter to primal instincts. Even more, Jesus' command to love our enemies appears to put us at risk from those who are likely to do us harm. Hospitality to strangers is an approach to difference that must be religiously cultivated. Instead of suspicion or maintaining a cautious distance, hospitality seeks to establish a positive relationship with the stranger. Although the two responses are closely related, this requires moving from *sympathy* for those who are hurting to *empathy* for those who are different. It entails a decision and choice to relate to strangers in the same way one would relate to a friend. This means affording the stranger the same consideration and benefits that normally accrue to those who over time have earned our trust. For Jesus the ultimate expression of hospitality was inviting others to join in his open table fellowship, what some refer to as his "open commensality."[23] The body of Christ distinguishes itself from other expressions of human community by how it eats together, inviting strangers to become friends in the intimate act of breaking bread together at table—both at the Eucharist and meals of fellowship.

A third virtue characterizing the church as Christ existing as community is *care for the physical needs of all*. This goes to the very core of elementary neighbor love. If the neighbor lacks the physical necessities for the very sustenance of life, providing these becomes our own fundamental ethical obligation. Among the most pressing physical needs for a humane standard of living are food, clean water, shelter, clothing, and basic medical care. Furthermore, we might add basic education as a prerequisite for building the capacity to secure and sustain these physical needs. The church of Jesus Christ affirms the embodied character of life. Because the human body cannot be separated from the soul, Christian care begins with the most urgent needs for physical life: adequate nutrition, clean water supplies, safe and secure housing, sufficient clothing, and access to basic medical treatment, including immunization from preventable diseases. Moreover, the church has a particular calling in a world of the HIV/AIDS epidemic that affects so many who are already poor.[24] Concern for spiritual care cannot neglect the priority of addressing physical needs. In recent decades, an emerging consensus asserts that it is indeed possible to alleviate extreme poverty through the provision of these elementary physical needs.[25] We lack not sufficiency of resources but rather the moral, economic, and political will to redistribute resources to those most in need. The church of Jesus Christ follows a foundational ethical imperative to press for this agenda.[26]

A fourth virtue follows closely from the previous, the demonstration of *preferential concern for the weak*. There are many issues that demand the church's attention. In particular we are drawn naturally toward those priorities that promise most to affect positively our own well-being and privileges. In the political process it is no fault to pursue one's own self-interest; in fact, this is assumed as the given state of affairs. The politics of Jesus Christ, however, push another agenda, preferential concern for "the least" (Matt 25:31-46). In order for God to be *for all people*, priority must be given to those whom the world neglects and deprives. This is not a negation of divine inclusivity; instead it reflects the insistence that for the sake of including all, the church begins with those most in need. It is, however, a reversal of business as usual. This means in the economic realm and political process that the church as the collective person Jesus Christ sets aside self-interest in order to lend focused attention to the situation of the most vulnerable and marginalized. A prophetic church lifts up the cries of the poor and defends the cause of the defenseless. In principle this also means attending to the needs of children, women, and persons with handicaps, those who often are reduced to silence in the prevailing hierarchies of power.

The fifth virtue entails *just economic and legal dealings with others*. For the body of Christ this means first examining its own economic life as the church and how it regulates its internal legal structure. Are those employed by the church granted just wages and benefits? Do retirees receive an adequate pension? Does the church invest in best business practices? Does church law provide protections for the most marginalized among its membership? Before the church begins to address the economic and legal structures of society, it must become circumspect by doing honest self-examination to put its own house in order. The prophets of Israel, including Jesus, held not only economic and political leaders but also religious officials accountable for their behavior. Turning to society, the church commits to shining a light on deceitful or dishonest business dealings, disclosing for public scrutiny one-sided transactions that take advantage of the weaker party. Likewise, the church raises its voice against legal proceedings that privilege the wealthy or strong at the expense of the poor or weak. This includes the insistence upon access to proper legal representation for those who cannot afford their own attorney.

Three Leaders for Social Justice

These five virtues come to expression in unique ways through the lives of three exemplary saints—Dorothy Day, Oscar Romero, and Mother Teresa—who embody the character of the body of Christ in action. Each of these figures was not only personally engaged but became significant leaders in movements for social justice.

Dorothy Day

Dorothy Day (1897–1980) was born in Brooklyn, baptized in the Episcopal Church, and raised in the metropolitan areas of San Francisco and Chicago. Although always a person of genuine religious sensibilities, for most of her early adulthood she lived a Bohemian lifestyle, considering Christianity bourgeois. During these years Day worked as a journalist, mainly in New York, especially for progressive or socialist newspapers. Already at this early stage in her life, she became a political activist in a circle that included artists, intellectuals, and political radicals. In 1926, while living with a beloved man, Day underwent a conversion to Christianity that forever altered the course of her life. Upon becoming pregnant, she discovered her need for God and experienced thereby what she described as "natural happiness."[27] Leaving behind her immediate past, Day sought baptism for her daughter in the Roman Catholic Church. Her own baptism soon followed in 1927. Her conversion led to Day's separation from the father of her child and to personal questioning about whether she had also turned her back on the causes for which she had been so actively engaged, in particular the needs of the poor. Years of spiritual wandering were to follow, as Day found herself "raising her child alone, while praying for some way of reconciling her faith and her commitment to social justice."[28]

Day continued her journalistic career, now also writing for Roman Catholic papers, such as *Commonweal*. Upon meeting Peter Maurin, a philosopher and political activist, in 1932, she discovered a soul mate who helped her conjoin Christian commitment with passion for the poor. In solidarity with the working class, *The Catholic Worker* began as a newspaper on May 1, 1933, and soon evolved into a movement to extend the radical hospitality of Jesus to the poor and destitute of New York during these years of economic depression. Together Maurin and Day sought to move beyond the denunciation of injustice to the inauguration of a new social order, taking seriously Jesus' promise that we encounter him in the person of our neighbor in need. Moreover, Day sought to actualize the church's social teachings in relationship to the Roman Catholic working class. *The Catholic Worker* office was renovated as a "house of hospitality" for the hungry, sick, and homeless, where the guests received the physical necessities of life, restoration of their human dignity, and the opportunity to participate in the cause. The fundamental spiritual attitude was one of voluntary poverty and manual labor. As the years went on, more than one hundred Catholic Worker houses were founded in communities both within the U.S. and across the world, mainly in cities but also as communal farms (which most closely accorded with Maurin's own imagination).

Not only does the life of Dorothy Day demonstrate dramatic concern for social justice, but she also acted as an advocate for nonviolence based on Jesus' teachings in the Sermon on the Mount. Beginning with World War II, subsequently during the Cold War, and including the war in Vietnam, Day engaged in social protest and acts of civil disobedience to witness to Christ's nonviolent alternative. Yet the daily witness of her faith centered on ministry among the poor in very personal interactions—welcoming others, addressing physical needs, showing in deed the love of Christ, and inviting them to join in community. Day understood finally that it was not by talk but by action that the world is changed: "I have long since come to believe that people never mean half of what they say, and that it is best to disregard their talk and judge only their actions."[29]

In many ways Day was a traditional Catholic in her piety. For example, she criticized the sexual revolution of the 1960s, having seen the debilitating effects of similar developments in the 1920s. She found spiritual support for her ministry in the liturgy of the church and in prayer, discovering a particular source of inspiration from the life of St. Therese of Lisieux. Day demonstrated loyalty to the Catholic Church and its social teachings, drawing radical implications for praxis from the church's teachings about liberating the poor and oppressed:

> What we would like to do is change the world—make it a little simpler for people to feed, clothe, and shelter themselves as God intended them to do. And to a certain extent, by fighting for better conditions, by crying out unceasingly for the rights of the workers, of the poor, of the destitute—the rights of the worthy and the unworthy poor, in other words—we can to a certain extent, change the world; we can work for the oasis, the little cell of joy and peace in a harried world. We can throw our pebble in the pond and be confident that its ever-widening circle will reach around the world.
>
> We repeat, there is nothing we can do but love, and, dear God—please enlarge our hearts to love each other, to love our neighbor, to love our enemy as our friend.[30]

In 1971 Day received the *Pacem in Terris* (Peace on Earth) award, named after the 1963 encyclical of Pope John XXIII. She, however, characteristically dismissed such acclaim saying: "Don't call me a saint. I don't want to be dismissed so easily."[31]

Dorothy Day authored an autobiography, *The Long Loneliness*, in 1952 and an account of the Catholic Worker movement, *Loaves and Fishes*, in 1963.[32] She directed the work of the Catholic Worker, a lay movement, for nearly fifty years. The ministry of the Catholic Worker fused together acts of charity in caring for the physical needs of the poor with advocacy for social justice. Although Day never held an official position in the church, her witness has become one of the most influential testimonies to Christian love in the twentieth century, "serving Christ not only through prayer and sacrifice but through solidarity with the poor and in struggle along the path of justice and peace."[33] She knew very well that the only way this work could be sustained for the long haul was through life together: "We have all known the long loneliness and we have learned that the only solution is love and that love comes with community."[34]

Oscar Arnulfo Romero

A different sort of conversion marked the life of Oscar Arnulfo Romero (1917–1980), the conversion from traditional Catholicism and conventional Christian piety to passionate defense of the poor in El Salvador. When Romero was elected archbishop of San Salvador in 1977, he was understood to be a preserver of the status quo. This no doubt satisfied the desires of the privileged classes, who wanted no interference with their policies of repressing dissent during these years of social upheaval. As he entered into the struggle facing the people of El Salvador, however, Romero was converted from endorsing the policies of the government to becoming a vigorous advocate for the poor and suffering. A key moment in this conversion process was the murder of his friend, Rutilio Grande, a progressive Jesuit priest who was an outspoken advocate for social justice. Romero presided at the funeral and was forced into deep and serious reflection about where to take his stand in the midst of the violence overtaking his country.

El Salvador had been ruled for generations by "fourteen families" who profited greatly at the expense of the poor majority. This oligarchy controlled not only the regional but also the national government. For Romero as archbishop, to break from supporting the traditional policies of the privileged classes set him on a course that would eventually lead to his death. One of the most influential and provocative platforms for Romero as archbishop was the weekly sermon he delivered which was broadcast on radio throughout the country. He used this venue to reveal the extent of the violence, human rights violations, and repression experienced by those who were demanding justice. Even more, he began to interpret the theology of the church as gospel for the poor:

> When we speak of the church of the poor, we are not using Marxist dialectic, as though there were another church of the rich. What we are saying is that Christ, inspired by the Spirit of God, declared, "The Lord has sent me to preach good news to the poor"—words of the Bible—so that to hear him one must become poor. (December 3, 1978)[35]

Such interpretation of the Scriptures, advocating God's preferential option for the poor in the categories of liberation theology, alienated Romero increasingly not only from the political establishment but also from many of his fellow bishops. If the political and social conditions in El Salvador required a choice between privilege and the poor, Romero had made his decision.

Week after week, Romero followed his conscience in defending the cause of the voiceless. This cost him dearly in terms of personal loneliness, alienation from colleagues, and even fear for his life. He was accused of transforming the Christian message into a radical political agenda. In an open letter to President Jimmy Carter of February 17, 1980, Romero advocated an end to U.S. military aid to the Salvadoran government and the cessation of all "military, economic, diplomatic, or other pressures, in determining the destiny of the Salvadoran people."[36] Ever more boldly, Romero continued to call for an end to poverty, social injustice, torture, and assassinations. On March 23, 1980, he went so far as to instruct members of the military to disobey orders that commanded them to violate the human rights of their fellow citizens:

> I would like to make an appeal in a special way to the men of the army . . . Brothers, you are part of our own people. You kill your own *campesino* brothers and sisters. And before an order to kill that a man may give, the law of God must prevail that says: Thou shalt not kill! . . . In the name of God, and in the name of our suffering people

whose laments rise to heaven each day more tumultuous, I beg you, I ask you, I order
you in the name of God: Stop the repression![37]

The confrontation between Romero and the prevailing powers raced toward its
seemingly inevitable climax.

On March 24, Romero was presiding at Mass in the chapel of the cancer hos-
pital of the Carmelite Sisters where he lived. As he stood behind the altar, a single
rifle shot rang out from the rear of the chapel which struck his heart. Romero
became the first bishop murdered at the altar since Thomas Becket in the twelfth
century. The Gospel reading for the service was John 12:23-26, which included
these words: "Unless the grain of wheat falls to the earth and dies, it remains only
a grain. But if it dies, it bears much fruit." The murder of Romero was rapidly
interpreted as his martyrdom by the poor of El Salvador and all those in solidarity
with them. Perhaps even more powerfully than before, Romero's witness revealed
the contradictions between Christian truth and the reality of injustice and violence. Already two weeks before his murder, he had commented on the possibility
of his assassination:

> I have frequently been threatened with death. I must say that, as a Christian, I do not
> believe in death but in the resurrection. If they kill me, I will rise again in the people
> of El Salvador. . . . Martyrdom is a grace from God that I do not believe I have earned.
> But if God accepts the sacrifice of my life, then may my blood be the seed of liberty,
> and a sign of the hope that will soon become a reality. . . . A bishop will die, but the
> church of God—the people—will never die.[38]

The truth of this prophecy has been enacted frequently in the liturgies of the
people. Across Latin America and indeed across the world, as the names of the martyrs are read, the people respond with the acclamation: "*Presente!*" Oscar Romero,
like Rutilio Grande and thousands of others martyred for the cause of justice and
peace, remains present and alive in the collective person Jesus Christ, the church.

In 1997 the cause of beatification and sainthood was opened for Romero in the
Roman Catholic Church, a process that continues. Pope John Paul I designated
Romero as "Servant of God" and he is honored by other Christian traditions as a
martyr of the faith. Jon Sobrino writes, "It was not simply that he imitated Jesus,
as do so many other Christians. No, he made the defense of the poor and oppressed
a specific and basic function of his episcopal ministry. His pastoral activity clearly
put him on their side. He denounced the destitution from which they suffered,
and its causes. He identified himself with them. He defended their interests."[39]
As with Dorothy Day, the life of Oscar Romero embodied the virtues of the body
of Christ in the cause of holiness as justice, demonstrating solidarity with the
oppressed and preferential concern for the poor.

MOTHER TERESA

Mother Teresa of Calcutta (1910–1997) walked a path of humble service to the destitute and hopeless, witnessing to the entire world of the love and compassion of Jesus. Born as Agnes Gonxha Bojaxhui to a family of Albanian descent, already at the age of twelve she experienced the call of God to serve as a missionary. Upon joining the Sisters of Loretto, she soon was sent to India to work as a teacher in the order's school in Calcutta. Deeply affected by the city's extreme poverty and suffering, in 1948 she was granted permission to follow God's call to take up a new ministry of primary care for the sick, homeless, and abandoned: "[God] wanted me to be poor with the poor and to love him in the distressing disguise of the poorest of the poor."[40]

Wearing a white sari with a blue border, she soon became known as Mother Teresa as she sought out the presence of Jesus in the poor, sick, and forgotten people on the streets of Calcutta. Joined by others in this service, including some of her former students, together they became the Missionaries of Charity in 1950. Early on, the Missionaries of Charity organized an open-air school for slum children. They saw their central purpose in caring for those children of God nobody else was prepared to receive. As the years unfolded, Mother Teresa organized centers of service around the world to care for the sick, homeless, and discarded ones. In particular her work became associated with a home for the dying in Calcutta. Here men, women, and children in the last stage of their lives were taken from the streets, bestowed with physical care, and welcomed with hospitality. "Those who had lived like 'animals in the gutter' were enabled, in Mother Teresa's home, to 'die like angels'—knowing that they were truly valued and loved as precious children of God."[41]

The Missionaries of Charity were sometimes subject to criticism for not engaging in the work of advocacy to change the social structures which led to extreme suffering. However, the work of advocacy, while having its own importance, was not understood as the *charism* of this order, which instead devoted itself, body and soul, to close encounter with the needs of particular persons:

> We have the specific task of giving material and spiritual help to the poorest of the poor, not only the ones in the slums but those who live in any corner of the world as well.
>
> To do this, we make ourselves live the love of God in prayer and in our work, through a life characterized by the simplicity and humility of the gospel. We do this by loving Jesus in the bread of the Eucharist, and loving and serving him hidden under the painful guise of the poorest of the poor, whether their poverty is a material poverty or a spiritual one. We do this by recognizing them (and giving back to them) the image and likeness of God.[42]

We discover in the work of Mother Teresa and the Missionaries of Charity a deep mystical awareness of Christ's real presence in the persons of the poor, sick, and dying.

Since her death some attention has been focused on Mother Teresa's religious doubt and struggles with the faith.[43] In many ways these revelations only help ground her more fully in the human predicament where we all "walk by faith, not by sight" (2 Cor 5:7). Regardless of her own personal struggles, however, God worked through her life to deliver love, mercy, and justice to "the least of these." In 1979 Mother Teresa was awarded the Nobel Peace Prize. Since her death in 1997, the Roman Catholic Church has initiated a process that has led to her beatification and is examining her future canonization as a saint. More importantly, the ministry of the Missionaries of Charity has continued to touch the lives of thousands through the 610 missions in 123 countries that were operating at the time of her death. When asked by people how they might join in her work, Mother Teresa typically asked them to minister to the poor in their own context:

> I want you to find the poor here, right in your own home first. And begin love there.
> Be that good news to your own people. And find out about your next-door neighbor.
> Do you know who they are? [44]

These words challenge us to live out the virtues of justice in our own communities where we live: solidarity with the oppressed, hospitality to strangers, care for the physical needs of others, and preferential concern for the weak.

Practicing Justice as Ministering Community

The biblical narrative of God's holiness and justice forms the character of the body of Christ and shapes God's people in the corresponding virtues. These virtues come to expression in the lives of those who live already now according to God's justice agenda. The character and virtues of the church as the body of Christ, Christ existing as church-community, are embodied in practices that reflect the Christian value of universal justice.

The first congregational activity that opens the door to justice is *the practice of hospitality*. Christian hospitality in the church begins with the recognition of God's radical hospitality to us! In Jesus Christ God has extended to us the invitation to join him at table. Nothing separates us from the love of God in Christ Jesus (Rom 8:39). Just as Jesus welcomed sinners and tax collectors—in effect all people—to come and eat with him, so the church—Christ existing as community—extends a blessed welcome to strangers and those in every kind of need to find a home in its midst.

While congregations generally view themselves as welcoming places, we need to do honest self-examination about what we mean by the term *friendly church*. Too often what we may really mean is: "If you become one of us, then we will be friendly to you." For a few people who share the same particular demographics of ethnicity, age, and class as most members of the congregation, it may be possible for them to become "like us." However, this excludes vast numbers of people from experiencing the hospitality that Jesus seeks to offer to those who are different from us. There are many persons who, due to core aspects of their identity, will never be "one of us," insofar as that would require a change of color, national origin, or culture. How can the church of Jesus Christ become that community which anticipates with excitement the new gifts that those different from ourselves will inevitably bring into our midst, rather than being just another community based on the conventional markers of human society?

Starting with worship, congregations need to learn the art of hospitality. How can we stretch our imaginations to anticipate the experience of those who might come as strangers to our church? This means not only reflecting on structural barriers that might prevent access to the congregation but, even more, it means deconstructing social barriers. Congregations well practiced in the art of hospitality have much to teach those less skilled. How can we not only become passive recipients of the people who walk in the door, but actively invite those who are different from us to know the friendship of Christ in our midst? This entails readiness to be changed by those who are different. Every serious relationship with another person changes everyone involved. How can we become ready and eager to be changed by what people new to us will bring to enrich our life together?

Beyond worship and the communion of the Lord's Table, congregations need to examine other communal eating practices. One of the basic signs of a welcoming and hospitable church involves how it gathers together at table to break bread.[45] How does your congregation engage in communal meals? Do you share good food lovingly prepared? Is there enough for all? How do people seat themselves in relation to their neighbors? Is there room at the table for outsiders? How can we grow in the hospitality we practice at the congregational dinners we already hold? How can we plan other meals that intentionally invite strangers into our midst, in order to build friendship?

A second core congregational ministry which serves justice is *the practice of charity and generosity*. There is incredible need for the church's generosity in sharing with others the basic necessities of life: food, clean water, shelter, clothing, and basic medical care. Moreover, many need access to fundamental education in order to be able to fend more ably for themselves. The opportunities for sharing our own means with those in need are many, both locally and afar. One ethical question often comes to the fore: How do we prioritize our giving? Yet another question may be even more critical: How do we learn to become more generous? On the local level, priority can be given to those ministries that allow members to offer not only financial support but active participation. Food pantries, housing shelters, used clothing distribution, domestic abuse support services, parish health clinics, and emergency aid are among those ministries organized locally and run by congregations, often ecumenically. Such forms of aid encourage church members to be the body of Christ in action. On a broader horizon, priority can be given to denominational efforts to relieve human suffering through hunger programs, development projects, health assistance, and crisis response. Those ministries organized and sponsored by denominations are among the most effective and economically reliable of all relief agencies. Information on the efforts of particular denominations is easily accessible on the respective websites.

The practice of charity and generosity begins with education about the reality of the need. This is accomplished most effectively by sharing first-hand accounts about particular situations. Congregations need to engage in sustained efforts at becoming knowledgeable about both chronic conditions of need and times of immediate crisis. Sermons, audio-visual presentations, forums, announcements, written materials, and online communications must consistently stress the connection between acts of charity and being the body of Christ. Church budgets should reflect the priority of benevolence giving by listing these line items first on the balance sheet and by increasing the percentage of congregational giving on an annual basis to a tithe and beyond, steadily increasing the percentage of the congregational budget given to works of charity. Special appeals also mobilize needed resources for works of mercy. These are again most effective when opportunities to give money are accompanied by ways to become personally involved. For sustaining and growing in generosity in response to the needs of others, it is vital for congregation members to gain personal experience in confronting the reality of human need.

A third congregational focus that serves God's justice is *the practice of healing ministry*. Congregations have long been at the forefront of healing ministry by praying for and visiting the sick. The church as a whole has also been attentive to the need for healing through the hospitals, agencies, and social ministry organizations that have been formed and sustained to promote human health. The healing ministry of Jesus Christ has been extended in these concrete ways to the lives of hundreds of millions of people over the generations. Yet the need for healing ministry continues in the present day. Concern for healing is one of the unique vocations of the church of Jesus Christ, in comparison to many other helping organizations. Healing ministry brings the church into immediate relationship to the unique needs of particular persons. By listening to, respecting, and praying for the yearnings of God's children, the Spirit continues to work miracles of healing. Such miracles affect not only physical but also emotional, spiritual, and social healing.

One ancient practice that is being restored with tremendous benefit in the life of many congregations is the service of healing as a dimension of Christian worship. Rites of healing allow worshipers to name their own need for healing and to focus on the needs of others for particular forms of healing. Such services mediate the healing power of Jesus in powerful ways that repair and sustain life. Liturgies of healing can allow for both the general participation of a worshiping congregation in the historic practice of the laying on of hands with prayer and more intimate personalized prayers for healing with a trusted confidant. The healing of persons has immediate implications for the healing of relationships and the healing of community. Wherever relationships and communities are healed, there also is an increase in justice. One further extension of the healing ministry by congregations involves the implementation of parish nursing programs. By incorporating the ministry of parish nurses into the life of the congregation, the church professionalizes a form of basic medical care and adds a dimension to holistic healing by uniting concern for medical health with spiritual well-being. Many denominations have models for organizing parish nursing programs.[46]

A fourth form of ministry with implications for the life of congregations is *the practice of restorative justice*. Restorative justice is distinct from and to be contrasted with retributive justice. Whereas retributive justice seeks to dole out punishment for past offenses, restorative justice aims at reestablishing the offender(s) into community. Restorative justice aims to repair and heal the harm caused to the victim(s) by the offender(s).[47] Restorative justice is best accomplished by an inclusive process, involving all affected parties, but with special safeguards to protect the victim(s) from further harm. Core principles of restorative justice include the convictions that (1) justice entails working directly with those parties most directly affected by an injury and that (2) those directly involved in the offense should have the opportunity to participate in the process to whatever degree they choose. Restorative justice often involves making reparations, rather than focusing on punishment. Reparations can include material payments, but especially seek to bring about relational healing and the restoration of community.

The practice of restorative justice has been employed with beneficial effects in several "Truth and Reconciliation" processes in countries ravaged by brutal conflict, for example, in South Africa following the end of apartheid and in Rwanda following the genocide. In South Africa, particular attention was paid to the testimony of victims, whose experiences were granted validation by the nature of the public process, which often included the physical presence of the offenders who had violated them.[48] The process aimed at attaining as much reconciliation between victims and offenders as possible, with offenders being given the opportunity to confess their guilt and in some cases being granted amnesty. The granting of amnesty has been one of the most controversial aspects of the truth and reconciliation processes. In the wake of the crimes of genocide, the challenges to any truth and reconciliation process are enormous insofar as vast numbers of victims were murdered and can no longer speak for themselves; yet such a process remains imperative for the emergence of an equitable post-genocide society.

Also in the arena of criminal justice, the principles of restorative justice have been employed constructively. Victims of crimes are offered the opportunity to participate in a process designed to restore offenders to community, with offenders taking responsibility for their actions and making reparations to those offended. Trained mediators structure any and every encounter between victims and offenders, especially to protect the vulnerability of victims. The participation of victims is always voluntary. Congregations with a calling in the area of prison ministry can especially benefit from instruction in the restorative justice process. Given the church's commitment to confession and absolution in the name of Jesus Christ, there is a striking affinity between the process of restorative justice and the church's ministry of reconciliation. What the church needs to learn from restorative justice is the imperative to protect victims every step of the way, for example, in cases dealing with sexual abuse in the church. The principles of restorative justice also have salutary implications for the mediation of some forms of church conflict. The church, with its emphasis on confession and forgiveness, does well to learn the practice of restorative justice as a process in which it refines its skills for mediating conflict.

A fifth ministry by which the church as the body of Christ promotes justice is *the practice of advocacy, holding accountable the privileged and those in authority*. As the biblical narrative recounts, the prophets spoke truth to those in power and held them responsible for misusing their power at the expense of the weak. The church takes up the prophetic mantle in advocating for equitable treatment of all those disadvantaged by their lack of economic resources and/or political influence. Typically, these two go hand in hand, economic wealth and political clout. The primary work of advocacy by the church is not to look out for its own self-interest, seeking advantages for itself as a religious organization. Instead, the church intentionally takes up the perspective of the poor and disenfranchised, analyzing economic exchanges and political transactions according to their impact on those in the system whose voices are weakest. Here again the work of advocacy organizations provides invaluable information and direction to the church as it engages in the practice of advocacy. Both offices of public policy within denominations and ecumenical advocacy organizations, like Bread for the World, provide accurate information, astute analysis, and constructive action steps that are highly effective in promoting the well-being of people in material need.[49] All the church's important works of charity must be accompanied by consistent engagement in advocacy, in order to address the root causes of human suffering and material deprivation.

In this chapter I have explored the creedal confession about the holiness of the church in relation to the church's social justice ministry. I have reflected on the biblical narrative linking God's holiness and the cause of justice. I have explored how this narrative forms the character of the body of Christ, instilling particular virtues and forming it as a justified and justice-making community in the world. I have shown how the virtues of justice have been concretely embodied in the lives of Dorothy Day, Oscar Romero, and Mother Teresa. Lastly, I have considered how congregations can serve God's justice by engaging in particular social ministry practices. In the next chapter I turn to the third classical mark of the church and explore how the confession of the church's catholicity moves the body of Christ into solidarity with the whole creation.

The Body of Christ Is Catholic

The Practice of Care for Creation

What does the Nicene Creed's confession of the church as "catholic" have to do with care for creation? Catholicity has to do with the church's expanse in time and *especially in space*. "The word 'catholic' . . . means: referring to or directed towards the whole, general."[1] Although "catholic" was not a word used to describe the church in the New Testament, it soon became a common descriptor to indicate that which holds together disparate local churches:

> The word is first applied to the Church in the New Testament times by Ignatius of Antioch (died *circa* 110): "Wherever the bishop is, there his people should be, just as, where Jesus Christ is, there is the Catholic Church" (*Smyrn.* 8:2). "Catholic Church" in this context means quite straightforwardly the whole Church, the complete Church, in contrast to local episcopal Churches. . . . [Catholic Church] refers here to the increasingly apparent reality of a whole Church, within which the individual Churches are bound up together, a general and all-embracing Church.[2]

It is this impulse toward encompassing the whole, toward universality, and toward generality that directs this inquiry into the relation of catholicity to care for creation.

Particularly after the emergence of Constantinian Christianity in the fourth century, the idea of catholicity took on three additional dimensions, those of orthodoxy, geography, and numerical increase. That the catholicity of the church came to entail orthodoxy in the face of heresy is well summarized by the famous reference from Vincent of Lérins (died c. 435):

> Moreover, in the Catholic Church itself, all possible care must be taken, that we hold that faith which has been believed everywhere, always, by all. For that is truly and in the strictest sense "Catholic," which, as the name itself and the reason of the thing declare, comprehends all universally. This rule we shall observe if we follow universality, antiquity, consent. We shall follow universality if we confess that one faith to be true, which the whole Church throughout the world confesses; antiquity, if we in no wise depart from those interpretations which it is manifest were notoriously held by our holy ancestors and fathers; consent, in like manner, if in antiquity itself we adhere to the consentient definitions and determinations of all, or at the least of almost all priests and doctors.[3]

Hans Küng describes the significance of the geographical and numerical senses that accrued to the word "catholic" in this way:

> The greater extent and numerical growth of the Church added to the senses of the words *"ecclesia catholica"* which we have noted, that is a total, all-embracing Church (the original ecclesiological meaning) and an orthodox Church (second polemical meaning) a new idea, that of a Church extending over the whole earth (geographical catholicity) and of a Church much larger in numbers than any other (numerical catholicity).[4]

For an ethical appropriation of "catholicity" for the life of the church in its social ministry, I will focus on the primal meaning of the word "catholic" as having to do with the whole, exploring the implications of this affirmation for the creation itself. In particular I will build upon the affirmation that catholicity involves, above all, the presence of Jesus Christ in the church: wherever Christ is present, there is also the catholic church.

> [T]he church's catholicity is determined by the universal, all-uniting presence of Christ. In this case what is meant is the church whole and entire, as it is in Christ. That includes its spatial catholicity—its presence in all parts of the inhabited earth (the *oikumene*) and its temporal catholicity—its presence in all periods of history.[5]

Jürgen Moltmann stresses the provisional character of the church's catholicity at the present time in anticipation of its eschatological fulfillment. The future eschatological goal of realized catholicity implies the mission of the church to the whole. The church's catholicity involves the universality and "unlimited breadth of its apostolic mission."[6]

> The church is catholic in its mission, because in its proclamation it appeals to people who do not belong to it, and because *it does not accept that there is any sphere which Christ*

would not have claimed for his own from the beginning. Thanks to its hope it cannot surrender any individual person *or any part of creation.*[7]

Moltmann identifies the core impulse of the catholic mission of God to restore not only humanity into the universal church but all of creation into an *apokatastasis panton*, the universal restoration of all things to God.[8] Over the course of history, the church has been far more articulate about God's universal mission to humanity than about the mission to the creation.[9] The horizon of creation has fallen into forgetfulness with the church's focus on human salvation. The urgency of the global ecological crisis, however, demands at this juncture in history that the full ramifications of the church's catholicity in relation to the creation be made explicit. We as human beings are in essence constituted of the self-same catholic matter as the universe itself.

The catholic impulse that directs the church's universal mission aims at the creation of a new heaven and new earth (Rev 21:1). Paul articulated the eschatological hope for God becoming "all in all" (1 Cor 15:28). The ultimate destiny of creation is not annihilation but transformation.[10] Moltmann interprets the biblical promises this way:

> God does not de-restrict himself in order to annihilate his creation, and in it to be "all in all." The primordial time and the primordial space of creation will end when creation becomes the temple for God's eternal Shekinah. The *temporal* creation will then become an eternal creation, because all created beings will participate in God's eternity. The *spatial* creation will then become an omnipresent creation, because all created beings will participate in God's omnipresence.[11]

"All created beings will participate . . ."! Insofar as God's eternal future is to incorporate the restoration of all things into God's presence, it is vital that our present conceptions of salvation and ecclesiology become commensurate with this expansive eschatological vision.

In the history of doctrine, both soteriology and ecclesiology conventionally have been constructed in an almost exclusively human-centric fashion. However, the slowly dawning recognition about the world as an ecological system and the urgency of the global ecological crisis require a far more expansive, even cosmic, construal of these central concepts. It is within the environment of a new heaven and new earth that eternal life unfolds for a recreated humanity.

> We are often inclined to relate the "environment" only to the thinking subject living in it, thus reducing the environment to a thing. Men and women tend towards anthropocentrism. They call nature—which after all is the home of many plants and animals—"*our* environment" or "*our* planetary house," as a way of appropriating it.

But we see the earth as the environment for plants, animals and human beings, the
sea as the environment for fish, and the air as the environment for birds. It was ecological wisdom when the author of the first creation account talked first of all about
the creation of environments, and only after that about the living things corresponding to them.[12]

Following this line of thought, the confession of a catholic church—meaning the
body of Christ extended throughout space and time—entails the incorporation of
all creation into Christ as the animating reality within whom "we live and move
and have our being" (Acts 17:28). Just as humanity exists "in Christ," so also the
creation itself is called to life in Christ. A catholic church, like humanity itself, is
located always within the environment of creation and lives in symbiosis with that
environment. Without the larger nexus of creation, there would be no humanity
and thereby no church. This is true not only in the present era but will also be true
eternally. Because of the dependence of humans on the well-being of creation, it is
imperative for humanity to relate to creation in a fundamental posture of stewardship and care.

This chapter explores the significance of the church's catholicity for the entire
creation. The impulse toward catholicity needs to be broadened to incorporate
the horizon of all creation, if for no other reason than that we as humans are
constituted of the same stuff as the rest of creation. The new creation certainly
does include a new humanity in Christ, but this new humanity only survives in
symbiotic relationship with the larger environment of which it has always been
a part. What has been implicit for generations must now become explicit: the
total dependence of humanity, and thus the church, upon a healthy ecosphere.
Shalom involves the restoration of life-giving relationships between humanity and
all creatures, plants, and elements. Shalom church attends to the complexity of
these relationships in an attitude of care.[13] I turn next to the biblical narrative that
undergirds these claims for the ethical responsibility of the body of Christ in the
stewardship of creation.

The Biblical Narrative: God's Care for Creation[14]

"In the beginning when God created the heavens and the earth . . ." (Gen 1:1). So
begins the Scripture's first creation narrative. Unlike those religions that denigrate
creation in favor of some kind of disembodied existence, biblical faith begins with
the fundamental affirmation of the very goodness of creation itself. Each dimension of creation was added by God in its proper niche; each dimension was created
good (Gen 1:4, 10, 12, 18, 21, 25, 31). Light, darkness, sky, earth, plants, sun,

moon, stars, sea creatures, birds of the air, living creatures, cattle, creeping things, wild animals, human beings—all are blessed by God as good! And to human beings, God gave a particular charge as those made in God's image: "Be fruitful and multiply, and fill the earth and subdue it; and have dominion over the fish of the sea and over the birds of the air and over every living thing that moves upon the earth" (Gen 1:28). What God intended as a command for human beings to act responsibly—stewarding and caring for the earth—has too often been interpreted by us as rationale for exploitation. Dominion is not domination. Dominion entails accountability to God who is the creator and *dominus* (Lord) of all created things!

The second creation narrative places Adam in the garden of Eden, a creature forged from the dust of the earth and animated by divine breath (Gen 2:7):

> And the Lord God planted a garden in Eden, in the east; and there he put the man whom he had formed. Out of the ground the Lord God made to grow every tree that is pleasant to the sight and good for food, the tree of life also in the midst of the garden, and the tree of the knowledge of good and evil. (Gen 2:9)

Here too God gives Adam a particular charge: "The Lord God took the man and put him in the garden of Eden to till it and keep it" (Gen 2:15). The Scripture again stresses how the human being is created with responsibility to care for God's creation. When no fitting helpmate for the man is identified among all the other living creatures, God creates woman as his partner, forming her from the very rib of the man (Gen 2:18-23). Eve becomes with Adam a keeper of the garden.

Together man and woman reside in the garden as God's splendid gift. Failing to recognize their limits, however, that they are creatures and not gods, all too soon they transgress the boundary God had established for them, eating the fruit of the forbidden tree, bringing disaster upon themselves with consequences for the whole creation:

> [C]ursed is the ground because of you; in toil you shall eat of it all the days of your life; thorns and thistles it shall bring forth for you; and you shall eat of the plants of the field. By the sweat of your face you shall eat bread until you return to the ground, for out of it you were taken; you are dust and to dust you shall return. (Gen 3:17-19)

Because human beings failed to obey the charge God had given them, not only do they fall into strife (Cain murders Abel) and face destruction (the punishment of the great flood), but the entire creation comes out of joint. While God chooses to deliver from the flood Noah and his family, together with pairs of all living creatures (male and female), to whom it is given to replenish the earth, the primordial narrative warns about the consequences of human sinfulness affecting the whole creation. Let the rainbow serve as a reminder of the covenant God made not only with humanity but "with every living creature" (Gen 9:12, 15, 16), never again to destroy the earth and its creatures by flooding!

The Bible is replete with other creation stories. Psalm 102 recounts: "Long ago you laid the foundation of the earth, and the heavens are the work of your hands" (v. 25). Psalm 104 rejoices in the heavens, the earth, the waters, and all their creatures:

> O Lord, how manifold are your works!
>> In wisdom you have made them all;
>> The earth is full of your creatures.
> Yonder is the sea, great and wide,
>> creeping things innumerable are there,
>> living things both small and great.
> There go the ships,
>> and Leviathan that you formed to sport in it.
> These all look to you
>> to give them their food in due season;
> when you give to them, they gather it up;
>> when you open your hand, they are filled with good things.
> When you hide your face, they are dismayed;
>> when you take away their breath, they die
>> and return to their dust.
> When you send forth your spirit, they are created;
>> and you renew the face of the ground. (vv. 24-30)

Notice both the delight in created goodness and the emphasis on how all creation is dependent upon God for its sustenance.

The prophet Isaiah also celebrated God as Creator:

> For thus says the Lord, who created the heavens (he is God!), who formed the earth and made it (he established it; he did not create it a chaos, he formed it to be inhabited!): I am the Lord, and there is no other. (Isa 45:18)
>
> For as the rain and the snow come down from heaven, and do not return there until they have watered the earth, making it bring forth and sprout, giving seed to the sower and bread to the eater, so shall my word be that goes out from my mouth; it shall not return to me empty, but it shall accomplish that which I purpose, and succeed in the thing for which I sent it. (Isa 55:10-11)

It is by the power of God's Word that creation came into existence at the beginning, and it is by the power of God's Word that creation continues to come into being and find its sustenance.

Also in the wisdom literature we find echoes of God's creative powers. The book of Proverbs adds the insight that it was through the mediation of Wisdom that God created the world (Prov 8:22-36). And in reply to Job's complaints, God thunders:

> Where were you when I laid the foundation of the earth?
> Tell me, if you have understanding.
> Who determined its measurements—surely you know!
> Or who stretched the line upon it?
> On what were its bases sunk,
> or who laid its cornerstone
> when the morning stars sang together
> and all the heavenly beings shouted for joy?
> Or who shut in the sea with doors
> when it burst out from the womb?—
> when I made the clouds its garment,
> and thick darkness its swaddling band,
> and prescribed bounds for it,
> and set bars and doors,
> and said, "Thus far shall you come, and no farther,
> and here shall your proud waves be stopped." (Job 38:4-11)

God is sovereign over the created order, whose wisdom transcends all human attempts at comprehension. All flesh exists to bless God's holy name (Ps 145:21).

One of the most significant promises of God to Israel involves the gift of the land, "a land flowing with milk and honey" (Exod 2:8):

> For the Lord your God is bringing you into a good land, a land with flowing streams, with springs and underground waters welling up in valleys and hills, a land of wheat and barley, of vines and fig trees and pomegranates, a land of olive trees and honey, a land where you may eat bread without scarcity, where you will lack nothing, a land whose stones are iron and from whose hills you may mine copper. You shall eat your fill and bless the Lord your God for the good land that he has given you. (Deut 8:7-10)

The people of God are to order their life on the land to provide for all, safeguarding through law the well-being of animals and birds (Exod 22:9-14; Deut 21:6-7; Deut 25:4) and allowing the earth to be renewed by the practices of Sabbath (Deut 5:12-14; Lev 25:1-7). The people of Israel will be rewarded by God for their obedience to the law through the fruitfulness of earth:

> If you follow my statutes and keep my commandments and observe them faithfully, I will give you your rains in their season, and the land shall yield its produce, and the

trees of the field shall yield their fruit. . . . And I will grant peace in the land, and you shall lie down, and no one shall make you afraid; I will remove dangerous animals from the land, and no sword shall go through your land. (Lev 26:3, 6)

Conversely, Israel will be punished for disobedience by devastations to the land and its produce (Deut 28:15-46).

Through the world of nature, God works weal and woe. The people make elaborate sacrifices to God of grain and animals (Jer 17:26; Leviticus 1), gifts of God precious to them. Israel demonstrates gratitude to God by offering the first fruits of the harvest as an act of thanksgiving (Lev 23:9; Deut 26:1-2). God is revealed through theophany and miracles in the creation: the burning bush (Exod 3:2-5), the parting of the sea (Exod 14:21), on the mountain (Exod 24:16-17), a cloud (Exod 40:34-38), the appearance of quail (Num 11:31), water from a rock (Num 20:7-12), the sending of snakes (Num 21:6-7), provision in the wilderness (Deut 8:1-3), the sun standing still (Josh 10:12-13), or water to quench thirst (Judg 15:18-19; 1 Kings 3:16-17). "The heavens are telling the glory of God; and the firmament proclaims his handiwork" (Ps 19:1). Conversely, God punishes evildoers through plagues wrought through the natural world (Exod 7:14-10:29; 1 Chron 21:11-17). Frequently in the writings of the prophets, God wreaks havoc in the creation as a means of dispensing justice: "I will utterly sweep away everything from the face of the earth, says the Lord. I will sweep away humans and animals; I will sweep away the birds of the air and the fish of the sea. I will make the wicked stumble. I will cut off humanity from the face of the earth, says the Lord" (Zeph 1:2-3; cf. Jer 12:10-13; Ezek 6:14; Hos 2:12; Joel 1:4-12; Amos 4:7-9; Hab 3:8-12; Hag 1:7-11).

The prophets of Israel anticipate the restoration of the shalom of creation in the coming messianic age:

I will open rivers on the bare heights, and fountains in the midst of the valleys; I will make the wilderness a pool of water, and the dry land springs of water. I will put in the wilderness the cedar, the acacia, the myrtle, and the olive; I will set in the desert the cypress, the plane and the pine together, so that all may see and know, all may consider and understand, that the hand of the Lord has done this, the Holy One of Israel has created it. (Isa 41:18-20)

The wild animals will honor me, the jackals and the ostriches; for I give water in the wilderness, rivers in the desert, to give drink to my chosen people. (Isa 43:20)

Animals will surrender their enmity with one another and with humanity:

The wolf shall live with the lamb,
    the leopard shall lie down with the kid,
the calf and the lion and the fatling together,

and a little child shall lead them.
The cow and the bear shall graze,
    their young shall lie down together;
    and the lion shall eat straw like the ox.
The nursing child shall play over the hole of the asp,
    and the weaned child shall put its hand on the adder's den.
They will not hurt or destroy
    on all my holy mountain;
for the earth will be full of the knowledge of the Lord
    as the waters cover the sea. (Isa 11:6-9)

Creation will yield its bounty for all, undoing the curse of primordial history:

He will give rain for the seed with which you sow the ground, and grain, the produce of the ground, which will be rich and plenteous. On that day your cattle will graze in broad pastures; and the oxen and donkeys that till the ground will eat silage, which has been winnowed with shovel and fork. (Isa 30:23-24)

The land itself shall display the shalom of God:

Then justice will dwell in the wilderness, and righteousness abide in the fruitful field. (Isa 32:16)
    I will make with them a covenant of peace and banish wild animals from the land, so that they may live in the wild and sleep in the woods securely. I will make them and the region around my hill a blessing; and I will send down the showers in their season; they shall be showers of blessing. The trees of the field shall yield their fruit, and the earth shall yield its increase. (Ezek 34:25-27)
    I will make for you a covenant on that day with the wild animals, the birds of the air, and the creeping things of the ground; and I will abolish the bow, the sword, and war from the land; and I will make you lie down in safety. (Hos 2:18)

God is to rule as the king of creation: "The earth is the Lord's and all that is in it, the world, and those who live in it" (Ps 24:1). Human beings are to live in obedience and accountability to God for the well-being of creation:

When I look at your heavens, the work of your fingers,
    the moon and the stars that you have established;
what are human beings that you are mindful of them,
    mortals that you care for them?
Yet you have made them a little lower than God,
    and crowned them with glory and honor.
You have given them dominion over the works of your hands;
    you have put all things under their feet,
all sheep and oxen,

and also the beasts of the field,
the birds of the air, and the fish of the sea,
    whatever passes along the paths of the seas.
O Lord, our Sovereign,
    how majestic is your name in all the earth! (Ps 8:3-9)

Humankind lives under the charge to steward the creation with responsibility for its health and well-being: "But let justice roll down like the waters, and righteousness like an ever-flowing stream" (Amos 5:24).

With the coming of Jesus, creation continues to play a prominent role in the narrative. A star in the sky marks the location of his birth (Matt 2:9). Jesus goes to the wilderness to face and overcome temptation from the hand of Satan (Matt 4:1). Mountains serve as the setting for dramatic revelations concerning Jesus: the Sermon on the Mount (Matt 5–7), the mount of transfiguration (Matt 17:1), and the mountain of the great commission (Matt 28:16). Jesus demonstrates authority over the chaotic waters, stilling a windstorm on the sea (Matt 8:23-26) and walking on water (Matt 14:25-27). The first disciples of Jesus are fishermen, called at the seashore as Jesus orchestrates a miraculous catch of fish (Luke 5:4-11). Jesus feeds the multitudes with a few fish and loaves of bread (Matt 15:32-38; John 6:1-15). With the coming of the Son of Man, great portents will occur in the sky (Matt 24:29-30). A cock crows as a sign of Peter's denial (Matt 26:34). During the hours of Jesus' crucifixion "darkness came over the whole land" (Matt 27:45). At his death the "earth shook, and the rocks were split" (Matt 27:51). Jesus' burial and first resurrection appearances take place in a garden, where he is at first mistaken for a gardener (John 19:41—20:18).

Creation imagery punctuates the teachings and parables of Jesus. Jesus demonstrates ready familiarity with the created environment and appeals to it regularly, lending insights into the nature of God's activity. Jesus' disciples are "the light of the world" (Matt 5:14), even as Jesus declares about himself: "I am the light of the world. Whoever follows me will never walk in darkness but will have the light of life" (John 8:12). God's generosity is revealed as "he makes his sun to rise on the evil and on the good, and sends rain on the righteous and on the unrighteous" (Matt 5:45). We are to store up for ourselves "treasures in heaven, where neither moth nor rust consumes" (Matt 6:20). In one of his most profound statements about human anxiety, Jesus teaches his followers:

> Therefore I tell you, do not worry about your life, what you will eat or what you will drink, or about your body, what you will wear. Is not life more than food, and the body more than clothing? Look at the birds of the air; they neither sow nor reap nor gather into barns, and yet your heavenly Father feeds them. Are you not of more

value than they? And can any of you by worrying add a single hour to your span of life? And why do you worry about clothing? Consider the lilies of the field, how they grow; they neither toil nor spin, yet I tell you, even Solomon in all his glory was not clothed like one of these. But if God so clothes the grass of the field, which is alive today and tomorrow is thrown into the oven, will he not much more clothe you—you of little faith? Therefore do not worry, saying, "What will we eat?" or "What will we drink?" or "What will we wear?" (Matt 6:25-31)

Here Jesus draws upon familiar examples from God's creation to address one of the most prevalent of human fears, pointing us to God's reliable providence: "You are of more value than many sparrows" (Matt 10:31).

Jesus also draws imagery from the common agrarian world. "A sower went out to sow" (Matt 13:3). Some seed falls on the path, other on the rocky ground, yet other among thorns. "Other seeds fell on good soil and brought forth grain, some a hundredfold, some sixty, some thirty" (Matt 13:8). Such is the kingdom of God! Or again, "The kingdom of heaven is like a mustard seed that someone took and sowed in his field; it is the smallest of all the seeds, but when it has grown it is the greatest of shrubs and becomes a tree, so that the birds of the air come and make nests in its branches" (Matt 13:31-32). Jesus and his followers fall into controversy when they pluck grain on the Sabbath (Mark 2:23-28). Sheep and shepherds also appear frequently in the teachings of Jesus: "Suppose one of you has only one sheep and it falls into a pit on the Sabbath; will you not lay hold of it and lift it out?" (Matt 12:11). Jesus is the Good Shepherd (John 10:14): "What do you think? If a shepherd has a hundred sheep, and one of them has gone astray, does he not leave the ninety-nine on the mountains and go in search of the one that went astray? And if he finds it, truly I tell you, he rejoices over it more than over the ninety-nine that never went astray" (Matt 17:12-13). Moreover, Jesus himself is referred to as the "Lamb of God" (John 1:29).

The sacraments, instituted by Jesus for the faith of his followers, make holy common elements of the created world—water, bread, and wine. Jesus himself was baptized in the waters of the Jordan River (Mark 1:9-10) and the risen Christ commands his disciples to go, make disciples, and baptize (Matt 28:19). According to Mark, they are told: "Go into all the world and proclaim the good news to the whole creation" (Mark 16:15). Jesus identifies himself as "the living water" (John 4:10-15). So too at the Last Supper Jesus blesses ordinary bread and wine, the fruit of the earth, and makes them sacred as his own body and blood (Matt 26:26-28). Jesus says: "I am the bread of life. Whoever comes to me will never be hungry, and whoever believes in me will never be thirsty" (John 6:35).

The entire New Testament affirms God as Creator of the world (Acts 4:24; 1 Cor 8:6) and rehearses God's wondrous deeds worked through nature in Israel (Acts 7:11, 30; 2 Cor 3:7-11; 2 Pet 2:4-9). God continues to work through the created world: Jesus ascends into heaven in a cloud (Acts 1:8-9); Peter receives revelation about the mission to the Gentiles in a vision about animals (Acts 11:4-9). The New Testament adds the conviction that creation took place through the mediation of Christ: "[F]or in him all things in heaven and on earth were created, things visible and invisible, whether thrones or dominions or rulers or powers— all things have been created through him and for him. He himself is before all things, and in him all things hold together" (Col 1:16-17). "He is the reflection of God's glory and the exact imprint of God's very being, and he sustains all things by his powerful word" (Heb 1:3).

According to Paul, God can be known through the created order: "Ever since the creation of the world his eternal power and divine nature, invisible though they are, have been understood and seen through the things he has made" (Rom 1:20). Paul goes on to develop theologically the nature of the fall into sin: "Therefore, just as sin came into the world through one man, and death came through sin, and so death spread to all because all have sinned. . ." (Rom 5:12). Sin has ongoing effects not only on humanity but on the whole creation: "For the creation waits with eager longing for the revealing of the children of God, for the creation was subjected to futility, not of its own will but by the will of the one who subjected it, in hope that the creation itself will be set free from its bondage to decay and will obtain the freedom of the glory of the children of God. We know that the whole creation has been groaning in labor pains until now, and not only the creation, but we ourselves, who have the first fruits of the Spirit, groan inwardly while we wait for adoption, the redemption of our bodies" (Rom 8:19-23).

Final redemption in Christ is not only a human affair, but has consequences for the entire cosmos: "For in him all the fullness of God was pleased to dwell, and through him God was pleased to reconcile to himself all things, whether on earth or in heaven, by making peace through the blood of the cross" (Col 1:19-20). God has revealed in Christ "a plan for the fullness of time, to gather up all things in him, things in heaven and things on earth" (Eph 1:10). At the eschaton, God will be "all in all" (1 Cor 15:28). This involves a new creation: "So if anyone is in Christ, there is a new creation: everything old has passed away; see, everything has become new!" (2 Cor 5:17). "But in accordance with his promise, we wait for new heavens and a new earth, where righteousness is at home" (2 Pet 3:13).

The imagery of the new creation is elaborated most explicitly in the book of Revelation. The tree of life is restored in "the paradise of God" (Rev 3:7). All creatures join in the chorus to sing God's praise: "Then I heard every creature in heaven and on earth and under the earth and in the sea, and all that is in them, singing, 'To the one seated on the throne and to the Lamb be blessing and honor and glory and might forever and ever' " (Rev 5:13). Although in the final apocalyptic battles the forces of evil render harm to the creation (Rev 7:1-3; 8:7-11; 16:20), ultimately a new creation will prevail by God's power:

> Then I saw a new heaven and a new earth; for the first heaven and the first earth had passed away, and the sea was no more. . . . And I heard a loud voice from the throne saying, "See, the home of God is among mortals. He will dwell with them; they will be his peoples, and God himself will be with them." (Rev 21:1, 3)
>
> Then the angel showed me the river of the water of life, bright as crystal, flowing from the throne of God and of the Lamb through the middle of the street of the city. On either side of the river is the tree of life with its twelve kinds of fruit, producing its fruit each month; and the leaves of the tree are for the healing of the nations. (Rev 22:1-2)

A restored creation is the setting for God's eternal shalom!

Human beings as part of God's new creation are "to present their bodies as a living sacrifice, holy and acceptable to God, which is your spiritual worship" (Rom 12:1). We are to have the mind of a servant, "the same mind . . . that was in Christ Jesus" (Phil 2:5). "But you are a chosen race, a royal priesthood, a holy nation, God's own people, in order that you may proclaim the mighty acts of him who called you out of darkness into his marvelous light" (1 Pet 2:9). As members of the body of Christ (1 Cor 12:12-27), we are to bear spiritual fruit: "[T]he fruit of the Spirit is love, joy, peace, patience, kindness, generosity, faithfulness, gentleness, and self-control" (Gal 5:22). God has placed human beings as the crown of creation, "subjecting all things under their feet" (Heb 2:5-8), making us stewards of the splendid universe God has created. Yet God will hold us accountable for "the thoughts and intentions of the heart. And before him no creature is hidden, but all are naked and laid bare to the eyes of the one to whom we must render an account" (Heb 4:12-13).

Character and Virtues in the Body of Christ: Caring for Creation

The extent of the Bible's references to God's creation has been overlooked and underdeveloped for generations in our preoccupation with what the biblical narrative means for humanity. Only with the emergence of ecological thinking in recent decades has the church begun to retrieve the significance of the first article of the creed about God's creation and the promised redemption of all things. Reinterpreting the catholicity of the church in relationship to the care of creation is both timely and urgent. The church as representative of humanity lives in dependence upon and solidarity with all that God has created. The biblical narrative forms the church with a particular character and instills the virtues needed for humanity to inhabit a sustainable place within the web of life. These virtues lead the church to engage in social ministry practices that embody stewardship of God's creation.

Eco-theology is an emerging field of theological reflection. Among the pioneers in this discussion is Larry Rasmussen, who concisely summarizes an emerging consensus about the significance of ecological science for theology:

> This, then, is present science's contribution as a story of origins: the stunning portrayal of a common creation in which we are radically united with all things living and nonliving, here and into endless reaches of space, and at the same time radically diverse and individuated, both by life-forms and within life-forms. And all of it is not only profoundly interrelated and inseparably interdependent but highly fine-tuned so as to evolve together. We are all—the living and not living, organic and inorganic—the outcome of the same primal explosion and same evolutionary history. All internally related from the very beginning, we are the varied forms of stardust in the hands of the creator God. (This latter judgment is obviously a theological, not scientific, one.) This reality is the most basic text and context of life itself, and thus of a life ethic.[15]

Because of the intricate interconnectedness of all things, living and inorganic, in a single ecological web of being, excesses on the part of humanity have consequences for all of creation. For centuries human beings have expanded their place in the ecosystem at the expense of other creatures. We have expropriated "resources" for our own use in utter disregard for the effects on other creatures and the earth itself, exceeding the limits of sustainability. We have fouled the environment with waste matter (for example, excessive carbon emissions) in ways that threaten the collapse of the whole life-supporting system.[16]

The challenge facing humanity in altering our habits is enormous. Virtually all aspects of contemporary life, including many of the things that enhance our comfort and convenience, are implicated in the charge of environmental degradation. Urban sprawl, transportation methods, communication systems, agricultural and animal husbandry practices, packaging of foods and products, pharmaceutical use, and the very mentality of consumerism each require thoroughgoing revision in light of the ecological crisis. The use of pesticides, herbicides, fertilizers, and other chemicals needs to be curtailed due to soil contamination and collateral effects on the various niches of the ecosystem. The burning of fossil fuels (especially oil and coal) has elevated carbon dioxide levels, destroying the protective layer of ozone, and leading to the devastating effects of global warming. Oceans and waterways are suffering from unprecedented pollution. Natural materials (water, forests, oil, topsoil, minerals) are being depleted at alarming rates. Species (for example, in the rain forests and oceans) are being eliminated at unprecedented rates, with long-term consequences for the entire ecosystem. Genetic engineering of plants and animals is being vigorously debated as to possible unforeseen harmful effects. Landfills are overflowing with non-renewable materials. Nuclear waste disposal presents a long-term problem, given the length of time it remains a threat to living beings. As might be predicted, marginalized populations and the poor suffer disproportionately from the effects of these and many other environmental problems.

Since first articulated in the devastating critique of Lynn White, responsibility for the environmental crisis has been attributed to the Judeo-Christian creation story and the claim that human beings have been granted "dominion" over creation by God.[17] An anthropocentric reading of the biblical narrative has led to devastating consequences for the natural world. Especially since the Industrial Revolution, the invention and uses of technology have expanded the human capacity to exploit and destroy the environment. White argued that the idea that the earth exists for human consumption is traceable to peculiarly Christian attitudes toward nature in the medieval period that finally are based on the Bible's assertion of (1) human dominion (that is, domination) over creation and (2) the setting apart of humanity from the rest of creation through the belief that humans are the only ones created in the image of God. If the church is to contribute to the remediation of the environmental crisis, it will require a dramatic constructive response to these charges and the implementation of an alternative eco-friendly paradigm.

Five Virtues

The biblical narrative—which underscores God as Creator, the created world as home to all creatures (including human beings), and human responsibility to care for our common home[18]—instills several core virtues in the character of the church as the body of Christ. The first of these virtues involves *the basic posture of praise and thanksgiving.* As creatures whose very existence is a gift of God and who have been placed in a world of incredible beauty and bounty, our fundamental stance to life in creation is that of gratitude. The liturgy offers plentiful opportunity for the body of Christ to practice and adopt the posture of praise: "Glory to God in the highest, and peace to God's people on earth. Lord, God, heavenly King, almighty God and Father, we worship you, we give you thanks, we praise you for your glory." The hymnody of the church reverberates with thanksgiving to God as generous Creator of all things: "Beautiful Savior, King of Creation"; "Praise to

the Lord, the Almighty, the King of Creation"; "How Great Thou Art!" These
and many other hymns adorn our lips and teach us to glorify God for the goodness
and beauty of creation. Moreover, the basic posture of praise and thanksgiving
becomes so ingrained in our fiber that our lives become acts of spiritual worship
(Rom 12:1).

The second virtue entails *loving the earth as our neighbor.* The two great commandments are to love God with all your heart, soul, and mind and to love your
neighbor as yourself (cf. Matt 22:37-39). However, we have thought rather narrowly by imagining our neighbors only to include other human beings. At this
juncture in human history the meaning of basic neighbor love must be expanded
to incorporate love for all living plants and animals that inhabit with us the earth,
seas, and sky. Neighbor love means approaching every element of creation with
sacramental respect. Each manifestation of creation has its own integrity and dignity. The creation has inherent value beyond whatever use human beings might
make of it. God has appeared to humanity in stars, clouds, mountains, and seas:
"The heavens are telling the glory of God" (Ps 19:1). Every aspect of creation is
rife to become a theophany of God's presence—not only wind, earthquake, or
fire but even the sound of sheer silence (1 Kings 19:12). In the words of William
Blake:

> To see a world in a grain of sand,
> And heaven in a wildflower,
> Hold infinity in the palm of your hand,
> And eternity in an hour.[19]

Or, even more radical, consider the opening lines of the poem, "Some Questions
You Might Ask," by Mary Oliver:

> Is the soul solid, like iron?
> Or is it tender and breakable, like
> the wings of a moth in the beak of the owl?
> Who has it, and who doesn't? [20]

The poets and mystics can assist our imaginations to honor, respect, and love the
earth and its creatures as our neighbors.

A third virtue is *readiness to learn a new paradigm for human participation in the
world.* We are accustomed to viewing ourselves as human beings at the center of
the universe. This conventional, human-centered or anthropocentric worldview
has proved itself not only sinful but also not sustainable. One classic definition of
sin is seeing the world as curved inward on oneself (*incurvitus in se*). Each of us as an
individual perceives the world egocentrically. Building on this proclivity, humans

collectively tend to interpret the world anthropocentrically. The challenge before us requires a paradigm shift so that we view ourselves as members of a community of beings within the web of life and see that what we do has consequences for all others in the ecosystem. Based on the biblical narrative in relationship to God's creation, the church is marvelously located to serve as a catalyst for the emergence of this new paradigm. In its interpretation of the world through sermons and educational offerings, leaders in the church can broaden horizons to see that humanity does not exist in isolation from creation but is indeed part of creation, dependent upon the well-being of creation for its own health. Not only that, but the church can teach that all members of God's creation—elements, plants, and living creatures alike—have their own integrity and intrinsic worth. These are not created for our exclusive use, but we exist in symbiosis with one another. When we make use of elements of creation or take the life of another life form, we do so in gratitude for the sacrifice that has been made for our sake.

A fourth virtue, closely related to the previous three, encompasses *stewardship as care for creation.* Contrary to prevailing stereotypes, stewardship is not only about money.[21] Instead stewardship has to do with responding to God's generosity by caring for all God has entrusted to us. Human beings finally are not "owners" of the earth. A profound translation of Psalm 24:1 reads: "God owns everything!" Theologically speaking, we do not own anything. In the words of an old adage: "You can't take it with you." All that we think we "possess" is in truth a trust from God for which we are responsible to care during our days on earth. The New Testament understands the role of the steward as a manager who is responsible to the real owner, God (cf. Luke 12:42-48). An attitude of stewardship is urgently needed in the relationship of human beings to creation. Whereas human beings have long acted more as exploiters of God's creation than as stewards, the creation is now exhibiting symptoms that demonstrate an absolute limit to such behavior.[22] We are faced with fundamental issues of sustainability; current patterns of human interaction with the creation are hastening the extinction of life forms, not only in many microcosms but eventually of the macrocosm itself.[23] As an alternative to the prevailing values and patterns of excessive consumption, the body of Christ is summoned to model the mind of the steward in relating to issues involving participation in God's creation. In particular, the church is called to serve as caretaker of all that pertains to its common life—real estate, building, and furnishings—exemplifying the way of the steward in all decisions rendered about their preservation and use.[24]

A fifth virtue involves *holding one another accountable for the care of creation.* The biblical narrative makes clear the charge given to humanity to till the garden and keep it (Gen 2:15). We are accountable ultimately to God for our stewardship of creation. But penultimately, it is also necessary for us to conform to a code of environmental ethics[25] and to obey established laws pertaining to the preservation of the environment.[26] These devices are necessary for guarding God's creation from the fallibility of our good intentions. As a contribution to the formulation of a code of environmental ethics, consider these eight principles articulated from the vantage point of deep ecology:

1. The well-being and flourishing of human and non-human life on earth have value in themselves (synonyms: intrinsic value, inherent worth). These values are independent of the usefulness of the non-human world for human purposes.

2. Richness and diversity of life forms contribute to the realization of these values and are also values in themselves.

3. Humans have no right to reduce this richness and diversity except to satisfy vital needs.

4. The flourishing of human life and cultures is compatible with a substantially smaller population. The flourishing of non-human life requires a smaller human population.

5. Present human interference with the non-human world is excessive, and the situation is rapidly worsening.

6. Policies must therefore be changed. These policies affect basic economic, technological, and ideological structures. The resulting state of affairs will be deeply different from the present.

7. The ideological change will be mainly that of appreciating life quality (dwelling in situations of inherent value) rather than adhering to an increasingly higher standard of living. There will be a profound awareness of the difference between bigness and greatness.

8. Those who subscribe to the foregoing points have an obligation directly or indirectly to try to implement the necessary changes.[27]

Social statements and social teachings from various church bodies can also serve as points of reference to hold us accountable for the care of creation.[28] The church in its catholicity has the responsibility of rendering its members and others accountable for their engagement with God's creation.

Three Lives Exemplifying Care for Creation

These five virtues come to expression in instructive ways through three Christian lives—Francis of Assisi, Chief Seattle, and Wendell Berry—who each exemplify the character of the body of Christ in caring for creation. Each of these figures not only personally engaged in the cause but also has made significant contributions to the emerging paradigm of care for creation.

FRANCIS OF ASSISI

Saint Francis (c. 1181–1226) was born in the city of Assisi, the son of a wealthy textile merchant.[29] Given his father's standing, Francis grew up as part of the privileged class and exercised his liberty as a troubadour, seeking pleasure and romance. Around the age of twenty he became a knight, thinking this would bring him glory and fame. Upon being captured, however, Francis spent a year in prison before he was released; thereafter he contracted a serious illness that threatened his life. These experiences were the occasion for a spiritual conversion. According to legend, as Francis was riding one day he encountered a leper. Moved by compassion, he not only gave his cloak to the leper but also kissed the poor man's disfigured face. From this moment, the life of Francis began to take on dramatically different contours, which put him in sharp conflict with the traditional values of his family.

The call of St. Francis occurred inside the decrepit chapel of San Damiano, where he heard the voice of Christ: "Francis, go and repair my church which is falling into ruins, as you can see!" Initially, Francis interpreted this command to entail the physical renovation of the dilapidated building. Only gradually did he comprehend that he was called to something far more comprehensive and challenging: the restoration of the Catholic Church to "the radical simplicity of the gospel," "the spirit of poverty," "the image of Christ in his poor," and the wonder of creation.[30] In order to finance the restoration of the building, Francis took from his father's goods and sold them. Incensed by Francis' activities, his father had him brought before the bishop for a hearing in the town plaza. Having confessed his fault, not only did Francis make restitution for what had been expropriated but in a dramatic display he removed his expensive clothing and gave them to his father, saying: "Hitherto I have called you father on earth; but now I say, 'Our Father, who art in heaven.'"[31] The peasant's frock with which the bishop covered Francis became the symbol of his new estate. During the next months, he lived as a beggar in the region surrounding Assisi. Hereafter he would consider himself married to Lady Poverty.

Francis embraced the vocation of preaching simplicity and poverty. Soon he assembled a community of followers, who would in time become the order of "lesser brothers" (Friars Minor), otherwise known as the Franciscans. Francis and his band lived in community and roamed the countryside, sharing the way of Christ, singing heartrending songs, and making a profound impression on many. In 1211 Francis received Clare of Assisi among his followers; thereby the female

Order of Poor Dames ("Poor Clares") had its origin. The ministry of Francis took him across the face of Europe and the Middle East, with chapters of the order organized in many locations. Francis was an advocate not only for poverty but also nonviolence. The prayer of St. Francis profoundly articulates the nature of his spirituality:

> Lord, make us instruments of your peace.
> Where there is hatred, let us sow love;
> where there is injury, pardon;
> where there is discord, union;
> where there is doubt, faith;
> where there is despair, hope;
> where there is darkness, light;
> and where there is sadness, joy.
> Grant that we may not so much seek to be consoled as to console;
> to be understood, as to understand;
> to be loved, as to love.
> For it is in giving that we receive;
> it is in pardoning that we are pardoned; and
> it is in dying that we are born to eternal life.[32]

While Francis left few extant writings, his life made a deep impression on many, leading to the telling of the plenteous legends by which he is known. According to tradition, in 1224 Francis received the stigmata, the marks of Christ's crucifixion on his hands and feet. Already in 1228, only two years after his death, he was declared a saint of the church. October 4 marks the feast of St. Francis of Assisi.

The aspect of the Franciscan legacy directly related to this chapter concerns his love for God's creation. Francis apprehended the sacramental character of creation which he celebrated with wonder and in song. He composed the "Canticle of Creation" in praise of all God has created, which human beings are to joyously celebrate:

> Be praised, my Lord, for all your creation
>   and especially for our Brother Sun,
>   who brings us the day and the light;
>   he is strong and shines magnificently.
>   O Lord, we think of you when we look at him.
> Be praised, my Lord, for Sister Moon, and for the stars
>   which you have set shining and lovely in the heavens.
> Be praised, my Lord,
>   for our Brothers Wind and Air and every kind of weather
>   by which you, Lord, uphold life in all your creatures.

Be praised, my Lord, for Sister Water,
   who is very useful to us,
   and humble and precious and pure.
Be praised, my Lord, for Brother Fire,
   through whom you give us light in the darkness:
   he is bright and lively and strong.
Be praised, my Lord,
   for Sister Earth, our Mother, who nourishes us and sustains us,
   bringing forth fruits and vegetables of many kinds and flowers of
      many colors.[33]

This song reflects the sheer delight of living in communion with all God has created. St. Francis "was the one who had more or less invented the drama of the crèche, with living animals, at a Christ Mass, outdoors, in the midst of the darkness of a great cave lit by candles or torches or both."[34] Francis is often depicted in mystical communion with flowers, birds, and other living creatures.[35] Many stories recollect his conversations with birds or animals. "Altogether his life and his relationship with the world—including animals, the elements, the poor and sick, as well as princes and prelates, women as well as men, represented the breakthrough of a new model of human and cosmic community."[36] Francis continues to teach the church to love all creatures as our neighbors and to care for God's creation as joyful stewards.

CHIEF SEATTLE

Seattle, Chief of the Suquamish (c. 1786–1866), was born in a village near Puget Sound.[37] During his childhood, he experienced the arrival of the first white people, trappers and traders, to the Northwest. Soon settlers were arriving in large numbers, which led to increasing tensions and conflicts with the Native American people. Having proved himself as a warrior and leader, Seattle became chief of his tribe already when he was in his early twenties. Seattle chose to navigate the challenges posed by the invading peoples through negotiation and peaceful engagement, rather than war. However, as was ever the case, this strategy only led to increasing marginalization and loss for his people. Around 1848 Seattle was baptized into the Roman Catholic Church; many other Native Americans also became Christian about this time.

In 1855 Chief Seattle signed the treaty which transferred ancestral lands to the U.S. government and established a reservation in the Northwest for Native Americans. Increasingly, Seattle had come to view the conflict between his people and the white population as a clash of cultures. This became manifest in an acute way in the diverging views of the relationship between humans and the creation.

Native American spirituality is grounded in the sacredness of the created world. The world was made by the Creator for all living beings to live together in harmony. Human beings and animals are often considered nearest kin, based on many Native American creation stories. The sky, earth, and underworld are inhabited by spirits who control the weather and otherwise influence human affairs. Of particular significance for this chapter is the spiritual wisdom that humans are to live in concord with the created rhythms of life. This sensibility is reflected in a famous speech of Chief Seattle:[38]

> Our religion is the traditions of our ancestors—the dreams of our old men, given them in solemn hours of the night by the Great Spirit; and the visions of our *sachems*, and is written in the hearts of our people. Your dead cease to love you and the land of their nativity as soon as they pass the portals of the tomb and wander away beyond the stars. They are soon forgotten and never return. Our dead never forget this beautiful world that gave them being. They still love its verdant valleys, its murmuring rivers, its magnificent mountains, sequestered vales and verdant lined lakes and bays, and ever yearn in tender fond affection over the lonely hearted living, and often return from the happy hunting ground to visit, guide, console, and comfort them. . . .
>
> Every part of this soil is sacred in the estimation of my people. Every hillside, every valley, every plain and grove, has been hallowed by some sad or happy event in days long vanished. Even the rocks, which seem to be dumb and dead as they swelter in the sun along the silent shore, thrill with memories of stirring events connected with the lives of my people, and the very dust upon which you now stand responds more lovingly to their footsteps than yours, because it is rich with the blood of our ancestors, and our bare feet are conscious of the sympathetic touch. Our departed braves, fond mothers, glad, happy hearted maidens, and even the little children who lived here and rejoiced here for a brief season, will love these somber solitudes and at eventide they greet shadowy returning spirits. And when the last Red Man shall have perished, and the memory of my tribe shall have become a myth among the White Men, these shores will swarm with the invisible dead of my tribe, and when your children's children think themselves alone in the field, the store, the shop, upon the highway, or in the silence of the pathless woods, they will not be alone.[39]

Shalom church can learn deep respect for and wonder at the intricacies of God's creation from such testimony and from the spiritual traditions of Native American peoples. On June 7, 1866, Chief Seattle died on a reservation near the city that received from him its name.

WENDELL BERRY

Poet, novelist, essayist, and culture critic, Wendell Berry (born 1934) is a contemporary figure who gives expression to an alternative vision of human engagement with the world, challenging the church in its care for creation. He was born in Henry County, Kentucky, where his family has lived and farmed since before the Civil War.[40] After graduating from the University of Kentucky, in 1965 Berry moved to the farm Lane's Landing, where he resides and farms to the present. Over the years, he has served as a teacher of creative writing and is best known for his writings, which include numerous volumes of poetry, essays, novels, and short stories. Although Berry was baptized in the Baptist Church and attends the Port Royal Baptist Church, he chooses to live at the margins of church life. However, this in no way makes his voice irrelevant to the agenda of the church in its care for creation.

What distinguishes the work of Berry is his fierce commitment to place. Our spiritual well-being and ethical obligations are inextricably grounded in our physical location in space. We are given to steward the place where we find ourselves. This obligation has been obliterated by the development of an economic system that knows virtually no responsibility for the well-being of particular localities. In his novels and stories, Berry therefore locates the characters and plot in a particular place, the fictional community of Port William, Kentucky, where the story unfolds among a community existing together over time. This is how we learn the meaning of life: by living in close community with each other both through ordinary days and in times of crisis, year in and year out. One virtue that derives from this authorial perspective is the value of staying in place; taking responsibility for the care of the land and community where we live. Berry advocates for "propriety": fitting our conduct to our place and circumstances.[41] Whether farming or living in the city, we must become attuned to the uniqueness of the place where we live.

One strong theme in Berry's work relates to sound agricultural practices. In many of his essays, he advocates sustainable farming methods, the use of appropriate technologies, conservation of the environment, frugality, and fundamental reverence for life.[42] Conversely, he is a severe critic of the logic of a global economy, including the industrialization of agriculture and the concomitant environmental degradation.

> [Technological progress] has provided the means by which both the productive and consumptive capacities of people could be detached from household and community and made to serve other people's purely economic ends. It has provided as well a glamour of newness, ease, and affluence that made it seductive even to those who suffered most from it. In its more recent history especially, this revolution has been successful in putting unheard-of quantities of consumer goods and services within the reach of ordinary people. But the technical means of this popular "affluence" has at the same time made possible the gathering of the real property and the real power of the country into fewer and fewer hands.[43]

Such a trenchant critique of the consequences of "progress" is developed in detail in Berry's analysis of contemporary society. Rather than measuring the good life in terms of "productivity," we will be restored to our senses only when we again orient ourselves to "the standard of nature" (that is, natural well-being) as the compass guiding the quality of human life.[44]

Berry's writing regularly takes on the character of a biblical prophet, calling for authentic repentance in his challenge to economic and ecclesial business-as-usual. Christianity has functioned as "the religion of the state and the economic status quo": "It has, for the most part, stood silently by while a predatory economy has ravaged the world, destroyed its natural beauty and health, divided and plundered its human communities and households."[45] Even Berry's poetry can assume this prophetic character, as in "Let Us Pledge":

> Let us pledge allegiance to the flag
> and to the national sacrifice areas
> for which it stands, garbage dumps
> and empty holes, sold out for a higher
> spire on the rich church, the safety
> of voyagers in golf carts, the better mood
> of the stock market. Let us feast
> today, though tomorrow we starve. Let us
> gorge upon the body of the Lord, consuming
> the earth for our greater joy in Heaven,
> that fair Vacationland. Let us wander forever
> in the labyrinths of our self-esteem.
> Let us evolve forever toward the higher
> consciousness of the machine.
> The spool of our engine-driven fate
> unwinds, our history now outspeeding
> thought, and the heart is a beatable tool.[46]

Berry holds the church accountable for selling its soul in the attempt to demonstrate its relevance and usefulness to modern society, when in fact thereby "Christianity connives directly in the murder of Creation."[47]

At the same time, Berry recognizes the authentic calling of the church, rooted in the creation stories and the teachings of Jesus:

> I take literally the statement in the Gospel of John that God loves the world. I believe that the world was created and approved by love, that it subsists, coheres, and endures by love, and that, insofar as it is redeemable, it can be redeemed only by love. I believe that divine love, incarnate and indwelling in the world, summons the world always toward wholeness, which ultimately is reconciliation and atonement with God.[48]

Berry contrasts this faith in the goodness of what God has created to modern superstitions (which are based as much as religion on assumptions that cannot be proved!) that are leading to nature's destruction.[49] Both his fiction and poetry exude a holy apprehension that God's creation is infused with this incarnate love, as illustrated in the closing lines from his poem, "The Wild Geese":

> Geese appear high over us,
> pass, and the sky closes. Abandon,
> as in love or sleep, holds
> them to their way, clear
> in the ancient faith: what we need
> is here. And we pray, not
> for new earth or heaven, but to be
> quiet in heart, and in eye,
> clear. What we need is here.[50]

In his substantial body of work, Wendell Berry reminds the church of its calling to take seriously the stewardship of creation and holds both church and society accountable for our failures.

Practicing Care for Creation as Ministering Community

The biblical narrative of God's creation molds the character of the body of Christ and forms God's people in the corresponding virtues. These virtues come to expression in the lives of those who are committed to care for God's creation in thanksgiving and responsibility. The character and virtues of the church as the body of Christ, Christ existing as church-community, are embodied in practices that reflect the Christian value of creation care.

First, congregations can exercise *the practice of wonder*. How awesome and marvelous is God's creation! The more we know about the intricacies of the ecological web, of which we are a part, the more amazing it becomes! Because the church is grounded in the confessional affirmation of God as Creator of heaven and earth, the church can serve as a forum for learning about and celebrating the wonders of all God has made. This means both exploring the story of the evolutionary history of the universe as it continues to unfold and discovering concretely manifestations of God's created beauty in the world around us. In Christian education offerings, the church can assist people to learn that *no contradiction exists* between the biblical narrative of creation and scientific theories about the natural world. The Bible is replete with stories that praise God as Creator of all that exists and that interprets the world around us as God's handiwork. The scientific accounts help us understand *how* God, at the beginning of the universe and continuously, engages in the creative, sustaining process. This approach is especially constructive when the church accompanies young people in their learning about biology and evolution in adolescence. Church members need spaces to integrate their religious and scientific knowing. Moreover, the church can sponsor events and excursions to explore the beauty and wonders of God's world: a night with an astronomer to behold the glory of the heavens, a trip to an aquarium to discover the hidden world alive under water, or an outing to experience the array of colors in the turning of the leaves on an autumn day. By living in wonder at God's creation, we draw near to the experiences of those who first crafted the biblical creation narratives.

Second, congregations can foster *the practice of simplicity.* The energy it takes—physical and emotional—to drive the contemporary lifestyle is excessive. Not only are we facing energy shortages in the natural world (water, topsoil, oil, etc.), but we also often face acute shortages of emotional energy in trying to keep up with the contemporary pace of life. The pace and pressures of life are among the factors that contribute greatly to increasing rates of clinical depression and the phenomenon of burnout. We have been carefully taught by consumer culture, especially through the omnipresence of advertising (which surrounds us from an early age onwards) that the meaning of life has to do with the consumption of products: "If only you purchase the latest style clothing, the newest car model, the next labor-saving device, this newly improved product, you will know happiness." Such are the promises ever before us. However, we should all know by now that as soon as we have the next best widget, our yearning does not cease. The promises of consumerism are empty, even idolatrous, because they tempt us to put faith and trust in objects rather than in God. Moreover, our over-consumption is despoiling God's creation.

Congregations can serve as enclaves for experiments in an alternative, simplified lifestyle. To engage in countercultural practices that resist consumerism, most of us need a community of peers who both encourage us and hold us accountable. For example, the movement to celebrate Christmas alternatively—especially rethinking the giving and receiving of presents—finds an appropriate home in congregations that desire to focus on the birth of Jesus as the real meaning of the season.[51] Also on other occasions (for example, birthdays, anniversaries, weddings, etc.), congregations can encourage generosity to people in need in lieu of giving presents (balloons or flowers) to those who do not need them. As a third example, congregations can encourage the communal sharing of underutilized machines, such as lawn mowers, carpet cleaners, or yard tractors. Christian congregations can stimulate serious reflection on a simpler lifestyle in their communications and by example.[52] Congregations can contribute to the care of creation by encouraging people to simplify the complexity of their lives by saying, "Enough!"[53]

Third, congregations can enhance the care for creation by *the practice of attending to the local place.* We have heard the slogan, "Think globally; act locally." This has led to the coining of a new term, the "glocal."[54] In the life of the congregation we remain knowledgeable and alert to global developments and trends, especially in relationship to the interdependency of the whole ecosystem.[55] By our interconnectedness as members of the global church, we have the opportunity to learn about the ecological challenges facing members of the church throughout the world.[56] This learning provides the comprehensive horizon for us, however, to take primary responsibility for the specific place where we are located. We practice attending to our local place by how we steward the heating and cooling of church buildings, the use of electricity and water, the landscaping of our yards, and even how we do lawn care. Some churches have opened their grounds for the cultivation of community gardens, or have turned part of their property into green spaces for public use. Certainly, congregations can encourage and model a lifestyle that takes seriously the reduction of waste and recycling.

Furthermore churches can educate about the difference even small changes can make for the sake of the whole. Among the "17 Sensible Steps" proposed by Wendell Berry for local community practice, here are the first four:

1. Always ask of any proposed change or innovation: What will this do to our community? How will this affect our common wealth?
2. Always include nature—the land, the water, the air, the native creatures— within the membership of the community.
3. Always ask how local needs might be supplied from local sources, including the mutual help of neighbors.
4. Always supply local needs *first.* (And only then think of exporting their products, first to nearby cities, and then to others.)[57]

Although the thought may appear counterintuitive, attending to the care of the local community contributes the most to the well-being of the whole. Congregations can encourage members to eat foods grown and use products developed in the nearby community. Congregations can inventory the abilities of members and call upon one another for practical help in work projects. Even in selecting furnishings for the church, the congregation can give preference to those items made from natural substances and procured from the surrounding region. Mindfulness about care for creation in the mundane decisions congregations make contributes inexorably to the paradigm shift needed among people across the globe.

Fourth, congregations can engage in *the practice of living sustainably*. "The principle of sustainability means providing an acceptable quality of life for present generations without compromising that of future generations."[58] Sustainability entails living within our collective means—both ecologically and economically. Yet achieving sustainability, especially when the number of variables is so enormously complicated, is a major challenge to human comprehension. For example, the goal of ecological sustainability raises an acute dilemma regarding economic viability:

> Protection of species and their habitats, preservation of clean land and water, reduction of wastes, care of the land—these are priorities. But production of basic goods and services, equitable distribution, accessible markets, stabilization of population, quality education, full employment—these are priorities as well.

We are forced to recognize the tension that exists among competing ethical priorities, in this instance between the need for social justice and care for creation.[59] For the last few centuries we have for the most part been able to discount the ecological costs in achieving an unprecedentedly high standard of living for many people, especially those in Europe and North America. Often this standard of living has been heavily subsidized by expropriating resources and labor from other parts of the world with little regard for environmental consequences. God's creation, however, is exhibiting alarming signs of rebellion against this abuse. Especially among impoverished populations, strategies must be devised that do not compromise a decent standard of living for all people, while achieving long-term sustainability for the creation.[60] In development work, business, and agriculture, a coordinated effort must be implemented to attain long-term sustainability of both the economy and the creation.

In addition to a regimen of simplicity, conservation, and recycling, another important contribution to attaining sustainability involves reducing our "carbon footprint." Because of the threats posed by global warming to many parts of the ecosphere, it is urgent that people become knowledgeable and conversant about the significance of their carbon footprint (or imprint). According to the United Kingdom Carbon Trust, a "carbon footprint is the total set of GHG (greenhouse gas) emissions caused directly and indirectly by an individual, organization, event or product."[61] There are useful assessment processes to measure or estimate the size of our carbon footprint, which consists of the total sum of our carbon dioxide and other GHG emissions.[62] Once the GHG amount is known, strategies can be devised to reduce or neutralize the effects. For example, alternative means of transportation (for example, walking, cycling, or the use of public accommodations) and the use of solar or wind energy sources can mitigate the total impact of one's carbon emissions.

Fifth, congregations can engage in *the practice of advocacy for the creation*. Parallel to the practice of advocating nonviolence or social justice, this involves the church in monitoring and supporting legislation that advances the protection of the environment from degradation and promotes the well-being of the natural world.[63] Areas for possible advocacy by the church include the following: air quality, water quality, soil erosion, global climate change, agriculture, urbanization, biodiversity, species protection, the use of pesticides and hazardous chemicals, waste management, remediation of contaminated land, sustainable development, and stewardship of public lands and natural resources. As with all advocacy efforts, receiving reliable and timely information is crucial for effectiveness. To this end, participation in an advocacy network, which can provide educational materials and action updates, is indispensable.[64]

One particular dimension of environmental advocacy that requires focused attention is the phenomenon of environmental racism.[65] This involves environmental policies that make people of color suffer disproportionately from the effects of contaminating agents and waste disposal.

> Environmental racism is racial discrimination in environmental policymaking. It is racial discrimination in the enforcement of regulations and laws. It is racial discrimination in the deliberate targeting of communities of color for toxic waste disposal and the [locating] of polluting industries. It is racial discrimination in the official sanctioning of the life-threatening presence of poisons and pollutants in communities of color.[66]

Moreover, environmental organizations need to be proactive in including people of color in their leadership and membership. It is imperative that concern for environmental racism be incorporated into the mainstream environmental movement and especially in the advocacy efforts by the church.

In this chapter I have linked the confession of the church's catholicity to ethical responsibility to care for creation, observing how the biblical narrative concerning God's creative activity informs and authorizes the church's stewardship of creation. I have explored how this narrative forms the character of the body of Christ, infusing particular virtues and sending the church to care for God's creation, pointing out how these virtues have been embodied in the lives of St. Francis of Assisi, Chief Seattle of the Suquamish, and Wendell Berry of Henry County, Kentucky. Finally, I have considered how congregations can serve the care of God's creation by engaging in particular social ministry practices. In the next chapter I turn to the fourth and last mark of the church, examining how the confession of the church's apostolicity equips the body of Christ to respect every human being as God's child.

The Body of Christ Is Apostolic
The Practice of Respect for Human Dignity

The apostolicity of the church involves the "sending" (Greek: *apostellō*) of the church to the ends of the earth. The first apostles were those sent by the crucified and risen Jesus Christ to be his messengers and representatives in a mission to all peoples. The Acts of the Apostles renders Luke's account of the earliest activity of the apostles after the crucifixion and resurrection, moving outward from Jerusalem to the entire surrounding world to convey the word and follow in the way of Jesus Christ.

The apostolic character of the church extends in time both backward to the New Testament and forward to the eschaton. First John 1:1 gives expression to the rootedness of the Christian message in the faithful transmission of teaching: "We declare to you what was from the beginning, what we have heard, what we have seen with our eyes, what we have looked at and touched with our hands, concerning the word of life. . . ." From the earliest time to the present, the authenticity of the tradition has been predicated on the reliable transmission of the message first received from the apostles of Jesus. Very early in church history, the veracity of the Christian *kerygma* was predicated on episcopal succession, that is, the guarantee of apostolicity was demonstrated through an unbroken chain of bishops (the historic episcopacy). Already in the second century Irenaeus of Lyons (c. 140–202) gave evidence for the legitimacy of the Christian message by reviewing the names of

the first twelve bishops of Rome, who were understood as the successors of Peter.[1]
Following this listing Irenaeus goes on to add:

> In this order, and by this succession, the ecclesiastical tradition from the apostles, and
> the preaching of the truth, have come down to us. And this is most abundant proof
> that there is one and the same vivifying faith, which has been preserved in the Church
> from the apostles until now, and handed down in truth.[2]

Roman Catholic ecclesiology builds a juridical case for the apostolic nature of the
church based on the primacy of the bishop of Rome (the pope) and an unbroken
succession of bishops from Peter to the present.[3] The matters of papal primacy and
historic episcopacy came to serve as warrant for the truth of the Christian message
in the Roman Catholic tradition.[4]

In contrast to the Roman Catholic argument for an apostolic succession based
on the historic episcopacy, most Protestant traditions have understood apostolicity
to be grounded on the church's faithfulness to the *teachings* of the apostles.

> The *church is apostolic* because everything it confesses about Christ comes from the
> apostles as witness, whose testimony to the life, death and resurrection of Jesus Christ
> has been transmitted by the Holy Scripture. In this continuity the Church recognizes
> and lives its fundamental identity with the Church of Christ's apostles on which it is
> built once and for all.[5]

Luther, for example, argued that it was the apostolic character of the Christian
gospel that connected the ministry of the church with the New Testament apostles.[6] Only when the gospel is proclaimed in accordance with the preaching of
the apostles as witnessed in the Bible does it deserve to be called apostolic. For
Luther this meant the centrality of the message of justification by grace through
faith in Jesus Christ alone. In a parallel way, Calvin pointed to the Holy Scriptures
as the foundation for the church's teaching. The church is apostolic insofar as it
preaches faithfully the Word of Jesus Christ as first announced by the apostles
and as comes to authoritative expression in the canon of Scripture. Apostolicity is
primarily measured by the conformity of the church's teaching to the message of
the apostles.

Not only does the meaning of apostolicity stretch backward to link the church
to the ministry of the earliest apostles, it also extends *forward* in the apostolic mission of the church in each new generation.

> The Church is *apostolic* by following the example of the apostles in continuing their
> mission to proclaim the gospel which is confirmed by the action and the gift of the
> Holy Spirit. It witnesses to and serves the reconciliation of humankind to God in

Jesus Christ. In obedience to the mandate of Jesus Christ the Church proclaims the divine salvation to the world.[7]

Apart from the mission it has received from Jesus Christ through the apostles, the church lacks apostolic character: "An apostolic church is a church which is sent, a church with a mission. It is not a body which expresses itself, but which bears witness to something it has received."[8] Apostolicity entails the church's participation in the mission of Jesus Christ in relationship to all people.

Hans Küng emphasizes the insufficiency of a merely juridical interpretation of apostolicity. Instead, the church remains apostolic only when it engages in dynamic mission to the world: "To be a Church and to have a mission are not two separate things. To be itself, the Church must follow the apostles in continually recognizing and demonstrating that it has been sent out to the world. In this sense apostolic succession not only means following the faith and confession of the apostles, it means, in consequence of that faith, following in the footsteps of the apostolic ministry."[9] Küng affirms the dynamic character of the one holy catholic apostolic church:

> This makes it clear that apostolicity, like unity, holiness and catholicity, is not a static attribute of the Church. Like them it is an historical dimension, a dimension which has constantly to be fulfilled anew in history. Apostolicity too must continually be achieved between the Church and the apostles, between the Church's preaching and the apostles' witness, between the Church's ministry and the apostles' commission.[10]

The church fulfills its apostolic mission when it grasps the significance of its calling to relate the message of God in Christ to all peoples. Apostolicity not only reaches backward to the time of Christian origins, it reaches forward to eschatological fulfillment.

What is the ethical character of the church's apostolic mission? It is grounded in the vital affirmation that every human person has been created in the image of God (*imago Dei*) and for that reason alone is deserving of infinite respect. The dignity of human persons begins with and is sustained by this fundamental assertion about human existence: each and every human being is created in God's image. In the ancient world, to encounter the image of a king (for example, on a signpost) was to be reminded of the sovereignty of the one to whom the populace owed allegiance. To avow that every person is created in God's image is to claim that when we encounter another human being (as a kind of sign), we are to be immediately reminded of the God who created her or him and to relate to that person with sacred respect. Emmanuel Levinas has argued that we most encounter the transcendent dimension in this world when beholding the face of another human being.[11]

> The other becomes my neighbor precisely through the way the face summons me, calls for me, begs for me, and in so doing recalls my responsibility, and calls me into question.[12]
>
> This summons to responsibility destroys the formulas of generality by which my knowledge (*savoir*) or acquaintance (*connaissance*) of the other man re-presents him to me as my fellow man. In the face of the other man I am inescapably responsible and consequently the unique and chosen one.[13]

The failure to acknowledge the dignity of each human person is the source of every crime against humanity: "The substitution of men for one another, the primal disrespect, makes possible exploitation itself."[14] Conversely, affirmation of human rights is grounded in the conviction that all persons "have been endowed by their Creator with certain inalienable rights"[15] by virtue of the dignity afforded those made in the image of God.

The apostolic mission of the body of Christ takes seriously the mandate that it is sent to respect and defend the dignity of every child created in God's own image. Furthermore, the church understands these selfsame children of God to be each and every one a person for whom Jesus Christ died and was resurrected. This recognition deepens and expands the nature of the church's apostolic mission. As Jesus Christ entered into human suffering to fulfill the mission of the triune God, so also the apostolic mission of the church involves the participation of the body of Christ in the places of human suffering in the world today.[16] Jürgen Moltmann thereby links the apostolate of Jesus Christ to the sharing of human suffering.[17]

> Participation in the apostolic mission of Christ therefore leads inescapably into *tribulation, contradiction and suffering.* The apostolate is carried out in the weakness and poverty of Christ, not through force or the strategies of force. Reserved and withdrawn men and women and closed societies are opened through the witness of apostolic suffering, and can only through this be converted to the future of the kingdom. Just as the apostle Paul pointed to his persecutions, tribulations, wounds and scars in order to prove his apostolate (1 Cor. 6 and 7), so persecutions and sufferings will also be the proof of the apostolic church. "The blood of the martyrs is the seed of the church," said the early church.[18]

This means that the apostolic mission of the church, in conformity with the mission of Jesus Christ, joins the body of Christ to a theology of the cross (*theologia crucis*).[19]

The church perceives its particular apostolic mission at exactly those places where human beings suffer, especially where suffering at the hands of others can be redressed. Moreover, as the apostolic church enters into the particular suffering of others, so it also becomes a sign of the hope for resurrection life: "For if we have been united with him in a death like his, we will certainly be united with him in a resurrection like his" (Rom 6:5). By the apostolic message of the cross and resurrection of Jesus Christ, the church brings solidarity and hope to all who are created in God's image.

The Biblical Narrative: God's Affirmation of Human Dignity

The whole biblical narrative regarding God's affirmation of human dignity is highly ambiguous. There is much biblical material that contradicts the following narrative elements—texts that have been employed to authorize violence, ethnocentrism, patriarchy, heterosexism, and even genocide.[20] As with every appeal to Scripture, hermeneutical decisions are made about which aspects of the biblical witness are to be considered normative for faith and life. In this book I am arguing that the biblical narrative about God's reconciliation and peacemaking, concern for justice, care for creation, and respect for human dignity are the normative ethical elements. If consequent ethical behavior serves as a central criterion for the value of the biblical traditions, then these four strands of tradition establish the normative trajectory for considering God's relation to the world, here regarding God's respect for human dignity.

Genesis begins with this assertion about human nature:

So God created humankind in his image,
    in the image of God he created them. . . ." (Gen 1:27)

The indispensable foundation for affirming human dignity and solidarity with those who suffer is contained in this seminal description of the nature of human beings as created in God's image. Psalm 8 builds on this theme, in wonder at God's creation of humankind: "Yet you have made them a little lower than God, and crowned them with glory and honor" (Ps 8:5). We rejoice in the wonder of human life as created by God: "I praise you, for I am fearfully and wonderfully made" (Ps 139:4). In the New Testament there is also clear affirmation of the status of human beings made in God's image (1 Cor 15:49). Jesus Christ is the image of God in the flesh: "He is the image of the invisible God, the firstborn of all creation" (Col 1:15; cf. also Heb 1:3). Moreover, the work of Jesus Christ is interpreted as restoring the image of God after the fall into sin (cf. 2 Cor 4:4). Through Christ, the image of God is being restored to fullness: "[You] have clothed yourselves with the new self, which is being renewed in knowledge according to the image of its creator" (Col 3:10). The consequence of Christ's work is described as the overcoming of conventional human barriers: "In that renewal there is no longer Greek and Jew, circumcised and uncircumcised, barbarian, Scythian, slave and free; but Christ is all and in all!" (Col 3:11).

Because of the status of human beings in creation, God expresses particular love and care for all people as children of God, and knows each one by name. The stewardship of names in biblical genealogies preserves the memory of individual persons otherwise forgotten (cf. Gen 11:10-30, 1 Chron 1:1—9:44, etc.).[21] In unanticipated ways, God defends the dignity of particular persons. Not only does God grieve for Abel at his murder by his brother (Gen 4:10), but God acts to protect Cain, the murderer (4:15). While Isaac inherited God's promise from his father, Abraham, God also continued to bless and preserve the legacy of Hagar and Ishmael (Gen 21:12-18). God incorporates Ruth from Moab into the covenant people and through her extends the line to David (Ruth 4:18-22). God defends the cause of Uriah against the intrigue of David, calling the king to accountability for the death of the innocent one (2 Sam 11:1—12:14). Through the prophet Elijah, God makes provision for the widow of Zarephath and revives her dead son (1 Kings 17:8-24). God heals Namaan, the commander of a foreign army, from leprosy (2 Kings 5:1-19). Esther is employed by God to deliver the Jewish people from the hands of their enemies (Esth 8:3-17). God calls individual prophets to service and gives each one oracles to speak as the Word of the Lord to the people of their times (Isa 6:1-8, Jer 1:4-19, Ezek 2:1—3:11, Zech 1:1-6).

In the New Testament Jesus calls particular persons to become his apostles and knows each of them by name, the twelve (Matt 10:1-4) and Paul (Acts 9:1-19). Jesus was befriended by those whose names are remembered to this day, for example, Mary, Martha, and Lazarus (John 11:1-44). Jesus joins the weeping of these two women at the death of their brother, his friend (11:33-35). Jesus calls people by name to follow him: "Zacchaeus, hurry and come down; for I must stay at your house today" (Luke 19:5). Jesus ministers to many individuals, responding to each one's needs, for example, the healing of Peter's mother-in-law: "He came and took her by the hand and lifted her up. Then the fever left her" (Mark 1:31). Even from the cross Jesus ministers to his own mother and the disciple whom he loved, mindful of their needs: "'Woman, here is your son.' Then he said to the disciple, 'Here is your mother'" (John 19:26-27). After his resurrection, Jesus appears to his disciples with concern for them also as individuals, for example, Thomas (John 20:24-29) or Peter (John 21:15-19). In the earliest church, seven men are chosen to serve as deacons (Acts 6:1-6): Stephen, Philip, Prochorus, Nicanor, Timon, Parmenas, and Nicolaus. At the conclusion of his letters, Paul extends greetings to members of the churches, whom he knows by name as co-workers in the gospel (for example, Rom 16:1-16). The Bible from beginning to end dignifies human persons as they are known and called by name.

If God's concern and respect extends to each person, then it is especially important to recognize how the biblical narrative validates the dignity of the marginalized. If God's love is for all persons, this is demonstrated in God's concern for those conventionally considered outsiders. As mentioned already in chapter 4, the biblical narrative extends the promises of God toward universal reconciliation: "In the days to come the mountain of the Lord's house shall be established as the highest of the mountains . . . ; all the nations shall stream to it" (Isa 2:2). Here we underscore how outsiders are valued in the grand narrative of divine acts. I already have made reference to Namaan, the Syrian, and Ruth, the Moabite, as ethnic foreigners who were included in God's work in profound ways. King Melchizedek of Salem brings a mysterious blessing to Abraham in the name of God Most High (Gen 14:17-24). Solomon receives praise and blessing from the Queen of Sheba: "Blessed be the Lord your God, who has delighted in you and set you on the throne of Israel! Because the Lord loved Israel forever, he has made you king to execute justice and righteousness" (1 Kings 10:9). The prostitute Rahab, a Canaanite woman, gives assistance to the Israelites and is delivered, along with her family, to become one of the descendents of David and Jesus (Josh 2:1-21; 6:22-25). Even Cyrus, King of Persia, is incorporated into the company of those serving God's purposes: "Thus says the Lord to his anointed, to Cyrus, whose right hand I have grasped to subdue the nations before him . . ." (Isa 45:1).

The New Testament has many texts where Jesus and the early church either made positive reference to or interacted with foreign people. At his birth Jesus is sought out by three wise men from the East (Matt 2:1-12). Jesus engages in spirited conversation with the Samaritan woman at the well and she is amazed at his respect for her: "How is it that you, a Jew, ask a drink of me, a woman of Samaria?" (John 4:9). A Syrophoenician woman not only interacts with Jesus, but challenges him to expand his horizons: "Sir, even the dogs under the table eat the children's crumbs" (Mark 7:28). Jesus responds to her faith by casting out an unclean spirit from her daughter. Jesus heals the servant of a centurion: "Truly I tell you, in no one in Israel have I found such faith" (Matt 7:10). In his teaching, Jesus makes provocative references about the expanse of God's favor by citing the miracle of Elijah for the widow at Zarephath and the healing of Namaan, the Syrian (Luke 4:24-30). In another challenging story, Jesus employs a Samaritan as the stunning example of what it means to be a good neighbor (Luke 10:25-37). Furthermore, Jesus held up a Samaritan as the paragon for what it means to be thankful (Luke 17:11-19).

After the resurrection, Jesus sends his apostles to proclaim the good news to all, making "disciples of all nations" (Matt 28:19). This is exactly what unfolds in the life of the early church. Philip preaches in Samaria, leading Simon the magician to baptism (Acts 8:4-25). He proclaims the good news to an Ethiopian eunuch, who is also moved to baptism (Acts 8:26-40). Peter receives a vision from God to bring the gospel to Cornelius, a centurion of the Italian Cohort, and his household (Acts 10:1-33). This encounter is instrumental in leading Peter into ministry among the Gentiles: "I truly understand that God shows no partiality, but in every nation anyone who fears him and does what is right is acceptable to him" (Acts 10:34). This leads soon after to the formal decision at the Council of Jerusalem to open the mission to the Gentiles (Acts 15:1-21). Paul engages thereafter in travels that take him as a missionary throughout the Gentile world in Asia Minor, Greece, and even to Rome—including all the places where we have records of his correspondence (Rome, Corinth, Galatia, Ephesus, Philippi, Colossae, and Thessalonica). In each of these churches Paul developed relationships with the persons named in his letters. The book of Revelation makes reference to further congregations in Asia Minor: Smyrna, Pergamum, Thyatira, Sardis, Philadelphia, and Laodicea. These examples underscore the divine respect afforded to people of every land in the biblical narrative.

Women play a disproportionate role in the biblical narrative, considering the patriarchal structure of the society from which the stories derive. Not only Ruth and Esther, but also Sarah (Gen 21:1-7), Rebekah (Gen 24:60-67), Rachel (Gen 29:31—30:24; Jer 31:15), Miriam (Exod 15:20-21), Deborah (Judg 4:4—5:31), and Hannah (1 Sam 2) are among the female actors in Israel's history. The ministry of Jesus is distinguished by the significant role that women play, beginning with his birth of the virgin mother Mary (Luke 1:26-38; 2:1-20): "Here I am, the servant of the Lord; let it be with me according to your word" (Luke 1:38). Jesus' mother (John 2:3) and sisters were among his followers (Matt 13:56). Mary Magdalene, Martha, and Mary were among the many women who were his disciples (Matt 27:56; Luke 10:38-42). Mary anoints Jesus' feet with perfume as a sign anticipating his burial (John 12:1-8). In this ministry Jesus praises the faith demonstrated by women (Mark 12:41-44; Matt 15:21-28).

Not only women but children receive a welcome in Jesus' company, uncharacteristic for a man of his time: "Let the little children come to me, and do not stop them; for it is to such as these that the kingdom of God belongs" (Luke 18:16). "And he laid his hands on them and went on his way" (Matt 19:15). "Truly I tell you, whoever does not receive the kingdom of God as a little child will never enter it" (Luke 18:17). Likewise God's love extends also to the elderly, for example, the promise made to the aged Abraham and Sarah (Gen 17:1—18:15) and Zechariah and Elizabeth (Luke 1:5-25).

God also confers dignity and respect on those who are sick or otherwise marginalized by society. God brings healing to Abimelech (Gen 20:17), Naaman

(2 Kings 5:1-19), and Hezekiah (2 Kings 20:1-11). Among the healings performed by Jesus are the cleansing of a leper (Matt 8:1-4), the Gadarene demoniac (Matt 8:28-34), a paralytic (Matt 9:2-8), two blind men (Matt 9:27-30), a mute demoniac (Matt 9:32-34), and a man with a withered hand (Matt 12:9-14). "Great crowds came to him, bringing with them the lame, the maimed, the blind, the mute, and many others. They put them at his feet, and he cured them, so that the crowd was amazed when they saw the mute speaking, the maimed whole, the lame walking, and the blind seeing" (Matt 15:30-31). Jesus both healed the sick and cast out demons from those possessed (Mark 1:21-26, Luke 7:21; 8:2-3). Not only did these healings address the particular infirmity but they conferred human dignity by restoring the persons healed to the community (Luke 5:14). The earliest church continued the ministry of healing in Jesus' name (Acts 3:1-10; 5:12-16; 9:32-43).

While in the biblical narrative it is taken for granted that God's promises were given to the Jewish people, in our time it is important to make this point explicit, due to attempts to read the Bible according to Christian supersessionism. The promises of God to Israel—through Abraham and David—are fulfilled in the coming of Jesus, the Jew. Jesus' twelve disciples were Jews, as were the crowds who followed him. Although Jesus engages in controversy with the Pharisees and scribes, this must be interpreted always as an inter-Jewish debate. Paul makes it clear that God has never revoked the promises made to the Jewish people (Rom 11:1); in fact Gentile followers of Jesus must understand themselves as branches "grafted" into the tree that is Israel (Rom 11:17-24). "[A]ll Israel will be saved" (Rom 11:26) in the mystery and glory of God (Rom 11:25-36). Given the history of Christian anti-Semitism, it is crucial to be emphatic about God's respect for the Jewish people, even as we emphasize the dignity God affords all people.

In chapter 5 we saw how the biblical narrative demonstrates God's particular concern for the poor and lowly: "The rich and the poor have this in common: the Lord is the maker of them all" (Prov 22:2). Neither ethnic origin, nor gender, nor age, nor illness, nor class is able to separate from God's love those who were created in God's own image (cf. Rom 8:38-39). God respects the dignity of each one as child of God. In spite of human disregard or cruelty against fellow human beings as it may appear in some biblical texts, the weight of Scripture defends the value and dignity of every person whom God created.

The extent of God's love is revealed most profoundly by how God chooses to enter into human suffering. God's compassion for humanity is often compared to that of parents for children (Ps 103:13; Isa 63:15-16; Jer 31:20): "How can I give you up, Ephraim? How can I hand you over, O Israel? . . . My heart recoils within me; my compassion grows warm and tender. I will not execute my fierce anger; I will not again destroy Ephraim; for I am God and no mortal, the Holy One in your midst, and I will not come in wrath" (Hos 11:8-9). God's mercy was extended to God's people, in spite of their waywardness: "The Lord, the God of their ancestors, sent persistently to them by his messengers, because he had compassion on his people and on his dwelling place. . . ." (2 Chron 36:15). God's compassion comes to expression in acts of forgiveness (2 Kings 23:13; Ps 25:6-7; Isa 55:7) and deliverance from enemies (Ps 40:11; Isa 30:18; Jer 42:12): "Then in the time of their suffering they cried out to you and you heard them from heaven, and according to your great mercies you gave them saviors who saved them from the hands of their enemies" (Neh 9:27). God's mercy is known through God's provision for Israel in the wilderness (Neh 9:19; Isa 49:10) and in the restoration of the exiles (Deut 30:3; Isa 14:1; Exod 39:25). "Return to the Lord, your God, for he is gracious and merciful, slow to anger, and abounding in steadfast love" (Joel 2:13).

The suffering of God for God's people is prefigured in the suffering of the prophets:

> In your forbearance do not take me away; know that on your account I suffer insult. Your words were found, and I ate them, and your words became to me a joy and the delight of my heart; for I am called by your name, O Lord, God of hosts. I did not sit in the company of merrymakers, nor did I rejoice; under the weight of your hand I sat alone, for you had filled me with indignation. Why is my pain unceasing, my wound incurable, refusing to be healed?" (Jer 15:15-18)

Psalm 22 brings to expression the depths of suffering for the cause of God: "I am poured out like water, and all my bones are out of joint; my heart is like wax; it is melted within my breast; my mouth is dried up like a potsherd, and my tongue sticks to my jaws; you lay me in the dust of death (vv. 14-15). This trajectory comes to its apex in Isaiah's song of the suffering servant:

> Surely he has borne our infirmities and carried our diseases; yet we accounted him stricken, struck down by God, and afflicted. But he was wounded for our transgressions, crushed for our iniquities; upon him was the punishment that made us whole, and by his bruises we are healed. (Isa 53:4-5)

God enters into the suffering of the God's people through the suffering of those bearing God's Word to the world.

This theology of vicarious suffering for the sake of others becomes one of the profound lenses for interpreting the meaning of the passion and death of Jesus, giving rise to the theology of the cross. Prior to his passion Jesus laments for Jerusalem (Luke 13:31-35). At the institution of the Last Supper, Jesus says: "This is my blood of the covenant, which is poured out for many" (Mark 14:24). In the classic text of John 3:16, we hear: "For God so loved the world that he gave his only Son, so that everyone who believes in him may not perish but may have eternal life." Paul, in particular, delves into the profundities of the theology of the cross: "But God chose what is low and despised in the world, things that are not, to reduce to nothing things that are, so that no one might boast in the presence of God. He is the source of your life in Christ Jesus, who became for us wisdom from God, and righteousness and sanctification and redemption" (1 Cor 1:27-30). Jesus' death on the cross works life in us: "God made you alive together with him, when he forgave us all our trespasses, erasing the record that stood against us with its legal demands. He set this aside, nailing it to the cross" (Col 2:13-14). In the words of the ancient Christ hymn: ". . . he humbled himself and became obedient to the point of death—even death on a cross" (Phil 2:8). Just as the death of Jesus works to erase our sins, so the resurrection of Jesus brings us life (2 Cor 4:7-12).

The biblical narrative discloses how God bestows respect and dignity on human beings as those created in God's own image. God knows each one by name. God defends the cause of those otherwise marginalized, including foreigners, women, children, the aged, and the sick. In order to be a defender of the dignity of all people, God pays particular attention to those who are threatened by marginalization. Jesus dignified human existence all the more through his incarnation in human flesh, revealing the perfected image of God in his own life and refurbishing the divine image in us as a gift. Not only has God granted us particular dignity by virtue of our creation in the image of God, but God has revealed divine passion for us by entering into the places of human suffering, ultimately on the cross: "No one has greater love than this, to lay down one's life for one's friends" (John 15:13).

Character and Virtues in the Body of Christ: Respect for Human Dignity

The affirmation of the human being made in the image of God is the foundation for sacred respect afforded each child of God. The extent of God's affirmation is disclosed by how God chooses to enter into human suffering, paradigmatically in the person and cross of Jesus Christ. The church as the body of Christ takes on the character of Jesus Christ by participating in his work of reclaiming God's image in us, especially as we enter into solidarity with the suffering of others (cf. 2 Cor 5:10-16).

One of the momentous developments in the defense of human dignity from the twentieth century is the formulation and adoption of the Universal Declaration of Human Rights.[22] Rights might be defined as "entitlements pertaining to those needs and desires that other people are obligated to fulfill, or to allow *you* to fulfill."[23] Never before have the nations of the world arrived at a consensus on those rights which befit all human beings, regardless of nationality, religion, ethnicity, language, gender, age, disability, sexual orientation, or class.[24] Regardless of how well the international community has been able to address violations of human rights in particular instances, the concept of human rights has established unprecedented standards for human decency and expectations for right conduct. Among the human rights named in the Universal Declaration are two types: (1) civil and political rights and (2) economic, social, and cultural rights.[25] Included among civil and political rights are life, liberty, security, equal protection under the law, conscience, fair trial, freedom of movement and thought, peaceful assembly, marriage, family, and privacy. Among economic, social, and cultural rights are food, water, education, housing, health care, work, and adequate working conditions. Some theorists argue for an emerging third category of rights: "group rights" (including the rights to peace, a healthy environment, and economic development).[26]

One of the central debates involves the intellectual grounding of human rights. While theorists hesitate to ground human rights in the particularity of a single religion, in the Judeo-Christian tradition the generation of human rights discourse begins with the clear theological affirmation that human beings are created in the image of God. Both in Judaism[27] and Christianity are clear warrants for human rights as grounded in God's very creation of human persons:

> Christians believe that human beings are made in the image of God, that every person is of intrinsic worth before God, and that every individual has a right to the fullest possible opportunities for the development of life abundant and eternal. Denial of rights and freedoms that inhere in an individual's worth before God are not simply a crime against humanity; they are a sin against God.[28]

While some theorists may hesitate to acknowledge this religious grounding, the affirmation of the *imago Dei* remains one of the primary intellectual foundations of human rights theory, likely the cornerstone. For this reason the members of the body of Christ can authentically and proactively join in the movement to support and defend the cause of human rights.

Constructive Christology builds upon Christ's incarnation, passion, and death to affirm the participation of God in human suffering.

> What happens to bodies is important to God, who—according to Christian faith— has shared human embodiment in every range of experience. In this distinctively Christian ontology of the human, we find the resources for a universal conception of human dignity: human beings participate in God's image, because God participates in humanity as a victim of human rights abuse.[29]

Not only are human persons of sacred worth as those created in God's image but God has dignified human existence by taking on human flesh in Christ's incarnation. Furthermore, God enters into human suffering in the persons of those who suffer, especially among those suffering through the deprivation of basic human rights. As we violate the human rights of one of the least of Christ's sisters and brothers, so we violate him. The theology of the cross has profound ramifications for the defense of human rights.

> For faith, we said, is that trust in God then frees us sufficiently from *self* to make us cognizant of and compassionate in relation toward the other—in particular, the other who suffers, who is hungry and thirsty, who is imprisoned; the other who "fell among thieves"; the other who knocks at our door at midnight in need. The church is a community of suffering because it is a community whose eyes have been opened to the suffering that *exists*.[30]

Exactly in the places where humans suffer due to the oppression of others, Jesus enters in solidarity to lend hope and work liberation. A cruciform church conforms to the Crucified One by meeting him in the very places of suffering where he chooses to be found.

In the defense of human rights, the church can join with other faith communities in affirming the provisions of the "Declaration toward a Global Ethic" adopted by the Parliament of the World's Religions: "We must treat others as we wish others to treat us. We make a commitment to respect life and dignity, individuality and diversity, so that every person is treated humanely, without exception."[31] Moreover, the body of Christ can join in appealing to all people of good will for the universal reception and defense of human rights:

> For human rights to have a greater impact, they have to appeal to people's imaginations and become properly part of their vocabulary. For human rights really to take hold, they will have to be understood and fully internalized.[32]

The church of Jesus Christ can play a pivotal role in this process, first, by reflecting these rights within its own ranks and, second, by advocating for and defending human rights wherever they are endangered.

Five Virtues

The biblical narrative—which claims God as paradigmatic for the affirmation of human dignity—inculcates five core virtues into the character of the church as the body of Christ. The first of these virtues is the *affirmation of the common humanity of all those created by God.* While God has created us wonderfully different in terms of our size, gender, color, intelligences,[33] personality, gifts, abilities, interests, etc., none of these differences can ever be allowed to become determinative of the fundamental value of any particular human person. To equate the image of God in us with any minimal capacities, for example, reasoning ability, is to jeopardize the status of the mentally disabled.

It is essential to define the human as inclusively as possible, apart from all distinguishing qualities and abilities. Gilbert Meilander goes to the heart of the matter when he argues: "To belong to humankind one need not exercise its distinguishing traits; one need only be begotten of human parents."[34] The strength of this definition is that it allows for no exclusions, either based on mental or physical disability, or on the basis of generation through emerging reproductive technologies (for example, artificial insemination, *in vitro* fertilization, embryo transfer, surrogacy, or even cloning). Human value is no respecter of human differences. The innovative ministry of Jean Vanier, the founder of the L'Arche (The Ark) movement, which respects the dignity of persons with developmental disabilities through life in intentional community, provides a stellar case for the affirmation of the common humanity of all those created by God.[35] The body of Christ values each child of God by virtue of creation and for no other reason.

A second virtue involves *respect for the dignity of the marginalized*. Political and social systems throughout Western history have afforded privileges to certain categories of persons (in particular "white" men) and have marginalized those excluded by those categories. Thus women have faced the institutionalization of sexism (patriarchy), people of color the institutionalization of racism, same-gendered persons the institutionalization of heterosexism, children and the elderly the institutionalization of ageism, and people of the southern hemisphere the institutionalization of colonialism. For each of these classes of persons, the consequences are not only a question of human equality. Rather, in every case the resulting discrimination negatively affects the economic status of the respective group. This means the disadvantaged groups also normally suffer the effects of classism. Moreover, in particular instances multiple forms of discrimination violate the same persons (for example, older black women). This phenomenon led womanist theologian Katie Geneva Cannon, to employ the term "triple jeopardy," insofar as black women suffer from the combined effects of racism, sexism, and poverty.[36] Because the privileges of Euro-American men have become embedded in the social fabric, deconstructing the "isms" requires the force of the law and persistence over time.

The church as the body of Christ consists of members from all of these marginalized groups. Within the body of Christ, we affirm that when "one member suffers, all suffer together with it" (1 Cor 12:26). The suffering of marginalized people requires intentional and dedicated commitment on the part of the church.[37] Sexism needs to be deconstructed through proactive measures to build an egalitarian community of women and men.[38] Racism needs to be dismantled through the exposure of white privilege and affirmative action to guarantee the full equality of people of color.[39] Heterosexism needs to be remedied in church and society, beginning with the attitudes and policies of religious communities.[40] The rights of children and the elderly must be protected against structural discrimination.[41] Postcolonial thought must continue to challenge and overcome the destructive legacy of colonialism.[42] The church seeks to remain vigilant in the face of all forms of discrimination against and marginalization of those made in God's image.

A third core virtue relates to the *commitment to build an inclusive church.* In 1963 Martin Luther King declared:

> We must face the fact that in America, the church is still the most segregated major institution in America. At 11:00 on Sunday morning when we stand and sing that Christ has no east or west, we stand at the most segregated hour in this nation. This is tragic. Nobody of honesty can overlook this.[43]

In the ensuing decades very little has happened to alter this assessment, although the U.S. has become increasingly diverse, both culturally and religiously.[44] For churches that originated as Northern European ethnic enclaves or in the era of ethnic and racial separation, white privilege has become deeply embedded in congregational life.[45] Although many congregations have good intentions about being "friendly" to newcomers, what they generally mean is "If you become like us, you are welcome." For people of other ethnic origins or for those whose native language is not English, however, they can never become "one of us."

The kingdom of God is no respecter of ethnicity or language. Congregations are called to anticipate the arrival of God's kingdom by reflecting the diversity of humanity. If congregations are to become earnest about inclusivity, it means they must be ready to be changed by what new people bring to enrich the mix of life together in community. This is one of the greatest challenges facing congregations that have grown accustomed to the status quo of ethnic uniformity. How can the church celebrate different ethnic traditions as each being God's gift? How can the church embrace ethnic differences as enriching the whole, rather than as threat? There are a variety of strategies that congregations can employ in the commitment to greater inclusivity. First, they can listen carefully to the expressed needs of the new ethnic groups living in their community. Second, they can develop ministries to address the urgent needs of new populations, for example, offering classes in English as a second language or immigration counseling. Third, they can open up their buildings for use by different ethnic populations. Fourth, they can invite the use of their building for worship by a congregation from another ethnic group and language. Fifth, they can seek in humility to integrate the life of their own congregation with the religious ministry of another ethnic population.[46] This final suggestion is the most difficult of all, because it means we will be changed inevitably and dramatically by this encounter. Are we ready to be changed?

The fourth virtue comes to expression in *defending human rights*. One of the most significant innovations in the history of human thought transpired in the wake of World War II and the ravages of modern warfare, including the dropping of atomic bombs on Hiroshima and Nagasaki by the U.S. and the Holocaust in Nazi Germany: the formulation of the Universal Declaration of Human Rights by the United Nations in 1948. We have already argued for the compatibility of human rights discourse with the affirmation of human dignity grounded in the conviction that every human being is created in the image of God. What remains is for the church to claim the emerging defense of human rights as its own heritage. The protection of human dignity through defending civil, political, economic, social, and cultural rights as articulated in the Universal Declaration is coherent with the core values of the biblical narrative (as rehearsed in this chapter) and the Christian tradition. The human rights named in this document can be interpreted as consequential for what it means to be created in God's image. Church leaders need to draw the connections between theology and human rights in order to make it an indispensable portion of the church's legacy.

The fifth virtue entails *immersion in the theology of the cross*. "Do you not know that all of us who have been baptized into Christ Jesus were baptized into his death?" (Rom 6:3). Martin Luther, in listing the characteristics of the church, included "the holy possession of the cross" as the seventh mark:

> [T]he holy Christian people . . . must endure every misfortune and persecution, all kinds of trials and evil from the devil, the world, and the flesh (as the Lord's Prayer indicates) by inward sadness, timidity, fear, outward poverty, contempt, illness, and weakness, in order to become like their head, Christ.[47]

The church's life is characterized especially by voluntarily assuming the suffering of others in the spirit of Christian freedom in conformity to what Christ has done for us on the cross. Exactly at the places where human beings or the creation itself "groans" in agony (cf. Rom 8:22-23), the body of Christ is called to participate in sharing the pain and witnessing to God's power in weakness (2 Cor 12:9). The theology of the cross contrasts starkly with the prevailing theology of glory that holds out to church members the counterfeit promise that they will only receive blessings from God because of their faith. The gospel of Jesus Christ frees us from such self-preoccupation in order to devote our lives to participation in the suffering of others. Because this is where Christ chooses to be encountered, immersion in the theology of the cross is also paradoxically the source of our greatest joy.[48]

Three Christian Lives Exemplifying Human Dignity

These five virtues are imaged for the shalom church by three Christian lives—Bartolomé de Las Casas, Sojourner Truth, and Desmond Tutu—who each demonstrates the character of the body of Christ in respecting human dignity.

BARTOLOMÉ DE LAS CASAS

Bartolomé de Las Casas (1484–1566) was born in Seville, Spain, and experienced as an eight-year-old child Columbus's return from the New World, accompanied by seven native "Indians."[49] In 1502 he made a first voyage to Hispaniola and then returned to Spain to undertake studies for the priesthood. After ordination he traveled to Cuba, where he served as a chaplain during the Spanish conquest. Although a priest, he was rewarded through the conquest with an *encomienda* (plantation), which was replete with Indian indentured laborers. However, Las Casas underwent a life-changing conversion in 1514, stirred by the cruel genocide being inflicted on the Indian people. Joining the Dominican order, his life was set on a course that would make him a harsh critic of the Spanish treatment of the Indians and a champion of their fundamental human rights. For the next five decades Las Casas facilitated communications between the New World and Spain through visits, preaching, correspondence, and books to defend the humanity of the Indian people and advocate for their just and humane treatment. In 1543 he was appointed Bishop of Chiapas in southern Mexico, a position he held for more than twenty years.

Over the course of his life Las Casas arrived at ever deeper insights into the shared humanity of all peoples. As a man of his era, his comments sometimes appear antiquated or even offensive by current standards. However, the overall clarity of his vision and the strength of his commitment to human dignity prevailed:

> You are all in mortal sin! You live in it and you die in it! Why? Because of the cruelty and tyranny you use with these innocent people. Tell me, with what right, with what justice, do you hold these Indians in such cruel and horrible servitude? On what authority have you waged such detestable wars on these people, in their mild, peaceful lands, in which you have consumed such infinitudes of them, wreaking upon them this death and the unheard-of havoc? How is it you hold them so crushed and exhausted, giving them nothing to eat, nor any treatment for their diseases, which you cause them to be infected with through the surfeit of their toils, so that they "die on you" [as you say]—you mean, you kill them—mining gold for you day after

day? And what care do you take that anyone catechize them, so that they may come
to know their God and Creator, be baptized, hear Mass, observe Sundays and Holy
Days? Are they not human beings? Have they no rational souls? Are you not obligated to love them as you love yourselves? Do you not understand this? Do you not
grasp this? How is it that you sleep so soundly, so lethargically?[50]

The Spaniards' lust for gold was particularly repugnant to Las Casas.[51] So outspoken were his views that they provoked strong resistance in Spain and threats were
made against his life. He denounced the inhumane treatment of the Indian people
based on their genuine humanity as those created by God. Accordingly, he insisted
upon the peaceful evangelization of the Indians as the true and only way.[52] Las
Casas fervently opposed those who advocated any use of violence or war as means
to spread the Christian message.

Las Casas has been criticized for not affording the same respect to African
slaves as he did to the Indian peoples.[53] Rooted in a time and culture that took for
granted the institution of slavery, earlier in his career he called for the replacement
of Indian slaves by those from Africa, even requesting them for local use. However,
by the late 1540s, upon learning that the African people were acquired through
violent raids that forced them to become the victims of untold cruelty through
the slave trade, Las Casas "became enlightened about the evils and injustice of the
system of black slavery as it was then practiced."[54]

> Thus the bishop of Chiapas now expanded his message to condemn not only the
> enslavement of Indians and Africans, but also the slave trade itself. . . . He was also
> the first of his time to speak out against the institution of slavery. He presaged the
> movement to condemn slavery that would not begin until the end of the sixteenth
> century.[55]

In the 1550s Las Casas added several chapters to his major book, *History of the
Indies*, detailing the sordid history of the Portuguese conduct of the African slave
trade, repenting of his previous ignorance and behavior, and calling for the end
of slavery as an institution. In this regard, Las Casas demonstrated the integrity
of his convictions by his capacity to expand his horizons in the defense of human
dignity for all those oppressed as slaves.

Not only was Las Casas a staunch defender of the human rights of the Indian
people, but he also claimed that Christ himself was manifest in the encounter with
these children of God. In the words of Gustavo Guttiérrez:

> Bartolomé had another penetrating intuition. He saw the Indian in this "other,"
> this one-different-from-the-Westerner, the poor one of the gospel, and ultimately
> Christ himself. This is without a doubt the very key to the Lascasian spirituality and

theology. It sketches Bartolomé's "intelligence of faith" with original strokes, giving it its own physiognomy among other theological reflections of the age. The right to life and liberty, the right to be different, the perspective of the poor—these are intimately connected notions in the experience our friar has of the God of Jesus Christ, in whom he believes with all his strength, a strength he therefore places at the service of the liberation of the Indian.[56]

In this regard, Las Casas bears a message for the ages, wherever human beings are denied fundamental respect and dignity. Considering the prevailing worldview of his times, Las Casas shines like a beacon of hope for the defense of human rights in every generation. His prophetic witness anticipated the preferential option for the poor that only came to expression 500 years after the Iberian conquest of the Americas. Concluding his long ministry as Bishop of Chiapas, Las Casas returned to Spain at the end of his life, where he died in 1566 at age 82. He has been remembered and acclaimed in following generations as "the Defender of the Indians."

Sojourner Truth

Sojourner Truth (c. 1797–1883) was born as a slave in Hurley, New York, and given the name Isabella by her parents. At age forty-six, however, she claimed for herself the name by which she became widely known, reflecting her vocation as abolitionist, women's rights advocate, preacher, and prophet. She learned Dutch as her first language, which left her with a heavy accent when she spoke English. Sojourner Truth was bought and sold several times; some of her masters were cruel and their beatings left her with permanent scars. Although she was one of nine siblings, Sojourner Truth scarcely knew them as they were sold away in the slave trade.

Her mother instructed her in the Christian faith in the evenings after the work was done. In her life narrative, Sojourner Truth recalled the words her mother taught her about God: "He lives in the sky . . . and when you are beaten, or cruelly treated, or fall into any trouble, you must ask help of him, and he will always hear and help you."[57] Her mother also taught her to obey the commandments and to pray the Lord's Prayer while kneeling. The many inhumanities of slavery are detailed in her narrative: slave auctions, malicious treatment (beatings and rape), and the sale of one of her five children as chattel (another died in infancy; all were slaves). In 1826 Sojourner Truth fled and escaped to freedom with her infant daughter, Sophia, leaving the others behind. Emancipation of slaves in New York took effect on July 4, 1827. When she learned that one of her children, Peter, had been sold illegally to an owner in Alabama, Sojourner Truth became the first black woman to go to trial against a white man and win the case. Following emancipation, she worked as a housekeeper in New York City for a Christian evangelist. During this time, she became devout in the Christian faith.

After changing her name in 1843 and joining the Methodist Church, Sojourner Truth became an itinerant preacher. In 1844 she joined the Northhampton Association of Education, a communal organization supporting pacifism, women's rights, and religious tolerance. While a member of this Massachusetts community, she met Frederick Douglass and William Lloyd Garrison, leaders in the abolitionist movement. When the Association disbanded in 1846, she worked for Garrison's brother-in-law as a housekeeper and during this time dictated her life story, which Garrison published in 1850. In this same year she purchased a house in Northhampton and gave a famous presentation at the first National Women's Rights Convention, held at Worcester.

Sojourner Truth is most well known for the magnificent and stirring address she delivered extemporaneously at a Women's Convention held at Akron, Ohio, in 1851. This became known as the "Ain't I a Woman?" speech and it articulates her convictions about equal rights for women, including African Americans:

> Well, children, where there is so much racket there must be something out of kilter. I think that 'twixt the Negroes of the South and the women at the North all talking about rights, the white men will be in a fix pretty soon. But what's all this here talking about?
>
> That man over there says that women need to be helped into carriages, and lifted over ditches, and to have the best place everywhere. Nobody ever helps me into carriages, or over mud-puddles, or gives me any best place! And ain't I a woman? Look at me! Look at my arm! I have ploughed and planted, and gathered into barns, and no man could head me! And ain't I a woman? I could work as much and eat as much as a man—when I could get it—and bear the lash as well! And ain't I a woman? I have borne thirteen children, and seen them most all sold off to slavery, and when I cried out with my mother's grief, none but Jesus heard me! And ain't I a woman?
>
> Then they talk about this thing in the head; what's this they call it? [member of audience whispers, "intellect"] That's it, honey. What's that got to do with women's rights or negroes' rights? If my cup won't hold but a pint, and yours holds a quart, wouldn't you be mean not to let me have my little half measure full?
>
> Then that little man in black there, he says women can't have as much rights as men, 'cause Christ wasn't a woman! Where did your Christ come from? Where did your Christ come from? From God and a woman! Man had nothing to do with Him.
>
> If the first woman God ever made was strong enough to turn the world upside down all alone, these women together ought to be able to turn it back, and get it right side up again! And now they is asking to do it, the men better let them.

Obliged to you for hearing me, and now old Sojourner ain't got nothing more to say.[58]

The oratorical skills of Sojourner Truth combined with her deep commitment to equal rights brought her before hundreds of audiences in the next decade. Sometimes the crowds were hostile, but she was never silenced by fear. During this time she worked with many others, including Harriet Beecher Stowe, for the end of slavery and for women's suffrage. She insisted always on linking these two causes together: "If colored men get their rights, and not colored women, colored men will be masters over women, and it will be just as bad as before."[59]

In 1857 Sojourner Truth moved with some members of her family to a house near Battle Creek, Michigan. During the Civil War she helped to recruit soldiers for the Union Army. In 1864 she worked in Washington, D.C., for the National Freedmen's Relief Association, providing assistance to former slaves, and during that same year she met President Abraham Lincoln. Even after the adoption of the Thirteenth Amendment to the Constitution, abolishing slavery, in 1865, Sojourner Truth continued to struggle for freedom and equality for all people, in her later years taking up the causes of prison reform and opposition to capital punishment. Although she gave her life for the cause of freedom, upon attempting to vote in the presidential election in 1872 she was turned away from the polls. Sojourner Truth died at her home in Battle Creek in 1883. Her last recorded words, spoken to a journalist shortly before her death, were: "Be a follower of Jesus Christ."[60]

Desmond Mpilo Tutu

Desmond Mpilo Tutu (born 1931) has served a vocation as priest, bishop, and archbishop in the Anglican Church of Southern Africa, becoming an eloquent and bold public leader in the movement to end apartheid in South Africa. He grew up under the specter of apartheid and knew firsthand the indignities and humiliations afforded those labeled "black." His father was a teacher and he followed in his father's footsteps after his university studies. However, he resigned his teaching position in protest following the passage of a bill that guaranteed a poor educational future for black South Africans. Soon his interests turned to the study of theology. In 1960 Tutu was ordained as a priest in the Anglican Church and he engaged in further theological studies from 1962 to 1966 in England. Upon returning to South Africa, he served as a lecturer in theology from 1967 to 1972, deepening the theological foundations that would ground him in the time to come in the fight against apartheid. After three years in London as the assistant director of a theological education fund for the World Council of Churches, Tutu was appointed Dean of the St. Mary's Cathedral in Johannesburg, the first black to hold this position.

Tutu next served as Bishop of Lesotho from 1976 to 1978. In May 1976 he wrote an open letter to Prime Minister John Vorster, appealing for peaceful change from the apartheid system:

> I am writing to you as one human person to another human person, gloriously created in the image of the selfsame God, redeemed by the selfsame Son of God who for all our sakes died on the Cross and rose triumphant from the dead. . . . I am, therefore, writing to you, Sir, as one Christian to another. . . . This Jesus Christ, whatever we may have done, has broken down all that separates us irrelevantly—such as race, sex, culture, status, etc. In this Jesus Christ we are forever bound together as one redeemed humanity, black and white together. . . .
>
> I am writing to you, Sir, because I have a growing nightmarish fear that unless something drastic is done very soon then bloodshed and violence are going to happen in South Africa almost inevitably. A people can take only so much and no more.[61]

The letter was never answered. The Soweto riots in 1976 verified Tutu's insights and marked the intensification of the pressures to end the apartheid system.

In 1978 Tutu became the first black General Secretary of the South African Council of Churches. This brought him into the center of the swirl of historical developments rapidly unfolding both nationally and internationally against apartheid. As a means of bringing about the needed change, Tutu joined the voices of those advocating economic boycott and disinvestment as strategies, in contrast to the U.S. policy of "constructive engagement." In 1985, the same year that Tutu was appointed Bishop of Johannesburg, both the U.S. and the United Kingdom stopped investments, leading to a crisis in the South African economy and pressuring the government to reform. Tutu helped organize peace marches that brought tens of thousands into the streets of Cape Town.

As General Secretary for the Council of Churches, Bishop Tutu (and even more after his appointment as Archbishop of Cape Town in 1986) was able to help coordinate the efforts of the Christian community in vigorous opposition to the evils of the apartheid system and toward reconciliation among the estranged parties. In many public events, he consistently communicated the human dignity of all people: "Say to yourselves in your heart, 'God loves me.' In your heart: 'God loves me, God loves me. . . . I am of infinite value to God. God created me for freedom.' "[62] Tutu coined the term "rainbow nation" to describe the emerging new South Africa, also naming his fellow citizens "the rainbow people of God."[63] Due to the steady pressures from within and without South Africa, including those from the Christian churches, peaceful resistance finally brought down the apartheid system, culminating in the national elections in 1994.

During the transition from the apartheid era, Tutu was a consistent advocate for reconciliation among all the people of South Africa. Among his many other forms of service Tutu served from 1987 to 1997 as President of the All Africa Council of Churches.

In 1995 Tutu was called upon to chair the Truth and Reconciliation Commission, which staged a high profile series of public hearings to investigate the crimes committed under the apartheid regime and especially to render vindication to the victims.[64] Although the work of the commission has been criticized for hiding the full truth about the viciousness of apartheid, most agree that the process was indispensable for furthering the reconciliation process toward the building of a post-apartheid South Africa. The value of the process is evidenced by how it has served as a model for other contexts which were seeking to recover from societal division and violence, such as Rwanda and the Solomon Islands.

As a consequence of his courageous witness throughout the anti-apartheid struggle and his unrelenting defense of human rights, Tutu has been described as "South Africa's moral conscience," the voice of the voiceless. He has articulated his theological position in terms of *ubuntu*, the African concept that affirms that people only form their identities in relationship to one another.[65] Among the many causes for which he has voiced concern are the Israeli-Palestinian conflict, poverty eradication, environmental justice, women's rights, gay rights, and the fight against HIV/AIDS. He has served as board member or patron for many humanitarian organizations. Included in the honors that Tutu has received over his lifetime of ministry are the Nobel Peace Prize (1984), the *Pacem in Terris* Award (1987), and the Gandhi Peace Prize (2005). He is also the recipient of many honorary degrees from prestigious international educational institutions. Based on his core commitment that all God's children are created in God's image, Desmond Tutu has given exceptional leadership to the body of Christ in the cause of respecting human dignity.

Practicing Respect for Human Dignity as Ministering Community

The biblical narrative of God's respect for human dignity shapes the character of the body of Christ and forms God's people in the commensurate virtues. These virtues come to expression in the lives of those who safeguard and defend human dignity wherever it is threatened. The character and virtues of the church as the body of Christ, Christ existing as church-community, are manifested in practices that reflect the Christian commitment to respecting human dignity within God's creation.

The first ecclesial practice involves *admiring the divine image in the face of the other*. By innate instinct we have the tendency to be suspicious or fearful of those who are different from us. It is therefore profoundly countercultural to approach those who are "other" as those made in the very image of God. This requires unlearning our aversion to those who appear to be outsiders and instead meeting them with "admiration."[66] The root of the Latin word translated as "admire" means "to wonder." We are summoned by the divine image in our neighbor to behold each one in wonder, not fear. Instead of dividing human beings into binary and dualistic categories—male/female, black/white, old/young, straight/gay, able/disabled[67]—the image of God in the other calls us to stand in awe of the mystery of the one whom God has created. Instead of seeing the other according to the categories by which we tend to classify others, we are to call each person by name, seeking to honor the depths of uniqueness that belong to every child of God.

In order for us to respect one another as the persons God made us to be, the body of Christ expresses particular admiration and welcome to those who are excluded or degraded in the surrounding society: singles, members of unconventional families, women, children, youth, the elderly, people of color, foreigners, gays and lesbians, and those with disabilities. Indeed, a congregation may find a particular ministry in reaching out to persons in populations of those who experience marginalization or suffer discrimination based on any of these or another category. For example, a congregation might reach out to a different ethnic population by listening carefully to the expressed needs of that group and opening up its church building for use by that community. Or the body of Christ might get serious about ministry to those suffering from hearing or visual impairments by developing ministry to the deaf or blind. Or a church might proactively seek to make its building physically accessible to those whose mobility is impaired and reach out to those confined to wheelchairs. These and similar ministries demonstrate profound respect for those who are different from the mainstream. Differences are not a reason for fear or contempt but rather an occasion for praising God who divined a world of splendid diversity.

A second practice, related to the previous, is *expecting to encounter Christ in the person of the vulnerable one*. Do we take Jesus Christ at his word, that he meets us in those persons whom the world dismisses or scorns (Matt 25:31-46)? It is not only our duty, as those grounded in Scripture, to acknowledge the divine image in our neighbor but to embrace the promise that, as we minister to those who are different from us, we will experience the presence of Christ! The paradigmatic text for this practice is the story of the Good Samaritan (Luke 10:25-37). Neither the priest nor the devout layman took the time to acknowledge the wounded man at the side of the road as neighbor. Instead it was an alien who not only recognized the personhood of the stranger but ministered to his needs. To this very day the church recalls the Christ-like character of how this Samaritan related to his neighbor in need. No doubt that in caring for the afflictions of this stranger, the Samaritan ministered to Jesus Christ himself!

How often in the experience of the church, we "have entertained angels without knowing it" (Heb 13:2) by going to visit a shut-in, listening to the story of a stranger on the street, or playing with a child! Mysteriously, Jesus Christ comes to meet us in our relationships with those with disabilities! Inexplicably, we are the ones to receive a divine blessing as we develop friendships with gay and lesbian persons! There is a sacramental quality to how Christ chooses to meet us in the company of those whom the world fails to acknowledge with the full dignity owed those created in God's image. By cultivating such relationships, the body of Christ is healed as it embraces those parts that make it whole.

A third practice entails *participating in the suffering of others*. The theology of the cross affirmed in this chapter leads us to the many places in this world where human beings suffer. It is tempting to truncate the breadth of the theology of the cross by relating it primarily to my own suffering or the suffering of those dear to me. There is an inevitability to human suffering that belongs to the human condition. Each of us faces discouragement, fragility, sickness, finitude, and mortality as dimensions of our common human circumstance. Moreover, it belongs to the character of God in Christ crucified to minister to us exactly when we must bear the cross in relation to our own personal suffering. However, the theology of the cross means even more than this. The way of the cross leads us beyond the parameters of our own suffering (or the suffering of those in our family or congregation) and opens to us the horizon of a world where people suffer unjustly at the hands of others. The theology of the cross summons the church of Jesus Christ to take a stand in exactly these places.

Wherever human dignity is threatened or the divine image is disregarded, here the church takes its stand. Each of the provisions of the Universal Declaration of Human Rights gives the body of Christ direction for where to join Christ in a suffering world: where rights are denied based on race, color, sex, language, political opinion, national origin, property, birth, or other status; where people are enslaved; where human beings suffer arbitrary arrest, torture, or are dealt cruel, inhuman, or degrading punishment; where the accused are denied due process under a rule of law; where the freedoms of movement, peaceful assembly, or speech are violated; where the right to a nationality is disavowed; where the right to marriage and family are not allowed; where the right to own property is refused;

where freedom of thought, conscience, or religion are jeopardized; where the right to work under fair conditions and at equitable compensation is threatened; where existence is endangered through insufficiency of food, water, shelter, health care, or social services; or where the right to education is ignored. One acute instance facing the church in North America involves the status of migrant laborers, particularly those from Central America. What obligation does the church of Jesus Christ have in providing sanctuary to these persons who are deprived of basic rights by their lack of legal immigration status?[68] In exactly such places of human suffering, the church of Jesus Christ chooses to take a stand, attending to the needs of the people and participating in their cause. The goal, however, is not merely to join the suffering but through participating in the suffering of others to alleviate it and rectify its causes.

A fourth and urgent practice is *principled opposition to genocide.* Tragically, the brutal reality of human genocide continues to plague our world. Genocide involves violent intentions and actions "to destroy, in whole or in part, a national, ethnical, racial, or religious group."[69] Instances of genocide in the modern world are shockingly many: Native Americans in North America, Armenians in the Ottoman Empire early in the twentieth century, the Jews of Europe in the Holocaust, Bosnians in the former Yugoslavia, the Tutsis in Rwanda, and particular ethnic tribes in Darfur, Sudan. The paradigmatic form of genocide is that of the Nazi persecution and murder of six million Jewish people during the Shoah in World War II. Building on the long history of anti-Semitism in Christianity and Western civilization, Hitler and the Nazi regime were enabled to dehumanize, label, vilify, blame, scapegoat, isolate, remove, and annihilate the Jewish population of Europe with only minimal resistance from the non-Jewish majority. Most of the German population participated in the genocide as bystanders, if not as sympathizers, including those who were members of the Protestant or Roman Catholic churches.[70] If we do not learn an alternative practice from the Holocaust, the church will be doomed to repeat its failures over and over again in the future.

The symptoms of genocide are identifiable: hate speech, racial profiling, intolerance, segregation, legal discrimination, separation, internment, and violence. Early detection of genocidal behavior by the global community is crucial to its prevention. Eight stages of genocide have been identified[71]:

1. Classification: people are divided into "us" and "them."
2. Symbolization: hate symbols are forced upon the identified population.
3. Dehumanization: language is used to deprive the identified group of humanity.

4. Organization: military or special squads are organized to control the enemy.
5. Polarization: propaganda is employed to perpetrate hatred.
6. Preparation: victims are identified and separated according to type.
7. Extermination: the dehumanized are "eliminated" from society.
8. Denial: perpetrators deny having committed any crimes.

The church of Jesus Christ can play a significant role in identifying, naming, and persisting in opposition to genocidal behavior. To this end the church needs to participate actively in global networks aimed at the early detection and prevention of genocidal violence.[72] Ending genocide requires securing reliable information, educating the public, and persistence in organizing efforts. The global character of the church equips it to make a major contribution to this undertaking.

A fifth practice involves the church in *advocating for human rights*. Effective advocacy remains a formidable challenge to the church in every quarter—whether for peace, justice, care of creation, or for human rights. The importance of the practice of advocacy will be underscored in the final chapter through a discussion of congregation-based community organizing. In this context, however, I emphasize the responsibility of the body of Christ to advocate for those whose human rights have been deprived by the unjust exercise of human authority. Because of the common humanity we share with all who are created in God's image, the church demonstrates solidarity and concern not only for those who are Christians but also for all people who face the violation of their basic human rights. Toward this end, we join together with people of other religious faiths and all people of good will to secure and defend the rights of all people. This involves advocacy both for civil and political rights and social and economic rights.

According to God's left-hand strategy, the Christian church can and should join forces with other humanitarian efforts in undertaking effective advocacy. This legitimizes the involvement of Christians in the broad spectrum of human rights organizations, including Amnesty International, Human Rights Watch, the Anti-Defamation League, Anti-Slavery International, Freedom House, and United Nations Global Compact. The strength of these organizations is demonstrated in educating members of the church about matters of human rights and building a sizable coalition of concerned persons to make a significant impact on decision makers.

This chapter has explored the meaning of the church's apostolicity for guarding human dignity. I have rehearsed the biblical narrative concerning God's respect for humanity and God's participation in human suffering on the cross and have explored how this narrative forms the character of the body of Christ, incarnates particular virtues, and sends the church to enter into human suffering and defend human rights. I have suggested how these virtues have been embodied in the lives of Bartolomé de Las Casas, Sojourner Truth, and Desmond Tutu. Lastly, I have considered how congregations can embody the theology of the cross by engaging in particular social ministry practices that promote profound respect for all those created in the image of God. In the eighth and final chapter I reflect on how the central themes of the last four chapters—reconciliation and peacemaking, social justice, care for creation, and respect for human dignity—together constitute the character of the body of Christ as shalom church. I also examine the many contradictions that afflict the integrity of the shalom church and acknowledge the unfinished agenda. Furthermore, I reflect on how congregation-based community organizing can serve as a significant instrument for more effective social ministry by the church. I conclude by reaffirming our vocation to share in God's mission as the shalom church through social ministry.

Part III

Praxis of the Shalom Church

Embodying Shalom Church
The Praxis of the Kingdom in a Torn Creation

God's mission—into which the church has been invited and called to partici-pate—is to mend the torn fabric of creation (*tikkun olam*). The outward manifes-tations of the tear are everywhere evident: violence in homes, on the street, and between nations; people who seek to survive without the most basic necessities of adequate food, water, shelter, or medical care; earth, sea, sky, and their creatures in acute distress; human beings denied fundamental respect and dignity at the hands of others. These are the most obvious signs that something is dramatically amiss in God's good creation. We read and hear about these conditions in the news and on the Internet. But there are also inward manifestations of the creation's anguish, hidden within the human heart: loneliness, isolation, shame, guilt, fear, anger, enmity, depression, despair, the sickness unto death. Each of these also signals the world's dis-ease, although only a sensitive observer may detect them.[1] The theo-logical term to describe the world's condition, sin, encompasses both the outward and inward realms.

The triune God is missionary in character, taking initiative to heal the human and cosmic condition of brokenness and disrepair. In this mission God has designed two distinct but interrelated strategies to restore wholeness. With the right hand, God offers the gospel of Jesus Christ to the world with the promise of the forgive-ness of sins, renovation of life, and eternal salvation. God commissions the church with the vocation of evangelizing, to proclaim the Word of grace as assemblies gather for worship and to share the message of God's love in Jesus Christ with the entire world. An evangelizing church seeks to participate faithfully in God's right-hand strategy. [2]

At the same time, God, with the left hand, seeks to rule the public world in peace, justice, and equity. Through this left-hand activity God seeks in often hidden ways to establish and maintain the structures that preserve life in the face of death. God provides the arenas of family, workplace, religious organization, and government to order the world justly and peaceably. Freed from self-preoccupation by the message of God's grace in Jesus Christ, the baptized enter the left-hand realm of God with one primary interest: to serve the neighbor. Those neighbors include the members of one's own family, colleagues at work, members of one's church, and the unknown faces of the general public. God commissions the church with the vocation of fostering shalom in these varied dimensions of the public world, engaging with concern for each one's welfare and advocating for the common good. The shalom church aims to keep good faith with God's left-hand strategy.

In Jesus Christ God became incarnate in the world to implement God's right- and left-hand strategies with concentrated energy, proclaiming the gospel of the kingdom and mending creation's tattered fabric (*tikkun olam*). God-in-the-flesh ministered to enfleshed human souls holistically. Before his death on the cross, the very body of the living Jesus Christ was imparted to his followers through a meal of bread and wine: "This is my body. This is my blood. Do this in remembrance of me." As Jesus' disciples received the body of Christ as food, they themselves became the living expression of Christ's body in the world. Each baptized person lives as a gifted member of the body of Christ, the church. Each one is needed for the healthy functioning of the entire body. All the parts, working together as one body, re-present the existence of Jesus Christ in the world. If the world is to encounter Jesus Christ today, this meeting occurs through an encounter with his extant body, the church.

How literally dare we take this imagery of the church as the body of Christ? Dietrich Bonhoeffer articulated an ecclesiology that dared to assert that in fact the church *is* Christ existing as church-community, the collective person Jesus Christ.[3] While acutely aware of its fallibility, Bonhoeffer challenged the church to claim its God-given identity and vocation in the world: to manifest Christ's corporate reality in time and space. "Now you are the body of Christ and individually members of it" (1 Cor 12:27).

> But speaking the truth in love, we must grow up in every way into him who is the head, into Christ, from whom the whole body, joined and knit together by every

ligament with which it is equipped, as each part is working properly, promotes the
body's growth in building itself up in love. (Eph 4:15-16)

Bonhoeffer's provocative insight into the nature of the church builds upon the
Pauline metaphor with radical aplomb! As the church gathers for Word and sacrament at worship, the Holy Spirit is at work forming this community as the actual
body of Christ in the world. The body of Christ is created in Christ's image. Even
more, this community assumes the very character of Jesus Christ. The church
assumes not only the "mind" of Christ (cf. Phil 2:5) but even the fundamental
nature of Christ.

If the church *is* the body of Christ, then it belongs to this body to reflect
Christ's nature in its public ministry. The four marks of the church (*notae ecclesiae*) denote the classical confession of the church's enduring character: one, holy,
catholic, apostolic. God in Christ has instilled in the church these distinguishing
traits, which have been confessed in the Nicene Creed over the generations. While
these four marks have been employed conventionally to describe the nature of the
church theologically and more recently to promote ecumenical rapprochement
among the divided churches, each of these classical marks also entertains an ethical dimension that grounds the body of Christ in social ministry. The oneness of
the church authorizes its engagement in the ministry of reconciliation and peacemaking. The holiness of the church summons it to advocate for just structures that
provide sufficiency in the basic necessities for human survival. The catholicity of
the church places it in solidarity with all God has created, bestowing responsibility for creation care. The apostolicity of the church sends it forth to afford profound respect to and defend the dignity of every child whom God has created in
the divine image, that is, all people.

As the body of Christ is enveloped by and immersed in the biblical story of
God's peacemaking, justice, care for creation, and respect for human dignity, the
church assumes the character of Jesus Christ who reflected these very qualities
in relationship with others and the creation itself.[4] The four interrelated biblical narratives recounted in chapters 4–7 serve as the womb for the gestation of
particular virtues that belong to Christ existing as church-community. Twenty
such virtues have been elaborated as distinguishing characteristics of the church
of Jesus Christ. These virtues have been illustrated by twelve brief biographies
of those who embody them concretely. In every case, not only have the selected
representatives demonstrated the respective virtues in their personal lives, but
they have belonged to or led social movements that defended and advocated for
these values in the public sphere. The embodied virtues next generate particular
practices by which congregations can participate in God's mission through social

ministry. Altogether twenty congregational practices have been described. While these are not exhaustive, they provide solid grounding for the vocation of the shalom church.[5] By organically linking the nature of the body of Christ with the character of Jesus Christ, we contend not only that the church *does* social ministry but that the church *is* social ministry by definition.

This final chapter addresses some of the tough issues and difficult challenges hindering a fuller embodiment of shalom church. First, I confront the historical legacy of the church and the numerous contradictions that undermine confidence in the capacity of the church to live up to the agenda outlined in this book. Second, I examine both the tensions between and the interconnections among the four central social ministry themes of the book (peacemaking, justice, care for creation, human dignity) to demonstrate how the four strands weave together to constitute the whole cloth of shalom church. Third, I explore particular issues of leadership and examine how the principles of congregation-based community organizing can enhance the ministry of the body of Christ as shalom church. The conclusion reminds us how the contemporary context for embodying shalom church is religiously pluralistic and, in the West, post-Christian. The body of Christ must learn to navigate uncharted territory as it engages the world in the spirit of shalom.

Confronting Contradictions

The entire history of the church is one long scandal. Analyzed from a critical angle, this assertion might serve as an accurate summary statement about the legacy of the Christian church in the world. The discrepancy between what the church purports to be and its actual accomplishments is stunning. Already in its earliest history, the life of the church was characterized both by increasingly harsh polemic, as the followers of Jesus separated from the Jewish mainstream, and by disputes with those whose teachings and practices were deemed inauthentic (that is, heresy). Evidence of the church in conflict is at hand already in the New Testament: Jesus' controversies with Pharisees and scribes ("the Jews" in John's Gospel), Jesus' trial and crucifixion by the Romans, Paul's controversies with opponents in several of his epistles, suspicions and accusations about false teachers in the Pastoral letters, and the highly charged, symbolic language against enemies in the book of Revelation. The contest was sometimes framed in terms of the forces of God versus the power of Satan, a battle against the principalities and powers. Such language has been used too often in later times to demonize opponents. And once an opponent has been demonized, any action can be rationalized against this enemy.

Each of the four central themes of this book is contradicted by warrants from the Bible itself. The conquest of the Holy Land is accompanied by horrible texts that authorize genocide against the Canaanite tribes.[6] The judges and kings employ graphic violence to slay their enemies, all at God's command. Violence against women sometimes appears routine.[7] Texts of judgment condemn God's opponents to the torments of hell. The people of God fail to extend hospitality to strangers or justice to the poor among them. God authorizes pestilence and plagues to punish the wicked. The goats who, unlike the sheep, fail to minister to the hungry, sick, or imprisoned are sentenced to eternal punishment. The earth, sky, waters, and their creatures are left devastated by human destruction. The sky turns to darkness, the moon to blood. The land is laid waste. Respect for others is refused and human dignity denied. While I have claimed that such texts are not to be viewed as normative for the life of the Christian church, they have been routinely cited over the course of church history to validate discrimination, exclusion, hatred, pogroms, violence, murder, war, and genocide. While we can claim the trajectories that promote peacemaking, justice, creation care, and human dignity as the normative tradition, the church itself has not and does not always guard against misuse of its Scripture for values and actions that contradict these commitments.

The long history of the church is also replete with patterns and events that mightily contradict the agenda of the shalom church. Particularly consequential has been the legacy of Christian anti-Semitism, which runs from its origins in the New Testament to the present century.[8] The polemic of Jesus and his earliest followers against their closest kin in the faith has given rise over the centuries to bitter defamation of Jewish persons, customs, and religion. After the assumption of the mantle of power in the fourth century under the Constantinian arrangement, Christianity has too often exercised its privilege in harmful and murderous ways against the Jewish people, all under the guise of biblical warrants. Discrimination against the Jews in the Middle Ages gave rise to pogroms and banishment.

Consider, for example, the shameful and blatant excoriation of the Jews by Martin Luther toward the end of his life, "On the Jews and Their Lies."[9] The Jewish people suffered repeatedly as identifiable scapegoats. Anti-Semitism became a normal dimension of Western civilization. This tradition of anti-Semitism was so much a part of the shared worldview that Hitler and the National Socialists could facilely appeal to this deep-rooted prejudice in executing their policies of systematic genocide with scarcely a whimper of opposition, even on the part of the church. Even after the Holocaust, anti-Semitism continues to raise its ugly head in detestable statements and stereotypes against the Jewish people. Holocaust denial is unimaginably frequent. The Jews remain a common object for irrational blame. Overcoming the legacy of anti-Semitism remains a major challenge facing the church still today.

Other major scandals in the history of the church include the crusades, the Inquisition, wars conducted in Christ's name, and the legacy of witch trials. Under the banner of Christendom, the Crusade movement represents an entire epoch of Christian history in the high Middle ages.[10] From the end of the eleventh century through the fourteenth century, popes and kings colluded in seeking to stem the spread of Islam, in particular seeking to conquer Jerusalem and liberate the Holy Land, and wage holy war against heretics and heathen. A Christian warrior caste, the knights, received blessing and material support from the church for the several military expeditions against the enemies. The knights bore on their cloaks the sign of the cross and were promised plenary indulgences for their sins. The Crusades symbolize the extent to which the church became militarized under the influence of Christendom. Instead of reaching out to pagans in mission, the crusades sought their destruction.

Building on the legacy of the Crusades, the church also engaged in battle against its internal enemies, those accused of heresy, by means of the Inquisition (the thirteenth to fifteenth centuries).[11] At its most severe, the Inquisition employed torture to secure "voluntary confessions" and the death penalty for obstinate heretics, especially by burning at the stake. The methods of the Inquisition were carried forward into the sixteenth and seventeenth centuries through the organization of witch trials, persecution, and burnings. As many as 60,000 "witches" lost their lives to this persecution. Witch trials were held by both Roman Catholic and Protestant authorities, including the witch trials at Salem, Massachusetts, in 1692.

The Protestant Reformation also can be held responsible for many forms of excess against enemies. Martin Luther engaged in horrific polemic against the peasants on the occasion of their protesting social injustice and uprising in 1525. The accumulated grievances of the peasants about their living conditions and rising hopes based on the Reformation led to riots and revolt, including attacks on monasteries and castles. Luther took issue with both the theology and tactics of the peasants, publishing intemperate and inflammatory denunciations of the peasants:

> A rebel is not worth rational arguments, for he does not accept them. You have to answer people like that with a fist, until the sweat drips off their noses. The peasants would not listen; they would not let anyone tell them anything, so their ears must now be unbuttoned with musket balls until their heads jump off their shoulders. Such pupils need such a rod.[12]

While Luther is not by any means solely responsible for the actions of the rulers against the peasants, his endorsement contributed to violent retaliation by the authorities and the slaughter of many. Moreover, later generations have employed Luther's judgment to justify repression of legitimate social protest. The Reformation also saw violent repression against Anabaptists and other representatives of the Radical Reformation, who did not share and even rejected the theological positions of the major reformers.[13]

Many other instances could be cited in Christian history for the failure of the church to act anything like the shalom church. In recent history we could document how the Christian tradition was co-opted by the German Christians in Nazi Germany[14], used to validate apartheid in South Africa,[15] and employed to justify hate crimes in the United States.[16] The Bible has been interpreted to rationalize the suppression of women, people of color, sexual minorities, and many other groups. Even more, citations of Scripture have been used as warrants to defend many forms of violence, from domestic violence to international war. While Christianity is not the only religion to fall prey to the misuse of its heritage, the power and influence of Christianity in history makes distortions of its authority particularly consequential and egregious.

Gerhard Ebeling goes so far as to argue that the four classical marks of the church are stated so definitively by the Nicene Creed in order to buttress the church as it sought to address the readily apparent contradictions between the empirical church and its God-intended existence:

> [T]he unity of the church had been so radically called into question that it had to be affirmed so emphatically. . . . Likewise, its apostolicity had to be emphasized because it was all too obvious that the church was drifting away from its apostolic origins. . . . The church's holiness had become so important because the signs of its unholiness were so strikingly obvious. . . . [Universality or catholicity] became such a focal point for the church because its own tendency to particularism was giving it so much trouble. These statements of perfection were actually prompted by the experience of the church's many imperfections. They are cries of protest against appearances being taken for the truth and judgments on what is ultimately true being made on the basis of what can be seen.[17]

If this is the case, then already at the composition of the Nicene Creed the assertion of the *notae ecclesiae* encompassed the recognition of the church's limitations and sinfulness.

It would prove futile for the church to defend its innocence in the face of this scandalous legacy. The only authentic response is for the church to acknowledge its tragic participation in human sinfulness, sinfulness that has affected not only individuals but the institutions and structures in which the church has been embodied over the centuries. The Christian faith holds that sinfulness infects human existence on every level, including ecclesial existence. For this reason the church can be emboldened to acknowledge its history of scandal and humbly confess its sins against God and humanity. If the scandals were, however, all that can be said about the value of the church, then we might only conclude that the Christian religion is bankrupt, as do the great despisers of religion in the contemporary world.[18]

One of the most authentic claims about Christian existence is that its character is *simul justus et peccator*, that is, the body of Christ in the world is simultaneously sinful and justified. Based on much of its empirical record, the church discloses its solidarity with the sinful human condition. However, based on God's forgiveness and grace, in particular as that has been revealed in Jesus Christ, the church yet dares to call itself justified for Christ's sake. This means that the legacy of the church cannot be reduced to its history of scandal; instead by the power of God through the Holy Spirit, the church also manifests the character of Jesus Christ to the world, however fragmentarily. While the body of Christ must be endlessly vigilant to guard against scandal, God nevertheless chooses to work through this modest instrument to pursue divine purposes. For this reason we dare confess that the body of Christ is simultaneously a scandal to the world and the shalom church. This twofold paradoxical claim allows the church to acknowledge and repent of its history of sinfulness, even while imploring God to manifest true shalom through its ministry.

Only because God chooses to continue to work through the paradoxical reality of the church can the body of Christ hope to serve as a sign and instrument of God's shalom in the world.[19] The church is a "sign community" wherever it witnesses to the world by its life together, however imperfectly, by demonstrating the character of Jesus Christ through peace, justice, creation care, and respect for human dignity. The church exists as God's "instrument" as it seeks to foster God's shalom agenda through its mission and engagement in the problems of society. In both functions, the church's scandalous history can itself become an asset as it allows God's spiritual power to become manifest in the world through its weakness (2 Cor 12:9).

> A church that protects itself against a search into its own sinfulness is a church that does not believe in its own message of reconciliation and that undermines its spiritual power to witness about this message for others in the world.[20]

The calling to serve God's shalom is not only something that the body of Christ aims to provide to others outside the church, but it remains an agenda for the church itself to manifest in its own ecclesial life. The more the church is able to re-present God's shalom in its own life together, the better it will be able to further its mission to the world. In order for the world to accept the work of the church as credible, the body of Christ will humbly seek to embody provisionally the work of the shalom church. This remains an urgent agenda for the body of Christ in its ministry and mission.

Exploring the Interfaces of the Shalom Church

Just as the four classical marks of the church combine together to constitute the theological character of ecclesial existence, so the ethical implications of these marks must be woven together in constituting the full character of the shalom church. This section explores some of the interconnections among the core themes of the book—peacemaking/reconciliation, justice, care for creation, respect for human dignity—toward developing a thick description of the agenda for the shalom church. Altogether the four ethical marks of the church constitute a set of six interfaces, each of which presents particular tensions and possibilities. The fabric of the shalom church might be figured according to the following diagram:

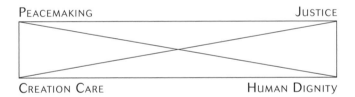

The Fabric of the Shalom Church

Seen together, the four components create six pairs of axes, each of which disclose important considerations for the church in its social ministry.

Axis One: Peacemaking—Justice. "No peace without justice!" This slogan discloses a fundamental truth about the social conditions necessary for true and lasting peace. Without sufficiency in the fundamental necessities of life—food, clean water, shelter, basic medical care—the seeds of discontent sprout and grow. In a world of electronic media, awareness of the gaping separation between economic elites and the billions decimated by extreme poverty is apparent to many. How many wars have been seeded by the pursuit of securing basic material needs? How much of historical and contemporary "terrorism" is linked to indignation over the disparity between the affluent and the desperate poor? Instead of privileging military solutions in situations of conflict, giving priority to the issues of economic and social justice very often would address the roots of the problems rather than the symptoms. It is counter-intuitive to envision humanitarian aid as the response to an outbreak of violence, but such an approach may frequently come much closer to an accurate analysis of root causes. This raises the perennial question about the priority placed by the nations of the world on economic development and education in relation to the percentage of budgets dedicated to military purposes, including military aid. Conversely, it is also true that there can be no justice without peace. Wherever violent conflict prevails, social justice becomes an early victim. With the possible exception of a very few profiteers, situations of violent conflict and war make all parties victims of injustice, starting with the sacrifice of the most basic human right to life, liberty, and security of person.

Axis Two: Creation Care—Human Dignity. This axis discloses some of the most acute tensions and difficult challenges facing the agenda of the shalom church. The social ministry of the church for centuries has unfolded with a strong anthropocentric bias. Citing the biblical warrant that human beings *alone* are created in the image of God, the rights of human beings have been privileged at the expense of the rest of creation. If the critique of Christian theology as the cause of the environmental crisis is not accurate in principle, Christian practice—until very recently—has lent credence to the hypothesis. Human beings—authorized by the Scriptural warrant to "have dominion"—have related to God's good creation as robbers, exploiting the riches of nature for their own short-sighted gain. How can theology reconceptualize the place of the human within the whole of creation? In this book I have proposed that the body of Christ relate to the creation with the equivalent of "neighbor love." The earth, sea, sky, and their creatures are our neighbors, due all of the requisites of care afforded to human neighbors. H. Paul Santmire advocates the concept of "partnership" as best encompassing the needful new relationship between humans and God's creation.[21] The challenge facing the church is to afford respect for nature the same urgency as respect for human dignity in a new paradigm of holistic shalom: "nature, human community, and church in differentiated and dynamic harmony, with the church called to celebrate and to embody the vision of divine *shalom*, of peace with justice, which is God's ultimate purpose—which is to say, God's eschatological purpose—for the whole universe."[22]

Axis Three: Peacemaking—Creation Care. With this axis we are summoned to expand our notion of what peace and reconciliation entail. Conventionally, we imagine peace as the absence of inter-human conflict. If there are no wars, there is peace. However, the peace of God entails not only reconciliation among human beings but also the reconciliation of human beings with creation itself. The integration of this insight theologically is long overdue. We find antecedents already (as I have noted in chapter 6) in the legacy of the prophets, who comprehended God's eschatological shalom as inclusive of restored harmony in the whole creation: "The wolf and the lamb shall feed together, the lion shall eat straw, like the ox; but the serpent—its food shall be dust! They shall not hurt or destroy on all my holy mountain" (Isa 65:25). The new heaven and new earth will promote the flourishing of all creatures in a creation restored to proper balance. Human desire learns to yield to the intrinsic needs of earth, sea, sky, and their creatures for life. This eschatological vision can become the basis for an earth-care ethic already in the present. One of the most urgent revisions of the traditional theological paradigm involves the full incorporation of creation care as a normal dimension of Christian self-understanding. This includes a conception of peace that honors the integrity of creation as one of its fundamental precepts. One of the silent victims of every war or violent conflict is the devastation wreaked on the creation itself. Trees, fields, streams, mountains, sky, and their creatures are due fundamental respect, which is ripped to shreds as collateral damage during times of human violence. No peace without the integrity of God's creation!

Axis Four: Justice—Human Dignity. There is a very close relationship between the cause of social justice and respect for human dignity. One might even assert that respecting human dignity is a crucial dimension of justice itself. Any execution of "justice" apart from actualizing the criterion that every human being is created in God's image is in danger of becoming a form of tyranny rather than an expression of justice.[23] Indeed, one can point to many historical instances where rhetoric about justice has served as the rationale for crimes against humanity (for example, the Soviet Union under Stalin or the "cultural revolution" in China). Does not every regime pursue its vested interests in the name of justice? Does not every form of repression take place in the defense of higher justice? For these reasons it is crucial that the pursuit of justice occurs through highly participatory processes that honor the dignity of those in whose name justice is sought. This means that the church in its social-justice ministry aims to facilitate grassroots involvement by those whose cause is being furthered. This begins with careful listening to those who suffer most from prevailing inequities and mobilizing these persons in efforts to attain a greater measure of justice. This approach might be described as "accompaniment."[24] "We understand *accompaniment* as walking together in a solidarity that practices interdependence and mutuality."[25] Only active participation in the cause of justice by those who are most disaffected can avoid the dangers of presumption and promote actual human dignity. The value of congregation-based community organizing as a strategy for accomplishing this aim will be discussed in the next section.

Axis Five: Peacemaking—Human Dignity. The test case for all peacemaking efforts is the degree to which they are able to incorporate and engage in the reconciliation process those whose views are most in conflict. I have considered the propensity of human beings to demonize and dehumanize their opponents in the dynamics leading to violence. On whatever scale of conflict—from interpersonal to congregational to international levels—there is a strong tendency to label, diminish, and deny humanity to "the other." Especially when the other party has acted in such a way as to cause harm, "we" become indignant and readily accuse "them" of subhuman motives. In processes of reconciliation and peacemaking a fundamental commitment involves maintaining the humanity of all participants. Where longstanding conflict is being addressed, this becomes a very difficult undertaking. But the only road forward toward reconciliation travels through acknowledgment of and engagement with the other as human, as deserving intrinsic respect and dignity. Apart from this provision, hopes for peace are small. Therefore reconciliation and peacemaking efforts need to bring together estranged parties face to face as an indispensable step. The mediation of conflict involves some form of personal encounter in order to realize the possibilities of reconciliation inherent in the basic affirmation of the other's human dignity. One of the compelling reasons for promoting dialogue, for example, between representatives of the world's religions or heads of state, is to foster personal relationships that mitigate against spirals of violence that begin with the denigration of the other's very humanity. Such relationships, based on mutual respect, are vital for preventing outbreaks of violence in the first place.

Axis Six: Justice—Creation Care. In situations of desperate poverty, survival becomes the decisive goal. Wherever human beings are reduced to foraging for their material existence on a daily basis, they understandably make use of every available resource to satisfy their own most elementary physical needs and those of their loved ones. For this reason those committed to the care of creation need to link their agenda to the achievement of sufficient, sustainable livelihood for all. One of the most devastating obstacles hindering the future development of those places that suffer from extreme poverty is the degradation of the natural environment—soil, vegetation, water supplies, air quality—that has occurred already. Only by implementing environmentally sound plans for the alleviation of poverty can the ecosphere recover from past abuse. Moreover, the lack of adequate environmental protection legislation, and thereby the requirement to pay the costs of environmentally sound production, can make the developing world a desirable location for businesses seeking to maximize profits, even at the expense of the health of creation. Both local and international laws are necessary to prevent such abuses to the ecosphere, another priority for the shalom church as it seeks to weave together social justice with creation care. Advances in integrating the cause of justice with good stewardship of God's creation can be further facilitated by attending to the particular and unique ecological circumstances of each local place. In planning human interactions with the environment, it is imperative to design approaches that honor the interdependence of human beings with nature in order to attain long-term sustainability.[26]

By exploring these six interfaces among the four core ethical dimensions of the shalom church, we begin to weave together into a single fabric what sometimes could be interpreted as competing agendas. The integrity of the shalom church depends upon the coordination of these four commitments into a holistic understanding. Thereby a more fulsome definition of shalom begins to emerge. Shalom involves God's mission to bring to pass truly life-giving relationships among God, human beings, and the entire creation. These relationships are characterized by life together in communion with God that is marked by peace, justice, care for creation, and respect for human dignity. Shalom manifests itself in harmonious and fulfilling relationships among all those whom God created to live together in community with the Trinity. These are the contours of the shalom that God seeks to realize at the coming of the kingdom. The praxis of the kingdom by the shalom church aims to approximate the reality of shalom already now in the midst of a torn creation. While the best that can be achieved within history are approximations, even these make significant and salutary differences for the salvation of God's people. God intends through the embodiment of shalom by the body of Christ to mend creation (*tikkun olam*), bestowing shalom all in all.

Praxis of the Kingdom and the Shalom Church

This book is intended to foster the praxis of the kingdom by the body of Christ as shalom church. The concept of "praxis" refers to theological method as the dynamic interplay between thought and engagement according to an action/reflection model.[27] The church as the body of Christ is formed by Scripture and liturgy to reflect Jesus' own praxis of the kingdom in its ministry and mission. Each of the last four chapters has concluded with five practices to guide social ministry in the life of congregations. This closing section continues to draw implications for praxis by further integrating the witness of the twelve representatives of shalom church into the whole argument, offering additional commentary on the place of advocacy in the life of the church, encouraging congregational involvement in congregationally-based community organizing efforts, and promoting the work of the body of Christ as ministering community.

The twelve exemplary witnesses to the praxis of the kingdom by the shalom church—Mahatma Gandhi, Martin Luther King Jr., A. J. Muste, Dorothy Day, Oscar Romero, Mother Teresa, Francis of Assisi, Chief Seattle, Wendell Berry,

Bartolomé de Las Casas, Sojourner Truth, and Desmond Tutu—offer concrete images of the praxis of the kingdom under the complexities of historical life and in difficult circumstances. Like the church of today, each of these figures was challenged to embody the praxis of the kingdom first incarnated by Jesus in their own place and time. Each one demonstrates how the powerful story of Scripture forms disciples to follow in the way of Jesus Christ. The narrative of the Bible, as we are immersed in its plotline, instills in us the virtues of the kingdom that characterize the shalom church. While each of the representative biographies has been employed to elucidate a particular dimension of the shalom church, we can readily see how their collective witness reinforces the entire fabric.

One of the most striking features of these biographical sketches underscores how thoroughly the virtues of the shalom church had become woven into the very stuff of these lives. Although each one faced external challenges and times of self-doubt, there is an overall lack of pretense and self-preoccupation in their witness. Each one faced the contingencies of their historical moment and simply did what was necessary for the sake of the neighbor as someone formed by the biblical narrative. These lives do not point to themselves but rather they point both to the way of Christ and also the needs of others. This lack of self-awareness about one's own "saintliness" may be a defining mark of the consistency of sainthood itself.

Moreover, each of these persons was selected to represent the work of the shalom church not because of their individual witness to particular virtues (as significant as these might be) but because they contributed as *leaders of movements* to the cause of shalom. This is a book not about heroic leadership by individuals but rather about mobilizing the church to collective responsibility in fostering God's shalom agenda. Each of the twelve figures contributed as leaders either to the common life of the church in its social ministry or to ecumenical movements for peace, justice, care for creation, and the respect of human dignity. This is a crucial point, insofar as the social ministry of the church is far more effective as the partnership of many, rather than the isolated work of the individual. We learn from these witnesses what leadership means as the art of mobilizing people to address their most difficult problems.[28]

Repeatedly, the role of advocacy has been stressed as a core practice for congregational social ministry. Advocacy accords with effectiveness in accomplishing the church's calling to participate in God's left-hand strategy for ruling the world, which includes the exercise of good and effective government by those holding offices of public trust. Martin Luther wrote:

> In sum, after the gospel and pastoral ministry there is no better purse or greater treasure on earth, or more generous alms, or a more beautiful endowment, or better good than a ruler who makes and upholds just laws.[29]

While the church's efforts in relieving immediate human suffering are always necessary and commendable, the scale of need transcends the capacity of the church to provide what is required through its own charitable outreach with limited resources.

It properly belongs to the social ministry of the body of Christ in the world to advocate for legislation and policies that maximize government efforts to order public life according to the way of peace, justice, care for creation, and respect for human dignity described in these pages. This advocacy needs to be carried out with partiality for the needs of the neighbor, especially for the most vulnerable members of human society and the creation itself, without privileging the church's or church member's own self-interest. Moreover, the arguments employed by the church need to be articulated with a rationale that appeals to the reasoning of those who might not share the church's Christian and biblical presuppositions. In engaging in advocacy efforts, the church is most effective when partnering with others who share common cause with them, both people of other religious faiths and all those of goodwill. This includes identifying regional or national advocacy organizations in which they can join and get involved. Teaching church members about the legitimacy of advocacy, and receiving their implicit authorization for and involvement in advocacy, remains one of the most urgent social ministry goals for the effectiveness of the shalom church.

In promoting the work of advocacy on the part of congregations, one very constructive approach is congregation-based community organizing. This is a well-honed approach for congregations to participate in influencing or formulating policies and legislation on a local, regional, or national level. Dennis Jacobsen, one of the most eloquent expositors of congregation-based community organizing, describes it this way:

> Congregation-based community organizing is rooted in the local congregation. The local congregation is the building block of the organization. Organizing must be linked to the faith and values of the local congregation, to its self-interest, to its needs for leadership training, to the realities of the neighborhood. Organizers must be attentive to the particular ethos and character of the local congregation. The pastor must be drawn into the center of the organizing effort; otherwise, the congregation as a whole will likely remain on the periphery.[30]

The principles of community organizing derive from the labor movement, especially as developed by Saul Alinsky. However, as adapted to the work of the church, these principles have been informed by the biblical narrative and Christian ethical reflection. The chief models of effective community organizations are based in major metropolitan areas and extend through networks located in multiple cities: The Gamaliel Foundation, the Industrial Areas Foundation (IAF), the Pacific Institute for Community Organization (PICO), and the Direct Action and Research Training Center (DART).[31] One of the challenges facing congregation-based community organizing is the formation of models and networks in the town and country contexts of rural congregations.

Congregations initiate their participation in community organizing networks by making a commitment to work in concert with one another in a local community. Several congregations (usually twenty or more) need to be committed to involvement, insofar as the cost in terms of money and time is significant. The process involves extensive training of pastors, staff, and a core team of church members in the arts of public engagement. This is followed by team members conducting extensive interviews ("one-on-ones") with large numbers of people in the congregational community. These interviews are designed to surface the most pressing issues facing the community and to identify the interviewee's self-interest in these issues. The term "self-interest" is one of the most easily misunderstood concepts in community organizing. In short, it is the measure of one's genuine personal interest and motivation for getting involved actively on behalf of a particular cause. After hundreds, if not thousands, of interviews have been conducted, the data are scrutinized to identify three or four issues where the level of self-interest warrants a focused investment of money and time to pursue them. The identified issues are researched, subjected to an analysis of the prevailing power dynamics, shaped into a conceivably winnable form, and informed by an action plan.

At a large public meeting, the issues are then announced and an organization is formed to address them. This newly formed organization then proceeds to strategize how to accomplish the established goals by mobilizing people into concerted action. "One-on-ones," that is, focused personal interviews, remain an indispensable component of the organizing process. The only way to provoke significant change is to organize a sufficient number of people whose efforts are coordinated together in demanding change. Key to success is an accurate assessment of the prevailing power dynamics and applying sufficient pressure ("agitation") to make the targeted change the most desirable option for those in authority.

Sustaining an effective organization is a major and long-term undertaking. It requires both wisdom and persistence to stay the course in the face of the predictable resistance to change on the part of power brokers who are benefitting from the status quo. In sum, congregation-based community organizing means active participation in the democratic process of political change. Too often the church has chosen to remain naïve about the real nature of the political process and how to achieve lasting change. The process of community organizing addresses this deficit and draws congregations into the center of God's left-hand strategy of caring for the needs of the neighbor. Leaders of congregations who are not poised to form a large-scale organization can nonetheless benefit from a clear understanding of the principles of community organizing and may apply them in addressing particular issues in their local and regional communities.

William Cavanaugh in *Torture and Eucharist*, his stunning analysis of the public witness of the church facing "disappearances" and torture in Chile during the Pinochet regime, analyzes what it means for the church to claim and assume its identity as the body of Christ in the world. This transpires as the church is immersed in the biblical narrative and participates in the Eucharist, which transforms it into the actual body of Christ:

> The church is a body, but not just *a* social body, one of a genus of other social bodies which can be described and plotted sociologically. The church is the true body of Christ, a *sui generis* gathering which deconstructs the necessity of divisions between public and private, body and soul. . . . The true body of Christ is wounded, marked by the cross. As the body of Christ, the church participates in the sacrifice of Christ, his bloody confrontation with the powers of this world. The church's discipline then is only the discipline of martyrdom, for Christ's body is only itself in its self-emptying. The church does not exist for its own sake; it is not predicated on its own perpetuation, as is the state. Its discipline is a constant dying to itself for the sake of others.[32]

The power of faith, which is the power of the imagination, undermines business-as-usual and frees the church as the body of Christ "to live inside God's imagination."[33] Life inside God's imagination is nothing other than life in the very kingdom of God. Through immersion in the biblical story as rehearsed in the ritual of the Eucharist, "the church is caught up in what is really real, the body of Christ."

In this book I have contended that the church not only "does" social ministry but, as the body of Christ in the world, the church "is" social ministry. Formed by the narrative power of Scripture and immersed in the sacramental power of worship, the church *is* nothing other than the real body of Christ in the world. This real body of Christ assumes the character of the collective person Jesus Christ, which is distinguished by the four classical notes of the church. These four marks—one, holy, catholic, apostolic—inhere in the very fiber of the church's corpus. Each of these marks of character subsumes an ethical imperative: peacemaking, justice, care for creation, respect for human dignity! Together these character marks constitute the substance of shalom church. This shalom church, following the praxis of the kingdom inaugurated by Jesus, incarnates what it means for *the body of*

Christ to live as ministering community. All those who are baptized, living together in Christian congregations, are invited to come under the influence of Holy Spirit and "become the true body of Christ, and to bring to light the suffering of others by making that suffering visible in their own bodies."[34] Thereby God mends the torn fabric of the creation (*tikkun olam*) and restores the wholeness, the *shalom*, for which we hunger.

CONCLUSION:
SHALOM CHURCH AND PEOPLE
OF OTHER FAITHS

The body of Christ undertakes its commission to serve God's shalom in a society and world marked by unprecedented diversity and a sometimes bewildering pluralism. This means the church cannot operate in an isolated bubble, but is called to enter the challenging arena of conflicting viewpoints and agendas with a commensurate public theology. If once the church could assume a posture of privilege, as under the conditions of Christendom, it can do so no longer. We have argued that the shalom church must be ready to forge coalitions and common cause with people of other religious faiths as well as with all people of good will who share similar commitments to the common good. In this conclusion to *Shalom Church*, we take a final look at some of the implications for interreligious dialogue and cooperation.

Not only does the church of Jesus Christ have to negotiate the complexities of a religiously plural globe, but the United States itself has become "the world's most religiously diverse nation."[1] In the face of the crises testing human and planetary survival—violence, poverty, environmental degradation, violations of human rights—it is imperative that people of different religious convictions identify shared ethical commitments and develop new cooperative strategies to promote the survival, if not thriving, of earth and its inhabitants. In this regard the initiatives of Hans Küng and colleagues in the Global Ethic project (in conjunction with the Parliament of the World's Religions) deserve increased attention and support from Christians. The Declaration toward a Global Ethic operates under the guiding presupposition that there can be no world peace without peace among the religions.

To further the cause of peace and reconciliation, representatives of the world's major religious traditions formulated and announced the Declaration toward a Global Ethic at the Parliament of the World's Religions in September 1993 as a statement of intent to strive together in affirming the fundamental principles of a common ethic:

> We are interdependent. Each of us depends on the well-being of the whole, and so we have respect for the community of living beings, for people, animals, and plants, and for the preservation of the Earth, the air, water and soil. . . .
>
> We must treat others as we wish others to treat us. We make a commitment to respect life and dignity, individuality and diversity, so that every person is treated humanely, without exception. . . . No person should ever be considered or treated as a second-class citizen, or be exploited in any way whatsoever. . . .
>
> We commit ourselves to a culture of non-violence, respect, justice, and peace. We shall not oppress, injure, torture, or kill other human beings, forsaking violence as a means of settling differences. . . .
>
> We must strive for a just social and economic order, in which everyone has an equal chance to reach full potential as a human being. . . . We must move beyond the dominance of greed for power, prestige, money, and consumption to make a just and peaceful world. . . . [2]

It is striking how closely this Declaration corresponds in its ethical agenda to the fourfold contours of the shalom church—respect for the preservation of the Earth, commitment to respect human life and dignity, commitment to a culture of non-violence, striving for a just social and economic order. The parallels run deep.

In his interpretation of the importance of the Global Ethic movement, Küng makes clear that the project is not about "a new global ideology, or even an attempt to arrive at one uniform religion."[3]

> It simply aims to make known what religions in West and East, North and South already hold in common, but is so often obscured by numerous 'dogmatic' disputes and intolerable self-opinionatedness. In short, the 'Declaration toward a Global Ethic' seeks to emphasize the minimal ethic which is absolutely necessary for human survival. It is not directed against anyone, but invites all, believers and also non-believers, to adopt this ethic and live in accordance with it.[4]

The focus of this effort is on mutual cooperation among members of the world religions and all people of good will on a common ethical agenda that is based on consensus positions among a wide spectrum of faiths. The contours of this effort conform to the commitments of shalom church.

Not only is there an emerging consensus about a shared ethical platform among people of different religious faiths, but there is another striking parallel to these ethical commitments that comes to expression in the Earth Charter, adopted by the United Nations Educational, Scientific, and Cultural Organization (UNESCO) in 2000. In the Preamble is stated:

> We must join together to bring forth a sustainable global society founded on respect for nature, universal human rights, economic justice, and a culture of peace.[5]

The Earth Charter proceeds to elaborate the significance of this fourfold agenda for the human community. Given the importance of forging coalitions in the pursuit of peace, justice, creation care, and respect for human dignity on the part of the shalom church, both the Declaration toward a Global Ethic and the Earth Charter provide promising bridges.

As a way forward in interreligious relations, representatives of the world religions might consider the value of having future dialogue focus primarily on exploring to what degree particular ethical commitments are held in common, that is, the commitments to peacemaking, social justice, caring for the earth, and defending human dignity. This process in some ways might resemble the consensual model followed by the World Council of Churches in seeking greater unity among different Christian church bodies. The leaders and peoples of the world religions might engage in dialogue around the following questions:

1. To what extent can your religious tradition recognize in these four ethical commitments an authentic expression of its convictions?
2. What consequences can your religious tradition draw from these four ethical commitments for its relations and dialogues with other religious groups, particularly with those which also recognize these commitments as expressions of authentic faith?
3. What guidance can your religious tradition take from these four ethical commitments for its rituals, educational, ethical, and spiritual life and witness?
4. What is the religious rationale, based on your core convictions, that makes necessary either agreement or disagreement with these four ethical commitments?[6]

By following such a method, interreligious dialogue could proceed to explore the religious beliefs that lead toward common ethical affirmations, rather than focusing on doctrines or beliefs that may primarily indicate significant differences. Interreligious dialogue in such a process would be both substantive, that is, concerning matters related to the survival of life in this world, and based on the search for common ground.[7]

This dialogue need not be reserved as the domain of "experts" in interreligious dialogue. Instead, the search for ethical common ground invites the participation of both religious leaders in local communities of faith and their members. For example, Paul Knitter has advanced the theme of human suffering as the basis for conversation among people from different religions as they gather in small groups.[8] He describes this process as a "dialogue of action" or a "dialogue of life." Given the evolution of U.S. society into such a religiously pluralistic environment, not only in major metropolitan centers but also across the heartland, new initiatives in interreligious dialogue based on the search for shared ethical commitments cannot only hasten new understanding of our interreligious neighbors but also foster hope for the survival, even flourishing, of Earth and all its creatures, including humankind.

APPENDIX: SUMMARY OF KEY THEMES

Twenty Virtues of the Shalom Church

1. Commitment to inclusivity
2. Love for enemies
3. Readiness to forgive
4. Repenting of violence
5. Nonviolent resistance
6. Solidarity with the oppressed
7. Hospitality to strangers
8. Care for the physical needs of all
9. Preferential concern for the weak
10. Just economic and legal dealings with others
11. Basic posture of praise and thanksgiving
12. Loving the earth as our neighbor
13. Readiness to learn a new paradigm for human participation in the world
14. Stewardship as care for creation
15. Holding one another accountable for the care of creation
16. Affirmation of the common humanity of all those created by God
17. Respect for the dignity of the marginalized
18. Commitment to build an inclusive church
19. Defending human rights
20. Immersion in the theology of the cross

Twelve Representatives of Shalom Church

1. Mohandas Gandhi
2. Martin Luther King Jr.
3. A. J. Muste
4. Dorothy Day
5. Oscar Romero
6. Mother Teresa
7. Francis of Assisi
8. Chief Seattle of the Suquamish
9. Wendell Berry
10. Bartolomé de Las Casas
11. Sojourner Truth
12. Desmond Tutu

Twenty Core Practices of the Shalom Church

1. Praying for peace
2. Interpreting the actions of others in the kindest way
3. Forgiving
4. Resisting violence
5. Advocating nonviolence
6. Hospitality
7. Charity and generosity
8. Healing ministry
9. Restorative justice
10. Holding accountable the privileged and those in authority
11. Wonder
12. Simplicity
13. Attending to the local place
14. Living sustainably
15. Advocacy for the creation
16. Admiring the divine image in the face of the other
17. Expecting to encounter Christ in the person of the vulnerable one
18. Participating in the suffering of others
19. Principled opposition to genocide
20. Advocating for human rights

STUDY GUIDE

Chapter One. For the Mending of Creation

For Personal Reflection

1. What words, metaphors, or expressions do you employ to describe God's purpose or mission in the world?
2. How do evangelizing and social ministry relate to one another in your understanding of what God is doing in the world?
3. What biblical texts are the most important to you as you think about God's involvement in the mending of creation (*tikkun olam*)? How can you employ these texts in your church leadership?
4. How have you engaged in the work of social ministry through advocacy? How does advocacy fit into your overall understanding of social ministry?
5. How do you evaluate your own personal involvement as a Christian in the political process? How might this be accomplished in the best possible way?

For Group Discussion

1. List and describe all the ways you have experienced the church at work in social ministry. Which of these have been the most effective?
2. Does the church's involvement in social ministry seem controversial to you? Why or why not?

3. What do you discern as the most urgent human need for social ministry in your community?

4. What are the greatest challenges your congregation faces in engaging in the ministry of evangelizing (God's right-hand strategy)? In the work of social ministry (God's left-hand strategy)?

5. How does your congregation encourage and support the baptismal vocation of its members in each of the four arenas of service: Family? Workplace? Church? Citizenship?

Chapter Two. Constructing Ecclesiology for Social Ministry

For Personal Reflection

1. Which New Testament images of the church most inform your own ecclesiology? What are the advantages and limitations of those preferred images?

2. Read and reflect carefully on Romans 12:3-8. What insights do you gain from this text about your own congregation and ministry?

3. What is the significance of receiving the body of Christ in the Lord's Supper as you think about your congregation as the body of Christ (cf. 1 Cor 10:16-17)?

4. Who are the "weaker" members of your congregation (cf. 1 Cor 12:22)? How do you seek to give special honor to those weaker members?

5. How does your congregation as the body of Christ manifest the character of Jesus Christ's love for the world? How can those in leadership foster that character?

For Group Discussion

1. How would you describe your ecclesiology? What images and metaphors are most common among the members of your congregation in picturing the life of the church?

2. What relationships and interconnections do you see between the three meanings of the body of Christ: Jesus Christ himself as God incarnate, the Lord's Supper, and the church?

3. How might Paul's wisdom about the church as the body of Christ in 1 Corinthians 12:12-31 guide the life of your congregation as you seek to live together in harmony and do God's will?

4. What does it mean that spiritual gifts are given to the body of Christ "for the common good"? How else might our gifts be put to use? Reflect on some ways the members of your congregation employ their gifts for the common good.

5. How does your congregation "equip the saints for the work of ministry, for building up the body of Christ" (Eph 4:12)?

Chapter Three. The Church as the Collective Person Jesus Christ

For Personal Reflection

1. Which relationships have been most formative in your life for making you the person whom you are? Which are the most life-giving relationships right now? Thank God for these persons.

2. What does Bonhoeffer mean by the term "collective person"? Think about the different groups to which you belong and compare the different personalities of these distinctive collective persons.

3. What does it mean to claim that "it is worship for which humanity and the creation were made"? What is the relationship between worship and everyday life? Can you think of instances where worship serves as "training for discipleship on earth"?

4. Which threads of the biblical narrative have been the most significant in shaping and forming your own character and virtues?

5. What does it mean for you to confess in the Nicene Creed, "We believe in one holy catholic apostolic church"? What does it mean to claim these four marks of the church as constituting the very character of the body of Christ?

For Group Discussion

1. What difference does it make to think of human beings as persons made for relationship instead of as independent individuals?

2. If your congregation is a collective person, what are some of the distinctive character traits of that person?

3. As the members of your congregation gather for worship, how is God instilling in you the character of Jesus Christ through Word and sacraments? What is your experience of this formation by the Spirit?

4. Which virtues do you hope will be passed on to the next generation? How does active participation in the body of Christ affect the acquisition of those virtues?

5. How does the confession of the church's unity influence Christian practice in the daily life? Confession of the church's holiness? Catholicity? Apostolicity?

Chapter Four. The Body of Christ Is One

For Personal Reflection

1. How important to you is the unity of the church? What do you think of the claim that Jesus' prayer for the oneness of the church (John 17:20-21) is deeply connected to Jesus' call to peacemaking (Matt 5:9)?

2. Which biblical stories are most significant to you in telling about God's work of reconciliation and peacemaking? What guidance do you take from these stories for living your life as a Christian?

3. Who are you experiencing as your enemy? How easy is it for you to dehumanize your enemies? How difficult is it to pray for and forgive them? Take a few minutes to pray for your enemies right now.

4. Consider the power of nonviolent resistance documented in this chapter or other instances you have witnessed. What spiritual preparation is necessary for those who engage in nonviolent direct action?

5. What do you think about pacifism as a Christian response to violence and war? What do you think are the limits of pacifism? What is right about pacifism?

For Group Discussion

1. How are the church's divisions a scandal before the face of the world? How can belief in the church's oneness embolden the body of Christ to serve as a sign of reconciliation in places of violence in our world? What difference does it make when the church lives up to its claim to oneness by serving as peacemaker?

2. Does the Bible finally authorize the use of violence or does it sanction nonviolent peacemaking? How do we, as lovers of peace, interpret the various stories in the Bible that depict extreme violence?

3. How have you seen or experienced the phenomenon of scapegoating? Why is it important for Christians, who believe in the power of the cross, to resist and oppose all forms of scapegoating violence?

4. What lessons should the church learn from the lives of the peacemakers—Mahatma Gandhi, Martin Luther King Jr., and A. J. Muste? What troubled you and what inspired you about their witness?

5. In which of the five peacemaking practices does your congregation already engage? How might your congregation better embody God's reconciling and peacemaking in its ministry and mission?

Chapter Five. The Body of Christ Is Holy

For Personal Reflection

1. How do you experience the holiness of God in your life? Can you recall profound moments when you encountered divine holiness? How were you changed as a result of those experiences?

2. Which signs of social injustice do you find the most troubling? Which biblical passages inspire you in the struggle against injustice?

3. Which of the five social ministry practices described in this chapter most naturally invite your own participation? Which of these practices most appeals to you as an area for future growth?

4. Mother Teresa said, ". . . find out about your next-door neighbor. Do you know who they are?" What wisdom do you discover in this quote for your own involvement in the cause of social justice?

5. What is your own need for healing? How could the healing ministry of the church better address your own need for physical, emotional, or spiritual healing?

For Group Discussion

1. What are the signs of God's sanctification at work in your congregation? How has God's holiness become manifest through the body of Christ in your community?

2. What is your understanding of the nature of God's kingdom? How is the kingdom of God as proclaimed by Jesus related to the yearning for social justice?

3. In which issues of social justice is your congregation already most involved? How might your congregation actualize more fulsomely the five virtues named in this chapter?

4. What motivates people like Dorothy Day, Oscar Romero, and Mother Teresa to risk their possessions, their health, and their lives for the sake of the poor? What prevents your congregation from risking more for the sake of others?

5. Evaluate your congregation's involvement in justice ministry. Are you primarily engaged in charitable giving? Where do members have an opportunity for personal involvement? To what degree are you also involved in advocacy work? Why do charity and advocacy need to go together?

Chapter Six. The Body of Christ Is Catholic

For Personal Reflection

1. What importance does it have to you that human beings, all earth's creatures, and all living things are constituted from the selfsame matter? What obligation to care for creation derives from the mutual interdependence of all created things?

2. If you were a psalmist, which wonders of God's creation would you write and sing about?

3. How might you better embrace a creation-centered approach to the world around you, in contrast to an overly anthropocentric approach? How might you differently structure your days to embrace the care of creation?

4. How connected are you to the local place where you live? Why is it important for people to accept ethical responsibility to love and care for their local place with Christian neighbor love?

5. What changes would be necessary for you to achieve a more environmentally sustainable lifestyle? How might you give leadership in encouraging others to live more sustainably?

For Group Discussion

1. How have you understood the meaning of the church's confession about a "catholic" church? Does it enhance your understanding or create new confusion to understand the catholicity of the church in relation to God's intention to restore the entire creation to its fullness in Christ?

2. Read together Matthew 6:25-31. What comfort do you receive from seeing the birds of the air and considering the lilies of the field? How do the promises of God about a plenteous creation relieve your anxiety about having enough?

3. In what ways does your congregation already practice stewardship of God's whole creation? What new steps should be implemented in the near future?

4. Many of the biographies examined in this book involved a conversion, for example, in the life of St. Francis. What kind of a conversion is needed for Christians to take seriously the importance of the care of God's creation as a virtue?

5. How might your congregation implement educational programs, small groups, or other activities that encourage simplicity of life? What value might this have in enhancing the Christian discipleship of your members?

Chapter Seven. The Body of Christ Is Apostolic

For Personal Reflection

1. How do you understand the apostolicity of the church's mission? How can the church become more effective in respecting the dignity of each human being created in God's image?

2. What does the theology of the cross mean to you? How does the cross of Jesus call you to special concern for those who suffer?

3. Why is it important to define humanity so as to make sure no one of human parentage is excluded? How have you seen others stripped of their humanity and what have been the consequences when that happens?

4. Those denied their human dignity need the solidarity of those who can offer bold and forthright advocacy. How have you ever raised your voice to defend the voiceless? How can you do this more effectively in the future?

5. In which relationships have you unexpectedly encountered Jesus Christ? Where have you "entertained angels" unaware?

For Group Discussion

1. Who are the ones in your community and across the world, whose human rights are in need of defense? How might the members of your congregation raise their voices on their behalf?
2. How does the conviction that each human being is made in God's image influence how you relate to others? How should it make a difference in the life of your congregation? In your outreach?
3. How much of God's wonderful diversity is reflected in the membership of your congregation? What steps might be taken to be proactive about increasing the various forms of diversity to better model the amazing diversity of peoples in God's kingdom?
4. What lessons do you learn from the witness of Bartolomé de Las Casas, Sojourner Truth, and Desmond Tutu for the ministry and mission of your congregation? Which virtues do they demonstrate that are worthy of fostering among the youth of the church?
5. How have you experienced the presence of Jesus Christ in times of your own suffering? Why is it important for the church to live out the theology of the cross in caring for the needs of those who suffer?

Chapter Eight. Embodying Shalom Church

For Personal Reflection

1. This book claims that the very character of the body of Christ makes it an evangelizing and shalom church. How compelling is the argument that the church of Jesus Christ is by definition an evangelizing church and a shalom church or no church at all?
2. Which arguments against Christianity do you find most convincing? How do you try to answer when people question the validity of Christian faith based on all the contradictions?
3. Which of the four central ethical themes—peacemaking, social justice, creation care, and respecting human dignity—is most important to you? How can you link this concern with aspects of the other three themes?

4. What is the difference between a leader who gets involved individually and a leader who knows how to mobilize others into action? How can you better focus your leadership on the mobilization of others?
5. What questions do you have about the principles and practices of congregation-based community organizing? How might you find out more about what this approach could mean in your own context?

For Group Discussion

1. What does it mean to be a "public" church? How does your congregation function as a public church?
2. Many people are put off by the church because of its hypocrisy. Which of the many contradictions in Scripture and the history of the church cause you the most concern?
3. In light of this book, put the meaning of "shalom" into your own words. How does the idea of shalom give expression to human longing and to God's purpose for the church?
4. The role of advocacy has been strongly emphasized in this book. As you reflect on the importance of advocacy by the church, what reservations remain? How might your congregation take the next step in learning the art of advocacy?
5. What would it mean for your congregation to claim its mission as sha- lom church? How can you better represent the body of Christ as social ministry?

BIBLIOGRAPHY

Chapter One. For the Mending of Creation

Bliese, Richard H., and Craig Van Gelder, eds. *The Evangelizing Church: A Lutheran Contribution.* Minneapolis: Fortress Press, 2005.

Carter, Craig A. *Rethinking Christ and Culture: A Post-Christendom Perspective.* Grand Rapids: Brazos, 2006.

Lazareth, William. *Christians in Society: Luther, the Bible, and Social Ethics.* Minneapolis: Fortress Press, 2001.

McCurley, Foster R., ed. *Social Ministry in the Lutheran Tradition.* Minneapolis: Fortress Press, 2008.

Moe-Lobeda, Cynthia D. *Public Church: For the Life of the World.* Minneapolis: Augsburg Fortress, 2004.

Niebuhr, H. Richard. *Christ and Culture.* New York: HarperCollins, 2001.

Rieger, Joerg. *Christ and Empire: From Paul to Postcolonial Times.* Minneapolis: Fortress Press, 2007.

Unruh, Heidi Rolland, and Ronald J. Sider. *Saving Souls, Serving Society: Understanding the Faith Factor in Church-Based Social Ministry.* Oxford: Oxford University Press, 2005.

Wallis, Jim. *The Great Awakening: Reviving Faith and Politics in a Post-Religious Right America.* New York: HarperCollins, 2008.

Wink, Walter. *The Powers That Be: Theology for a New Millennium.* New York: Random House, 1998.

Chapter Two. Constructing Ecclesiology for Social Ministry

Braaten, Carl E., and Robert W. Jenson, eds. *Marks of the Body of Christ.* Grand Rapids: Eerdmans, 1999.

Davis, Thomas J. *This Is My Body: The Presence of Christ in Reformation Thought.* Grand Rapids: Baker, 2008.

Dunn, James D. G. *The Theology of Paul the Apostle.* Grand Rapids: Eerdmans, 2006.

Kim, Yung Suk. *Christ's Body in Corinth: The Politics of a Metaphor.* Minneapolis: Fortress Press, 2008.

Martin, Dale B. *The Corinthian Body.* New Haven: Yale University Press, 1995.

Minear, Paul S. *Images of the Church in the New Testament.* Louisville: Westminster John Knox, 2004.

Schroer, Silvia, and Thomas Staubli. *Body Symbolism in the Bible.* Translated by Linda M. Maloney. Collegeville, Minn.: Liturgical, 2001.

Solberg, Mary M. *Compelling Knowledge: A Feminist Proposal for an Epistemology of the Cross.* Albany: State University of New York Press, 1997.

Stark, Rodney. *The Rise of Christianity: How the Obscure, Marginal, Jesus Movement Became the Dominant Religious Force.* Princeton: Princeton University Press, 1996.

Yorke, Gosnell L. O. R. *The Church as the Body of Christ in the Pauline Corpus: A Re-Examination.* Blue Ridge Summit, Pa.: University Press of America, 1991.

Chapter Three. The Church as the Collective Person Jesus Christ

Bass, Dorothy C. *Practicing Our Faith: A Way of Life for a Searching People.* San Francisco: Jossey-Bass, 1997.

Bonhoeffer, Dietrich. *Ethics.* Edited by Clifford J. Green. Translated by Reinhard Krauss, Charles C. West, and Douglas W. Stott. Dietrich Bonhoeffer Works in English. Minneapolis: Fortress Press, 2005.

———. *Life Together and Prayerbook of the Bible.* Edited by Geffrey B. Kelly. Translated by Daniel W. Bloesch and James H. Burtness. Dietrich Bonhoeffer Works in English. Minneapolis: Augsburg Fortress, 1996.

———. *Sanctorum Communio: A Theological Study of the Sociology of the Church.* Edited by Clifford J. Green. Translated by Reinhard Krauss and Nancy Lukens. Dietrich Bonhoeffer Works in English. Minneapolis: Augsburg Fortress, 1998.

Cavanaugh, William T. *Torture and Eucharist: Theology, Politics, and the Body of Christ.* Oxford: Blackwell, 1998.

Dykstra, Craig. *Growing in the Life of Faith: Education and Christian Practices.* 2nd ed. Louisville: Westminster John Knox, 2005.

Green, Clifford J. *Bonhoeffer: A Theology of Sociality.* Grand Rapids: Eerdmans, 1999.

Haight, Roger. *Historical Ecclesiology.* Vol. 1 of *Christian Community in History.* New York: Continuum, 2004.

———. *Comparative Ecclesiology.* Vol. 2 of *Christian Community in History.* New York: Continuum, 2005.

———. *Ecclesial Existence.* Vol. 3 of *Christian Community in History.* New York: Continuum, 2008.

Hauerwas, Stanley, and Samuel Wells, eds. *The Blackwell Companion to Christian Ethics.* Oxford: Blackwell, 2004.

MacIntyre, Alasdair. *After Virtue: A Study in Moral Theory.* 2nd ed. South Bend, Ind.: University of Notre Dame Press, 1984.

Chapter Four. The Body of Christ Is One

Bailie, Gil. *Violence Unveiled: Humanity at the Crossroads.* New York: Crossroad, 1995.

Childs, James M., Jr. *The Way of Peace: Christian Life in Face of Discord.* Minneapolis: Fortress Press, 2008.

Confessing the One Faith: An Ecumenical Explication of the Apostolic Faith. Faith and Order Paper No. 153. Geneva: World Council of Churches, 1991.

Gandhi, Mahatma. *The Essential Gandhi: An Anthology of His Writings on His Life, Work, and Ideas.* Edited by Louis Fischer. 2nd ed. New York: Vintage, 2002.

Girard, René. *Things Hidden Since the Foundation of the World.* Translated by Stephen Bann and Michael Metteer. Chicago: Stanford University Press, 1987.

Hentoff, Nat, ed. *The Essays of A. J. Muste.* New York: Simon and Schuster, 1967.

King, Martin Luther, Jr. *A Testament of Hope: The Essential Writings of Martin Luther King, Jr.* Edited by James Melvin Washington. San Francisco: Harper & Row, 1986.

Maguire, Daniel C. *The Horrors We Bless: Rethinking the Just-War Legacy.* Minneapolis: Fortress Press, 2007.

Simpson, Gary M. *War, Peace, and God: Rethinking the Just-War Tradition.* Minneapolis: Augsburg Fortress, 2007.

Welch, Sharon D. *Real Peace, Real Security: The Challenges of Global Citizenship.* Minneapolis: Fortress Press, 2008.

Chapter Five. The Body of Christ Is Holy

Beckmann, David, and Arthur Simon. *Ending Hunger in God's World.* Mahwah, N.J.: Paulist, 1999.

Brockman, James R. *Romero: A Life.* Maryknoll: Orbis, 2003.

Brubaker, Pamela K., Rebecca Todd Peters, and Laura A. Stivers, eds. *Justice in a Global Economy: Strategies for Home, Community, and World.* Louisville: Westminster John Knox, 2006.

Day, Dorothy. *Dorothy Day: Selected Writings.* Edited by Robert Ellsberg. Maryknoll: Orbis, 2001.

Jung, L. Shannon. *Food for Life: The Spirituality and Ethics of Eating.* Minneapolis: Fortress Press, 2004.

McKibben, Bill. *Deep Economy: Economics as If the World Mattered.* Oxford: Oneworld, 2007.

Nessan, Craig L. *Give Us This Day: A Lutheran Proposal for Ending World Hunger.* Minneapolis: Augsburg Fortress, 2003.

Peters, Rebecca Todd. *In Search of the Good Life: The Ethics of Globalization.* New York: Continuum, 2004.

Teresa, Mother. *No Greater Love.* Foreword by Thomas Moore. Novato, Calif.: New World Library, 2002.

Zehr, Howard. *The Little Book of Restorative Justice.* Intercourse, Pa.: Good Books, 2002.

Chapter Six. The Body of Christ Is Catholic

Boff, Leonardo. *Francis of Assisi: A Model for Human Liberation.* Translated by John W. Diercksmeier. Maryknoll: Orbis, 2006.

Bonzo, J. Matthew, and Michael R. Stevens. *Wendell Berry and the Cultivation of Life: A Reader's Guide.* Grand Rapids: Brazos, 2008.

Bullard, Robert D., ed. *Confronting Environmental Racism: Voices from the Grassroots.* Cambridge, Mass.: South End, 1999.

Edwards, Andres R. *The Sustainability Revolution: Portrait of a Paradigm Shift.* Gabriola Island, B.C.: New Society, 2005.

Hessel, Dieter, and Larry Rasmussen, eds. *Earth Habitat: Eco-Injustice and the Church's Response.* Minneapolis: Fortress Press, 2001.

Jefferson, Warren. *The World of Chief Seattle: How Can One Sell the Air?* Summertown, Tenn.: Native Voices, 2001.

McFague, Sallie. *A New Climate for Theology: God, the World, and Global Warming.* Minneapolis: Fortress Press, 2008.

McKibben, Bill. *The End of Nature.* New York: Random House, 2006.

Rasmussen, Larry L. *Earth Community, Earth Ethics.* Maryknoll: Orbis, 1996.

Santmire, H. Paul. *Ritualizing Nature: Renewing Christian Liturgy in a Time of Crisis.* Minneapolis: Fortress Press, 2008

Chapter Seven. The Body of Christ Is Apostolic

Amesbury, Richard, and George M. Newlands. *Faith and Human Rights: Christianity and the Global Struggle for Human Dignity.* Minneapolis: Fortress Press, 2008.

Clapham, Andrew. *Human Rights: A Very Short Introduction.* New York: Oxford, 2007.

Battle, Michael. *Reconciliation: The Ubuntu Theology of Desmond Tutu.* Cleveland: Pilgrim, 1997.

Gutiérrez, Gustavo. *Las Casas: In Search of the Poor of Jesus Christ.* Translated by Robert R. Barr. Maryknoll: Orbis, 1993.

Hall, Douglas John. *The Cross in Our Context: Jesus and the Suffering World.* Minneapolis: Fortress Press, 2003.

Nessan, Craig L. *Many Members yet One Body: Committed Same-Gender Relationships and the Mission of the Church.* Minneapolis: Augsburg Fortress, 2004.

Painter, Nell Irvin. *Sojourner Truth: A Life, A Symbol.* New York: Norton, 1997.

Spink, Kathryn. *The Miracle, the Message, the Story: Jean Vanier and L'Arche.* Mahwah, N.J.: Paulist, 2006.

West, Traci C. *Disruptive Christian Ethics: When Racism and Women's Lives Matter.* Louisville: Westminster John Knox, 2006.

Westhelle, Vítor. *The Scandalous God: The Use and Abuse of the Cross.* Minneapolis: Fortress Press, 2006.

Chapter Eight. Embodying Shalom Church

DeYoung, Curtiss Paul. *Living Faith: How Faith Inspires Social Justice.* Minneapolis: Fortress Press, 2007.

Duchrow, Ulrich. *Shalom: Biblical Perspectives on Creation, Justice, and Peace.* Geneva: World Council of Churches, 1989.

Hoehn, Richard A. *Up from Apathy: A Study of Moral Awareness and Social Involvement.* Nashville: Abingdon, 1983.

Jacobsen, Dennis. *Doing Justice: Congregations and Community Organizing.* Minneapolis: Fortress Press, 2001.

Küng, Hans, and Karl-Josef Kuschel, eds. *A Global Ethic: The Declaration of the Parliament of the World's Religions.* Translated by John Bowden. New York: Continuum, 1993.

Maguire, Daniel C. *A Moral Creed for All Christians.* Minneapolis: Fortress Press, 2005.

Moe-Lobeda, Cynthia D. *Healing a Broken World: Globalization and God.* Minneapolis: Fortress Press, 2002.

Peters, Rebecca Todd, and Elizabeth Hinson-Hasty, eds. *To Do Justice: A Guide for Progressive Christians.* Louisville: Westminster John Knox, 2008.

Rieger, Joerg, ed. *Opting for the Margins: Postmodernity and Liberation in Christian Theology.* Oxford: Oxford University Press, 2003.

Welch, Sharon D. *After Empire: The Art and Ethos of Enduring Peace.* Minneapolis: Fortress Press, 2004.

NOTES

Chapter One. For the Mending of Creation

1. Frederich Buechner, *Wishful Thinking: A Theological ABC* (New York: Harper & Row, 1973), 95, in defining "Vocation."

2. As often as this book refers to "the mission of the church" or "the church's mission" it is to be understood as the church's intended participation in *God's mission*.

3. Cf. Richard H. Bliese and Craig Van Gelder, eds., *The Evangelizing Church: A Lutheran Contribution* (Minneapolis: Fortress Press, 2005), in which I am a contributing author.

4. See Norma Cook Everist and Craig L. Nessan, *Transforming Leadership: New Vision for a Church in Mission* (Minneapolis: Fortress Press, 2008), vii–viii, regarding the term *life-giving relationship*.

5. H. Paul Santmire, *Ritualizing Nature: Renewing Christian Liturgy in a Time of Crisis* (Minneapolis: Fortress Press, 2008), employs the concept of shalom to describe God's intention for restoring the whole creation to wholeness; see pp. 91, 167, 181, and 227.

6. "Transforming Theology and Life-giving Civilization," World Council of Churches Consultation at Changseong, Korea, August 17, 2007, Final Document, 1.

7. "Alternative Globalization Addressing People and Earth (AGAPE) Consultation on Linking Poverty, Wealth, and Ecology: African Ecumenical Perspectives," World Council of Churches Consultation at Dar es Salaam, Tanzania, November 5–9, 2007, Final Report, 10.

8. "Transforming Theology and Life-giving Civilization," 1.

9. While the Bible also contains "texts of terror" that contradict this justice trajectory, this book claims as normative the biblical traditions that reveal God as the protagonist for peace, justice, care for creation, and human dignity.

10. Craig L. Nessan, "Reappropriating Luther's Two Kingdoms," *Lutheran Quarterly* 19 (Autumn 2005): 302–311.

11. Dennis Jacobsen, *Doing Justice: Congregations and Community Organizing* (Minneapolis: Fortress Press, 2001), 1–12.

12. Walter Wink, *The Powers That Be: Theology for a New Millennium* (New York: Random House, 1998) is a one-volume summary.

13. The danger of such a worldview is that it can easily lead to the demonization of enemies rather than love for enemies in the spirit of Jesus.

14. *Evangelical Lutheran Worship* (Minneapolis: Augsburg Fortress, 2006), 95.

15. Martin Luther, "The Freedom of a Christian," in *Martin Luther's Basic Theological Writings*, ed. Timothy F. Lull; 2nd ed. (Minneapolis: Fortress Press, 2005), 386–411.

16. I am particularly indebted for the retrieval of Luther's two-kingdoms paradigm to the creative analysis and interpretation by Ulrich Duchrow, *Christenheit und Weltverantwortung: Traditionsgeschichte und systematische Struktur der Zweireichelehre* (Stuttgart: Klett-Cotta, 1983), 439–573; and Ulrich Duchrow, Wolfgang Huber, and Louis Reith, eds, *Umdeutungen der Zweireichelehre Luthers im 19. Jahrhundert: Texte zur Kirchen- und Theologiegeschichte* (Gütersloh: Gerd Mohn, 1976).

17. Other church bodies in particular contexts also may operate in this fashion, for example, when the Roman Catholic Church engages in advocacy according to the logic of Christendom.

18. On the meaning of *care*, see Craig L. Nessan, *Beyond Maintenance to Mission: A Theology of the Congregation*, 2nd ed. (Minneapolis: Fortress Press, 2010), 104–6.

19. Gustaf Wingren, *Luther on Vocation*, trans. Carl Rasmussen (Eugene, Ore.: Wipf & Stock, 2004).

20. See Karen L. Bloomquist, *The Dream Betrayed: Religious Challenge of the Working Class* (Minneapolis: Fortress Press, 1989).

21. Lee Hardy, *The Fabric of This World: Inquiries into Calling, Career Choice, and the Design of Human Work* (Grand Rapids: Eerdmans, 1990).

22. See Cynthia D. Moe-Lobeda, *Public Church: For the Life of the World* (Minneapolis: Augsburg Fortress, 2004).

Chapter Two. Constructing Ecclesiology for Social Ministry

1. Cf. Richard H. Bliese and Craig Van Gelder, eds., *The Evangelizing Church: A Lutheran Contribution* (Minneapolis: Fortress Press, 2005).

2. Rodney Stark, *The Rise of Christianity: How the Obscure, Marginal, Jesus Movement Became the Dominant Religious Force* (Princeton: Princeton University Press, 1996), 73–94.

3. Paul S. Minear, *Images of the Church in the New Testament* (Philadelphia: Westminster, 1960).

4. Hans Conzelmann, *1 Corinthians: A Commentary on the First Epistle to the Corinthians*, trans. James W. Leitch; Hermeneia (Philadelphia: Fortress Press, 1975), 207.

5. Dale B. Martin, *The Corinthian Body* (New Haven: Yale University Press, 1995), 102.

6. Ibid., 103.

7. Ibid., 248. Martin notes that the one significant limit to Paul's overcoming hierarchy has to do with male-female relationships.

8. Cf. ibid., 58–59, 92–96.

9. Cf. ibid., 86.

10. Mary M. Solberg, *Compelling Knowledge: A Feminist Proposal for an Epistemology of the Cross* (Albany: State University of New York Press, 1997).

11. Dietrich Bonhoeffer, *Discipleship*, trans. Barbara Green and Reinhard Krauss; Dietrich Bonhoeffer Works in English (Minneapolis: Fortress Press, 2001), 43–91.

Chapter Three. The Church as the Collective Person Jesus Christ

1. Dietrich Bonhoeffer, *Sanctorum Communio: A Theological Study of the Sociology of the Church*, ed. Clifford J. Green; trans. Reinhard Krauss and Nancy Lukens; Dietrich Bonhoeffer Works in English (Minneapolis: Fortress Press, 1998).

2. Ibid., 50.

3. Ibid., 55f.

4. Ibid., 70.

5. Ibid., 80.

6. Ibid., 83.

7. Ibid., 86.

8. Cf. ibid., 99.

9. See ibid.,103–6.

10. Ibid., 105.

11. Ibid., 134.

12. Cf. ibid., 136–38 (note 29).

13. Ibid., 140. Bonhoeffer quotes Kattenbusch in support of his argument.

14. Ibid., 141.

15. Dietrich Bonhoeffer, *Ethics*, ed. Clifford J. Green; trans. Reinhard Krauss, Charles C. West, and Douglas W. Stott; Dietrich Bonhoeffer Works in English (Minneapolis: Fortress Press, 2005), 93.

16. *Sanctorum Communio*, 178. Bonhoeffer quotes Luther (Luther's Works, American Edition 11:412).

17. Ibid., 211

18. Ibid., 215

19. Ibid., 228f.

20. Stanley Hauerwas and Samuel Wells, eds., *The Blackwell Companion to Christian Ethics* (Oxford: Blackwell, 2004), 16.

21. Ibid.

22. Ibid., 18.

23. Ibid., 19.

24. Ibid., 5.

25. Ibid., 7.

26. Ibid., 25.

27. Bonhoeffer, *Sanctorum Communio*, 243.

28. Cf. ibid., 280.

29. Ibid.

30. Cf. ibid., 288.

31. Ibid., 280.

32. Bruce C. Birch and Larry L. Rasmussen, *Bible and Ethics in the Christian Life* (Minneapolis: Augsburg, 1989), 74.

33. Foundational for the focus on character and virtues has been the work of Alasdair MacIntyre, *After Virtue: A Study in Moral Theory*; 2nd ed. (Notre Dame: University of Notre Dame Press, 1984).

34. Stanley Hauerwas, *The Peaceable Kingdom: A Primer in Christian Ethics* (Notre Dame: University of Notre Dame Press, 1983), 39.

35. Craig Dykstra, *Growing in the Life of Faith: Education and Christian Practices*; 2nd ed. (Louisville: Westminster John Knox, 2005).

36. Dorothy C. Bass, *Practicing Our Faith: A Way of Life for a Searching People* (San Francisco: Jossey-Bass, 1997).

37. Hauerwas, *The Peaceable Kingdom*, 33.

Chapter Four. The Body of Christ Is One

1. *Confessing the One Faith: An Ecumenical Explication of the Apostolic Faith*; Faith and Order Paper 153 (Geneva: World Council of Churches, 1991), 12.

2. Karl Baus and Eugen Ewig, eds., "Die Kirche von Nikaia bis Chalkedon: Die Reichskirche nach Konstantin dem Grossen," in *Handbuch der Kirchengeschichte*, ed. Hubert Jedin (Freiburg: Herder, 1985), 2.1:23–24.

3. For example, Johann Auer, *Kleine Katholische Dogmatik 8: Die Kirche—Das allgemeine Heilssakrament* (Regensburg: Friedrich Pustet, 1983), 289–293.

4. Francis Schüssler Fiorenza and John P. Galvin, eds., *Systematic Theology: Roman Catholic Perspectives* (Minneapolis: Fortress Press, 1991), 2:42–43. One notable exception is Hans Küng, *The Church*, trans. Ray and Rosaleen Ockenden (New York: Sheed and Ward, 1967), 263–359.

5. Kurt Aland, *A History of Christianity: From the Beginnings to the Threshold of the Reformation*, trans. James L. Schaaf (Philadelphia: Fortress Press, 1985), 1:164–172.

6. Michael A. Fahey, "Church," in Fiorenza and Galvin, eds., *Systematic Theology*, 2:42f.

7. Küng, *The Church*, reflects this emphasis.

8. Cf. Craig L. Nessan, *Beyond Maintenance to Mission: A Theology of the Congregation*; 2nd ed. (Minneapolis: Fortress Press, 2010), chap. 11, "Ecumenism: That All May Be One."

9. Tertullian, "The Prescription against Heretics," trans. Peter Holmes, in *The Ante-Nicene Fathers*, ed. A. Roberts and J. Donaldson (reprint; Grand Rapids: Eerdmans, 1975), 3:454 (20).

10. Walter M. Abbott, ed., *The Documents of Vatican II* (New York: Guild, 1966), 15 (*Lumen Gentium* 1; revised translation).

11. Michael Schmaus, *Dogma: The Church—Its Origen and Structure* (London: Sheed and Ward, 1972), 4:87, quoting the Second Vatican Council, "Constitution on the Church" (*Lumen Gentium*), 13.

12. Conrad Bergendoff, *The One Holy Catholic Apostolic Church* (Rock Island: Augustana Book Concern, 1954), 97–98.

13. N. T. Wright, *Jesus and the Victory of God* (Minneapolis: Fortress Press, 1996), 268–74.

14. Ibid., 274.

15. Richard A. Horsley, *Jesus and the Spiral of Violence: Popular Jewish Resistance in Roman Palestine* (Minneapolis: Fortress Press, 1993), 149–66.

16. Raymund Schwager, *Must There Be Scapegoats? Violence and Redemption in the Bible*, trans. Maria L. Assad (San Francisco: Harper & Row, 1987).

17. John and Mary Schramm, *Things That Make for Peace: A Personal Search for a New Way of Life* (Minneapolis: Augsburg, 1976).

18. Craig L. Nessan, "The Ethics of Forgiveness," *The Clergy Journal* 81/6 (April 2005): 3–4.

19. For this and the following, see Craig L. Nessan, "Sex, Aggression, and Pain: Sociobiological Implications for Theological Anthropology," *Zygon* 33/3 (1998): 443–54.

20. René Girard, *Violence and the Sacred*, trans. Patrick Gregory (Baltimore: Johns Hopkins University Press, 1979).

21. René Girard, *Things Hidden Since the Foundation of the World*, trans. Stephen Bann and Michael Metteer (Chicago: Stanford University Press, 1987).

22. Mark I. Wallace and Theophus H. Smith, eds., *Curing Violence: Essays on René Girard* (Sonoma, Calif.: Polebridge, 1994).

23. Santhosh J. Sahayadoss, "Martin Luther's Theology of the Cross and Its Significance for Creating a Culture of Peace," in *Doing Theology in a Global Context: A Festschrift for the Reverend Professor Dr. Hans Schwarz on the Occasion of His 70th Birthday*, ed. Craig L. Nessan and Thomas Kothmann (Bangalore: ATC, 2009), 259–66.

24. Walter Wink, *The Powers That Be: Theology for a New Millennium* (New York: Doubleday, 1999), 101–2.

25. M. K. Gandhi, *Nonviolent Resistance (Satyagraha)* (New York: Schocken, 1961), 375. As the subtitle indicates, this book is a primer on the philosophy and methods of nonviolent resistance, *satyagraha*, the power of truth.

26. Robert Ellsberg, *All Saints: Daily Reflections on Saints, Prophets, and Witnesses for Our Time* (New York: Crossroad, 1997), 54.

27. Martin Luther King Jr., *The Papers of Martin Luther King, Jr.*, ed. Clayborne Carson, Peter Holloran, Ralph Luker, and Penny A. Russell (Berkeley: University of California Press, 1992), 1:135–136.

28. "Martin Luther King Jr.," in *Wikipedia: The Free Encyclopedia*, April 15, 2009, http://en.wikipedia.org/wiki/Martin_Luther_King,_Jr.#March_on_Washington.2C_1963

29. Martin Luther King Jr., "Letter from Birmingham City Jail," in *A Testament of Hope: The Essential Writings of Martin Luther King, Jr.*, ed. James Melvin Washington (San Francisco: Harper & Row, 1986), 297.

30. Martin Luther King Jr., "I Have a Dream," in ibid., 219.

31. Martin Luther King Jr., "I See the Promised Land," in ibid., 286.

32. Ellsberg, *All Saints*, 72.

33. Nat Hentoff, ed., *The Essays of A. J. Muste* (New York: Simon and Schuster, 1967), 201.

34. Ibid., 372f.

35. "A. J. Muste," in *Wikipedia: The Free Encyclopedia*, April 16, 2009, http://en.wikipedia.org/wiki/A.J._Muste

36. Craig Dykstra and Dorothy C. Bass, "A Theological Understanding of Christian Practices," in *Practicing Theology: Beliefs and Practices in the Christian Life*, ed. Miroslav Volf and Dorothy Bass (Grand Rapids: Eerdmans, 2002), 18.

37. Martin Luther, "The Small Catechism," trans. Timothy J. Wengert, in *The Book of Concord: The Confessions of the Evangelical Lutheran Church*, ed. Robert Kolb and Timothy J. Wengert (Minneapolis: Fortress Press, 2000), 353.

38. "Confession and Forgiveness," *Evangelical Lutheran Worship* (Minneapolis: Augsburg Fortress, 2006), 96.

39. Dietrich Bonhoeffer, *Letters and Papers from Prison* (New York: Macmillan, 1971), 46.

40. Dietrich Bonhoeffer, *Life Together/Prayerbook of the Bible*, trans. Daniel W. Bloesch and James H. Burtness; ed. Geffrey B. Kelly; Dietrich Bonhoeffer Works in English (Minneapolis: Fortress Press, 1996), 108–18.

41. Norma Cook Everist, *Church Conflict: From Contention to Collaboration* (Nashville: Abingdon, 2004).

42. Gil Bailie, *Violence Unveiled: Humanity at the Crossroads* (New York: Crossroad, 1995).

43. Steven J. Kirsh, *Children, Adolescents, and Media Violence: A Critical Look at the Research* (Thousand Oaks, Calif.: Sage, 2006).

44. Wink, *The Powers That Be*, 42–62.

45. http://www.forusa.org/

Chapter Five. The Body of Christ Is Holy

1. For the classic treatment of the idea of the holy, see Rudolf Otto, *The Idea of the Holy*; trans. John W. Harvey (Oxford: Oxford University Press, 1958).

2. James Muilenburg, "Holiness," in *The Interpreter's Dictionary of the Bible*, ed. George Arthur Buttrick (Nashville: Abingdon, 1962), 2:616–617.

3. *Confessing the One Faith: An Ecumenical Explication of the Apostolic Faith*; Faith and Order Paper 153 (Geneva: World Council of Churches, 1991), 88.

4. Hans Küng, *The Church*, trans. Ray and Rosaleen Ockenden (New York: Sheed and Ward, 1967), 325.

5. This is also true of the references to believers as a "holy nation" (1 Pet 2:9) and "holy temple" (Eph 2:21).

6. Martin Luther, "The Freedom of a Christian," in *Career of the Reformer 1*, ed. Harold J. Grimm; trans. W. A. Lambert; Luther's Works, American Edition (Philadelphia: Fortress Press, 1957), 31:333–377.

7. Rodney Stark, *The Rise of Christianity: How the Obscure, Marginal Jesus Movement Became the Dominant Religious Force in the Western World in a Few Centuries* (San Francisco: HarperCollins, 1997), 161.

8. Ibid., 213–215.

9. St. Cyprian, "The Life and Passion of Cyprian, Bishop and Martyr," trans. Ernest Wallis; in *The Ante-Nicene Fathers*, ed. A. Roberts and J. Donaldson (reprint: Grand Rapids: Eerdmans, 1975), 5:556 (9).

10. Kurt Aland, *A History of Christianity: From the Beginnings to the Threshold of the Reformation*, trans. James L. Schaaf (Philadelphia: Fortress Press, 1985), 1:330–333.

11. Ibid., 1:388–391.

12. Leonardo Boff, *Francis of Assisi: A Model for Human Liberation*, trans. John W. Diercksmeier (Maryknoll: Orbis, 2006).

13. Kurt Aland, *A History of Christianity: From the Reformation to the Present*, trans. James L. Schaaf (Philadelphia: Fortress Press, 1985), 2:251–255.

14. Walter Rauschenbusch, *A Theology for the Social Gospel* (Louisville: Westminster John Knox, 1997); and Gustavo Gutiérrez, *A Theology of Liberation: History, Politics, and Salvation*, trans. Matthew J. O'Connell (Maryknoll: Orbis, 1988).

15. Küng, *The Church*, 344.

16. Stevan L. Davies, *Jesus the Healer: Possession, Trance, and the Origins of Christianity* (New York: Continuum, 1995).

17. N. T. Wright, *Jesus and the Victory of God* (Minneapolis: Fortress Press, 1996), 413–28.

18. Gordon W. Lathrop, *The Pastor: A Spirituality* (Minneapolis: Fortress Press, 2006), 77–79.

19. Shannon Jung, *Sharing Food: Christian Practices for Enjoyment* (Minneapolis: Fortress Press, 2006), 38–54.

20. Carl E. Braaten and Robert W. Jenson, eds., *Union with Christ: The New Finnish Interpretation of Luther* (Grand Rapids: Eerdmans, 1998).

21. L. Shannon Jung, *Food for Life: The Spirituality and Ethics of Eating* (Minneapolis: Fortress Press, 2004), 88–94.

22. Robert S. Wistrich, ed., *Demonizing the Other: Antisemitism, Racism, and Xenophobia* (London: Routledge, 2003).

23. John Dominic Crossan, *Jesus: A Revolutionary Biography* (New York: HarperCollins, 1994), 66–71.

24. Donald E. Messer, *Breaking the Conspiracy of Silence: Christian Churches and the Global AIDS Crisis* (Minneapolis: Fortress Press, 2004).

25. Jeffrey D. Sachs, *The End of Poverty: Economic Possibilities for Our Time* (New York: Penguin, 2005).

26. Craig L. Nessan, *Give Us This Day: A Lutheran Proposal for Ending World Hunger* (Minneapolis: Augsburg Fortress, 2003).

27. Robert Ellsberg, *All Saints: Daily Reflections on Saints, Prophets, and Witnesses for Our Time* (New York: Crossroad, 1997), 520.

28. Ibid.

29. Dorothy Day, *The Long Loneliness: An Autobiography* (New York: Harper and Row, 1952), 107.

30. Robert Ellsberg, ed., *By Little and By Little: The Selected Writings of Dorothy Day* (New York: Knopf, 1983), 98.

31. *Dorothy Day: Don't Call Me a Saint*; a film by Rebecca Larson (2006). Information at http://www .dorothydaydoc.com/home.html.

32. Dorothy Day, *Loaves and Fishes* (New York: Harper & Row, 1963).

33. Ellsberg, *All Saints*, 519.

34. Day, *The Long Loneliness*, 286.

35. James R. Brockman, ed. and trans., *The Violence of Love: The Pastoral Wisdom of Archbishop Oscar Romero* (San Francisco: Harper & Row, 1988), 124.

36. Oscar Romero, *Voice of the Voiceless: The Four Pastoral Letters and Other Statements*, trans. Michael J. Walsh (Maryknoll: Orbis, 1985), 189.

37. James R. Brockman, *The Word Remains: A Life of Oscar Romero* (Maryknoll: Orbis, 1982), 217.

38. Romero, *Voice of the Voiceless*, 50f.

39. Jon Sobrino, "A Theologian's View of Oscar Romero," in Romero, *Voice of the Voiceless*, 30.

40. As quoted in Ellsberg, *All Saints*, 393.

41. Ibid.

42. Mother Teresa, *Mother Teresa in My Own Words*, ed. José Luis González-Balado (New York: Gramercy, 1996), 108.

43. Mother Teresa, *Mother Teresa: Come Be My Light: The Private Writings of the Saint of Calcutta*, ed. Brian Kolodiejchuk (New York: Doubleday, 2007).

44. Mother Teresa, "Nobel Peace Prize Lecture," in *Mother Teresa: A Complete Authorized Biography*, by Kathryn Spink (San Francisco: HarperSanFrancisco, 1997), 299.

45. Nancy Tatom Ammerman with Arthur Emery Farnsley, *Congregation and Community* (Piscataway, N.J.: Rutgers University Press, 1997), 337–38.

46. For example, see the materials provided by the Presbyterian Church (U.S.A.), http://www.pcusa.org/ nationalhealth/parishnursing/ May 15, 2009.

47. Howard Zehr, *The Little Book of Restorative Justice* (Intercourse, Pa.: Good Books, 2002).

48. Desmond Tutu, *No Future without Forgiveness* (New York: Doubleday, 1999).

49. Bread for the World can be accessed at http://www.bread.org/ and, while especially focusing on adequate nutrition, provides a comprehensive agenda for addressing the material needs of all persons for food, clean water, shelter, clothing, and basic medical care.

Chapter Six. The Body of Christ Is Catholic

1. Hans Küng, *The Church*, trans. Ray and Rosaleen Ockenden (New York: Sheed and Ward, 1967), 296.

2. Ibid., 297.

3. Vincent of Lérins, *The Commonitory of Vincent of Lérins: For the Antiquity and Universality of the Catholic Faith Against the Profane Novelty of All Heresies*, trans. C. A. Huertley; The St. Pachomius Orthodox Library, http:// voskrese.info/spl/lerins.html, May 21, 2009, Chapter 2.

4. Küng, *The Church*, 298.

5. Jürgen Moltmann, *The Church in the Power of the Spirit: A Contribution to Messianic Ecclesiology*, trans. Margaret Kohl (New York: Harper & Row, 1977), 348.

6. Ibid., 349.

7. Ibid.; emphasis added.

8. Jürgen Moltmann, *The Coming of God: Christian Eschatology*, trans. Margaret Kohl (Minneapolis: Fortress Press, 1996), 237.

9. Cf. Michael Schmaus, *Dogma: The Church—Its Origen and Structure* (London: Sheed and Ward, 1972), 4:85.

10. Moltmann, *The Coming of God*, 270–72.

11. Ibid., 294.

12. Ibid., 300.

13. Milton Mayeroff, *On Caring* (New York: HarperPerrenial, 1971).

14. A valuable resource for the biblical narrative on the care of creation is *The Green Bible: New Revised Standard Version* (New York: HarperCollins, 2008).

15. Larry L. Rasmussen, *Earth Community, Earth Ethics* (Maryknoll: Orbis, 1996), 265.

16. Cf. Al Gore, *An Inconvenient Truth: The Planetary Emergence of Global Warming and What We Can Do about It* (New York: Rodale, 2006).

17. Lynn White, "The Historic Roots of Our Ecological Crisis," *Science* 155 (March 10, 1967): 1203–1207.

18. Shannon Jung, *We Are Home: A Spirituality of the Environment* (Mahwah, N.J.: Paulist, 1993).

19. William Blake, "Auguries of Innocence," in *The Poetry and Prose of William Blake*, ed. David V. Erdman (New York: Doubleday, 1965), 481.

20. Mary Oliver, "Some Questions You Might Ask," in *New and Selected Poems* (Boston: Beacon, 1992), 65.

21. For a trenchant critique of reducing the meaning of stewardship to money and an argument for a moratorium on the use of the word *stewardship* until a constructive definition can be articulated, see H. Paul Santmire, *Ritualizing Nature: Renewing Christian Liturgy in a Time of Crisis* (Minneapolis: Fortress Press, 2008), 251–57.

22. Already in 1972, professors and systems analysts argued that the planetary system was approaching the limits of human exploitation. This research was updated thirty years later in Donella H. Meadows, Jorgen Randers, and Dennis L. Meadows, *Limits to Growth: The 30-Year Update* (White River Junction, Vt.: Chelsea Green, 2004).

23. Andrés R. Edwards, *The Sustainability Revolution: Portrait of a Paradigm Shift* (Gabriola Island, B.C.: New Society, 2005).

24. Cf. Luke Gascho, *Creation Care: Keepers of the Earth* (Scottsdale, Pa.: Herald, 2008).

25. See, for example, *Common Declaration of John Paul II and the Ecumenical Patriarch His Holiness Bartholomew I*, "Common Declaration on Environmental Ethics," June 10, 2002, http://www.vatican.va/holy_father/john_paul_ii/speeches/2002/june/documents/hf_jp-ii_spe_20020610_venice-declaration_en.html, June 4, 2009.

26. For a summary of statutes in the U.S., see United States Environmental Law, Wikipedia, http://en.wikipedia.org/wiki/United_States_environmental_law, June 4, 2009.

27. Arne Naess, "The Deep Ecological Movement: Some Philosophical Aspects," *Philosophical Inquiry* 8 (1986): 1–2.

28. For example, "Caring for Creation: Vision, Hope, and Justice," A Social Statement of the Evangelical Lutheran Church in America, adopted August 28, 1993 (Chicago: ELCA, 1993).

29. For the following account, see Robert Ellsberg, *All Saints: Daily Reflections on Saints, Prophets, and Witnesses for Our Time* (New York: Crossroad, 1997), 432.

30. Ibid.

31. Ibid.

32. A Prayer Attributed to St. Francis, *Lutheran Book of Worship* (Minneapolis: Augsburg, 1978), 48.

33. Text adapted from the website of The Catholic Doors Ministry, http://www.catholicdoors.com/prayers/english3/p02704.htm, June 5, 2009.

34. Santmire, *Ritualizing Nature*, 6.

35. Cf. Leonardo Boff, *Saint Francis: A Model for Human Liberation*, trans. John W. Diercksmeier (Maryknoll: Orbis, 1982), 34–46.

36. Ellsberg, *All Saints*, 433.

37. For this and the following, Ellsberg, *All Saints*, 248–249.

38. An intense controversy surrounds this speech. Later paraphrases of the speech, seeking to enhance its relevance for the ecological movement, have distorted its meaning. The following quote is taken from the earliest recorded version by Henry A. Smith in 1887.

39. "Chief Seattle's Speech: Version by Dr. Smith," in Warren Jefferson, *The World of Chief Seattle: How Can One Sell the Air?* (Summertown, Tenn.: Native Voices, 2001), 87ff.

40. For this and the following, see Kyle Childress, "Good Work: Learning about Ministry from Wendell Berry," *The Christian Century* 122 (March 8, 2005): 28–33.

41. Wendell Berry, *Life is a Miracle: An Essay against Modern Superstition* (Washington, D.C.: Counterpoint, 2001), 13–22.

42. In this regard, Berry makes frequent reference to the work of Wes Jackson, President of The Land Institute, http://www.landinstitute.org/vnews/display.v, June 10, 2009.

43. Wendell Berry, *What Are People For?* (San Francisco: North Point, 1990), 185–86.

44. Ibid., pp. 207–210.

45. Wendell Berry, *Sex, Economy, Freedom & Community* (New York: Pantheon, 1992), 114–15.

46. Wendell Berry, "Let Us Pledge," *The Amicus Journal* 12/3 (Summer 1990): 33; reprinted in *Harper's Magazine* 281 (November 1990): 42.

47. Berry, *Sex, Economy, Freedom & Community*, 115.

48. Wendell Berry, *Another Turn of the Crank* (Washington, D.C.: Counterpoint, 1995), 89.

49. Cf. ibid., 77.

50. Wendell Berry, *Collected Poems—1957–1982* (San Francisco: North Point, 1985), 156.

51. For ideas about celebrating an alternative Christmas, see http://www.buynothingchristmas.org/alternatives/index.html, June 11, 2009.

52. One excellent resource for congregational use is Bob Sitze, *Starting Simple: Conversations about the Way We Live* (Herndon, Va: Alban Institute, 2007).

53. John V. Taylor, *Enough Is Enough: A Biblical Call for Moderation in a Consumer-Oriented Society* (Minneapolis: Augsburg, 1977).

54. Manfred Lange employed the term, "glocalization," in 1990. The word derives from the sense of the Japanese word, *dochakuka*, meaning "global localization." http://en.wikipedia.org/wiki/Glocalization, June 11, 2009.

55. See Rebecca Todd Peters, *The Search for the Good Life: The Ethics of Globalization* (New York: Continuum, 2004), especially chap. 5: "Globalization as Localization," 105–38.

56. Ibid., 114–123.

57. Berry, *Another Turn of the Crank*, 19.

58. For this and the following quote, "Caring for Creation," 7–8.

59. Cf. Rasmussen, *Earth Community, Earth Ethics*, 155–73.

60. An excellent resource that considers sustainable development holistically is *Guiding Principles for Sustainable Development* (Geneva: Lutheran World Federation, 2002).

61. For this and the following, see "Carbon Footprint," http://en.wikipedia.org/wiki/Carbon_footprint, June 11, 2009.

62. Helpful assessment tools are available on the Internet, for example, see http://www.carbonfootprint.com/, June 12, 2009.

63. One point of reference for this work is the World Charter for Nature, adopted by the United Nations in 1982, http://www.orgone.org/articles/ax7unwc1.htm, July 1, 2009.

64. For a comprehensive listing of organizations and resources on earth care, see Edwards, *The Sustainability Revolution*, 141–81. In addition to denominational advocacy offices, there are several ecumenical groups organized for promoting the care of creation, for example, Earth Ministry, http://www.earthministry.org/, June 12, 2009.

65. Dwight N. Hopkins, "Holistic Health & Healing: Environmental Racism & Ecological Justice," *Currents in Theology and Mission* 36 (February 2009): 5–19.

66. Benjamin F. Chavis, "Foreword," in *Confronting Environmental Racism: Voices from the Grassroots*, ed. Robert D. Bullard (Boston: South End, 1999), 3.

Chapter Seven. The Body of Christ Is Apostolic

1. Irenaeus, *Against Heresies*, in *The Apostolic Fathers with Justin Martyr and Irenaeus*, ed. A. Cleveland Coxe; *The Ante-Nicene Fathers*, ed. A. Roberts and J. Donaldson (reprint; Grand Rapids: Eerdmans, 1989), 414–16 (3:1-3).

2. Ibid., 826 (3:3).

3. Michael Schmaus, *Dogma: The Church—Its Origen and Structure* (London: Sheed and Ward, 1972), 4:174–188.

4. Cf. Johann Auer, *Kleine Katholische Dogmatik*, vol. 8 of *Die Kirche: Das allgemeine Heilssakrament* (Regensburg: Friedrich Pustet, 1983), 295–297.

5. *Confessing the One Faith: An Ecumenical Explication of the Apostolic Faith.* Faith and Order Paper 153 (Geneva: World Council of Churches, 1991), 89.

6. For this and the following, see Conrad Bergendoff, *The One Holy Catholic Apostolic Church* (Rock Island: Augustana Book Concern, 1954), 12–17.

7. *Confessing the One Faith*, 89.

8. Bergendoff, *One Holy Catholic Apostolic*, 20.

9. Hans Küng, *The Church*, trans. Ray and Rosaleen Ockenden (New York: Sheed and Ward, 1967), 358.

10. Ibid.

11. Cf. Emmanuel Levinas, *Totality and Infinity: An Essay on Exteriority*, trans. Alphonso Lingis (Pittsburgh: Duquesne University Press, 1969), 197–201, 291.

12. Emmanuel Levinas, "Ethics as First Philosophy," in *The Levinas Reader*, ed. Sean Hand (Oxford: Blackwell, 1989), 83.

13. Ibid., 84.

14. Levinas, *Totality and Infinity*, 298.

15. "The Declaration of Independence," in *The Constitution of the United States*, ed. Edward Conrad Smith (New York: Barnes & Noble, 1972), 24.

16. Cf. Jürgen Moltmann, *The Church in the Power of the Spirit: A Contribution to Messianic Ecclesiology*, trans. Margaret Kohl (New York: Harper & Row, 1977), 338–39.

17. Cf. ibid., 357–61.

18. Ibid., 361.

19. Mary Solberg, *Compelling Knowledge: A Feminist Proposal for an Epistemology of the Cross* (Albany: State University of New York Press, 1997).

20. Cf. Richard Amesbury and George M. Newlands, *Faith and Human Rights: Christianity and the Global Struggle for Human Dignity* (Minneapolis: Fortress Press, 2008), 104–7.

21. The lists of names are primarily of the male leaders of families, reflecting the patriarchal ordering of society at the time; however, the theological claim is that God knows each one by name, including women and children.

22. For the full text of the Universal Declaration of Human Rights, originally adopted by the General Assembly of the United Nations on December 10, 1948, see http://www.un.org/en/documents/udhr/, June 29, 2009.

23. Amesbury and Newland, *Faith and Human Rights*, 25.

24. I am here intentionally omitting race as a distinguishing marker, insofar as race has been demonstrated as a social construct with no basis as a physical characteristic of human being. See Theodore W. Allen, *The Invention of the White Race*; vol. 1: *Racial Oppression and Control* (New York: Verso, 1994). While racism is very real as a social construction, race is not a category grounded in human being itself.

25. For the following listing, see Andrew Clapham, *Human Rights: A Very Short Introduction* (New York: Oxford, 2007), 48.

26. Amesbury and Newlands, *Faith and Human Rights*, 36.

27. Ibid., 80–81.

28. National Council of Churches of Christ in the United States, "Human Rights: The Fulfillment of Life in the Social Order" (1995), as quoted by C. Dale White, *Making a Just Peace: Human Rights and Domination Systems. Reflections on the 50th Anniversary of the Universal Declaration of Human Rights* (Nashville: Abingdon, 1998), 18.

29. Amesbury and Newlands, *Faith and Human Rights*, 112–13.

30. Douglas John Hall, *The Cross in Our Context: Jesus and the Suffering World* (Minneapolis: Fortress Press, 2003), 152.

31. From the "Declaration toward a Global Ethic," released by The Parliament of the World's Religions on September 4, 1993, in *A Global Ethic: The Declaration of the Parliament of the World's Religions*, ed. Hans Küng and Karl-Josef Kuschel; trans. John Bowden (New York: Continuum, 1993), 14–15.

32. Clapham, *Human Rights*, 160.

33. It is important to acknowledge multiple intelligences, not just the conventional measures of intellectual reasoning ability. See Howard Gardner, *Multiple Intelligences: New Horizons in Theory and Practice* (New York: Basic Books, 2006).

34. Gilbert C. Meilander, *Faith and Faithfulness: Basic Themes in Christian Ethics* (Notre Dame: Notre Dame University Press, 1991), 44.

35. Jean Vanier, *Community and Growth* (Mahwah, N.J.: Paulist, 1989). See also Kathryn Spink, *The Miracle, the Message, the Story: Jean Vanier and L'Arche* (Mahwah, N.J.: Paulist, 2006).

36. Katie Geneva Cannon, *Black Womanist Ethics* (Atlanta: Scholars, 1988), 66, 174.

37. One acute dilemma relates to the ethical deliberation of abortion, where the concrete circumstances of the mother may collide with the rights of the unborn. Respect for the dignity of the marginalized entails both efforts to reduce the number of abortions and support for the full rights of women. Cf. Robert M. Baird and Stuart E. Rosenbaum, eds., *The Ethics of Abortion: Pro-Life Versus Pro-Choice*; 3rd ed. (New York: Prometheus, 2001).

38. Rosemary Radford Ruether, *Sexism and God-Talk: Toward a Feminist Theology* (Boston: Beacon, 1993).

39. Joseph Barndt, *Dismantling Racism: The Twenty-First Century Challenge to White America* (Minneapolis: Fortress Press, 2007).

40. Marvin M. Ellison and Judith Plaskow, eds., *Heterosexism in Contemporary World Religion: Problem and Prospect* (Cleveland: Pilgrim, 2007).

41. Diane C. Olson and Laura Dean F. Friedrich, *Weaving a Just Future for Children: An Advocacy Guide* (Nashville: Discipleship Resources, 2008), and Erdman B. Palmore, Laurence Branch, and Diana K. Harris, eds., *The Encyclopedia of Ageism* (Binghamton, N.Y.: Haworth, 2005).

42. Catherine Keller, Michael Nausner, and Mayra Rivera, eds., *Postcolonial Theologies: Divinity and Empire* (Atlanta: Chalice, 2004).

43. Martin Luther King Jr., in discussion following a speech at Western Michigan University in 1963. http://www.wmich.edu/library/archives/mlk/q-a.html, June 30, 2009.

44. Diana Eck, *A New Religious America: How a "Christian Country" Has Become the World's Most Religiously Diverse Nation* (New York: Harper Collins, 2001).

45. See the trenchant critique of worship and white superiority in Traci C. West, *Disruptive Christian Ethics: When Racism and Women's Lives Matter* (Louisville: Westminster John Knox, 2006), 112–40.

46. An excellent resource is Charles R. Foster, *We Are the Church Together: Cultural Diversity in Congregational Life* (Valley Forge, Pa.: Trinity Press International, 1996).

47. Martin Luther, "On the Councils and the Church," in *Church and Ministry 3*, ed. Eric W. Gritsch; Luther's Works, American Edition; ed. Helmut T. Lehmann (Philadelphia: Fortress Press, 1966), 41:164.

48. One of the most fascinating theological developments in the last few decades is the increasing number of monographs devoted to the theology of the cross. These include Jürgen Moltmann, *The Crucified God*, trans. R. A. Wilson and John Bowden (New York: Harper and Row, 1974); Alister E. McGrath, *Luther's Theology of the Cross: Martin Luther's Theological Break* (Oxford: Blackwell, 1990); Charles B. Cousar, *The Theology of the Cross: The Death of Jesus in the Pauline Letters* (Minneapolis: Fortress Press, 1990); Gerhard O. Forde, *On Being a Theologian of the Cross* (Grand Rapids: Eerdmans, 1997); Mary Solberg, *Compelling Knowledge: A Feminist Proposal for an Epistemology of the Cross* (Albany: State University of New York Press, 1997); Douglas John Hall, *The Cross in Our Context: Jesus and the Suffering World* (Minneapolis: Fortress Press, 2003); Deanna A. Thompson, *Crossing the Divide: Luther, Feminism, and the Cross* (Minneapolis: Fortress Press, 2004); John D. Caputo, *The Weakness of God: A Theology of The Event* (Bloomington: Indiana University Press, 2006); Vitor Westhelle, *The Scandalous God: The Use and Abuse of the Cross* (Minneapolis: Fortress Press, 2006); S. Mark Heim, *Saved From Sacrifice: A Theology of the Cross* (Grand Rapids: Eerdmans, 2006); Anna Madsen, *The Theology of the Cross in Historical Perspective* (Eugene, Ore.: Wipf and Stock, 2007); David A. Brondos, *Fortress Introduction to Salvation and the Cross* (Minneapolis: Fortress Press, 2007); Phil Ruge-Jones, *The Word of the Cross in a World of Glory* (Minneapolis: Augsburg Fortress, 2008); Theodore W. Jennings Jr., *Transforming Atonement: A Political Theology of the Cross* (Minneapolis: Fortress Press, 2009).

49. For this and the following, see Robert Ellsberg, *All Saints: Daily Reflections on Saints, Prophets, and Witnesses for Our Time* (New York: Crossroad, 1997), 306–7.

50. Bartolomé de Las Casas, *Historia*, 3; chap. 4 contains the text of this sermon. The translation is from Gustavo Gutiérrez, *Las Casas: In Search of the Poor of Jesus Christ*; trans. Robert R. Barr (Maryknoll: Orbis, 1993), 29.

51. See Bartolomé de Las Casas, *The Only Way*, ed. Helen Rand Parish; trans. Francis Patrick Sullivan (Mahwah, N.J.: Paulist, 1992), 133.

52. Ibid., 68–116.

53. For a helpful discussion of this issue, see Paul S. Vickery, *Bartolomé de Las Casas: Great Prophet of the Americas* (Mahwah, N.J.: Paulist, 2006), 84–90.

54. Ibid., 88.

55. Ibid., 90.

56. Gutiérrez, *Las Casas*, 456.

57. Soujourner Truth, "Narrative of Sojourner Truth, a Northern Slave: Emancipated from Bodily Servitude by the State of New York in 1828," in *Slave Narratives*, eds. William L. Andrews and Henry Louis Gates Jr. (New York: Library of America, 2000), 578.

58. Sojourner Truth, "Ain't I a Woman," speech in modern dialect, http://en.wikipedia.org/wiki/Ain%27t_I_a_Woman%3F, July 2, 2009.

59. Adapted from Ellsberg, *All Saints*, 515.

60. For the preceding and this quote, see http://en.wikipedia.org/wiki/Sojourner_Truth, July 2, 2009.

61. Desmond Tutu, *The Rainbow People of God: The Making of a Peaceful Revolution* (New York: Doubleday, 1994), 7, 10.

62. Ibid., 183.

63. Ibid., 185–89.

64. Desmond Tutu, *No Future without Forgiveness* (New York: Doubleday, 1999).

65. Michael Battle, *Reconciliation: The Ubuntu Theology of Desmond Tutu* (Cleveland: Pilgrim, 1997).

66. Mark Kline Taylor, *Remembering Esperanza: A Cultural-Political Theology for North American Praxis* (Maryknoll: Orbis, 1990), 200–8.

67. Rosemary Radford Ruether, *Liberation Theology: Human Hope Confronts Christian History and American Power* (New York: Paulist, 1972), 16–22.

68. James A. Oines, "Sanctuary as Civil Initiative" (Unpublished paper, Dec. 14, 2007).

69. Clapham, *Human Rights*, 36. This definition is from the *Convention on the Prevention and Punishment of the Crime of Genocide*, Article II, adopted by the United Nations General Assembly on December 9, 1948.

70. Victoria J. Barnett, *Bystanders: Conscience and Complicity during the Holocaust* (Westport, Conn.: Praeger, 1999).

71. Gregory H. Stanton, "The 8 Stages of Genocide," Genocide Watch, http://www.genocidewatch.org/aboutgenocide/8stagesofgenocide.html, July 8, 2009. Originally presented as a briefing paper at the U.S. State Department in 1996.

72. One excellent resource is provided by the U.S. Holocaust Memorial Museum, http://www.ushmm.org/genocide/take_action/, July 8, 2009.

Chapter Eight. Embodying Shalom Church

1. Cf. Robert D. Putnam, *Bowling Alone: The Collapse and Revival of American Community* (New York: Simon & Schuster, 2000).

2. Cf. Richard H. Bliese and Craig Van Gelder, eds., *The Evangelizing Church: A Lutheran Contribution* (Minneapolis: Fortress Press, 2005), 124–27.

3. Cf. Clifford J. Green, *Bonhoeffer: A Theology of Sociality* (Grand Rapids: Eerdmans, 1999), 19–66.

4. Stanley Hauerwas, *A Community of Character: Toward a Constructive Christian Social Ethic* (Notre Dame: University of Notre Dame Press, 1981).

5. See the Appendix for a concise summary of the twenty virtues, twelve representative biographies, and twenty congregational practices.

6. Cf. Mieke Bal, *Death and Dissymmetry: The Politics of Coherence in the Book of Judges* (Chicago: University of Chicago Press, 1988).

7. Phyllis Trible, *Texts of Terror: Literary-Feminist Readings of Biblical Narratives* (Philadelphia: Fortress Press, 1984).

8. For a concise review, see "A Time for Recommitment: Building the New Relationship between Jews and Christians," Statement by International Council of Christians and Jews (Council of Centers of Jewish-Christian Relations, 2008/2009), http://www.ccjr.us/index.php/dialogika-resources/documents-and-statements/interreligious/565-iccj09july5.html, July 21, 2009.

9. Martin Luther, "On the Jews and Their Lies (1543)," in *The Christian in Society 4*, ed. Franklin Sherman; trans. Martin H. Bertram; Luther's Works, American Edition (Philadelphia: Fortress Press, 1971), 47:121–306.

10. Christopher Tyerman, *God's War: A New History of the Crusades* (Cambridge: Belknap, 2006).

11. Toby Green, *Inquisition: The Reign of Fear* (New York: St. Martin's, 2007).

12. Martin Luther, "An Open Letter on the Harsh Book against the Peasants (1525)," in *The Christian in Society 3*, ed. Robert C. Schultz; trans. Charles M. Jacobs; Luther's Works, American Edition (Philadelphia: Fortress Press, 1967), 46:65.

13. George Huntston Williams, *The Radical Reformation* (Philadelphia: Westminster, 1962).

14. Susannah Heschel, *The Aryan Jesus: Christian Theologians and the Bible in Nazi Germany* (Princeton: Princeton University Press, 2008).

15. John W. DeGruchy and Charles Villa-Vicencio, eds., *Apartheid Is a Heresy* (Grand Rapids: Eerdmans, 1983).

16. Michael Barkun, *Religion and the Racist Right: The Origins of the Christian Identity Movement* (Chapel Hill: University of North Carolina Press, 1996).

17. Gerhard Ebeling, *Dogmatik des christlichen Glaubens* (Tübingen: Mohr Siebeck, 1985), 3:369–370. The English translation is from *One Holy, Catholic and Apostolic Church: Some Lutheran and Ecumenical Perspectives*, ed. Hans-Peter Grosshans (Minneapolis: Lutheran University Press and Lutheran World Federation, 2009), 26.

18. For example, Christopher Hitchens, *God Is Not Great: How Religion Poisons Everything* (New York: Hachette, 2007).

19. Roger Haight, *Ecclesial Existence*; Christian Community in History 3 (New York: Continuum, 2008), 99–109.

20. David Patterson and John K. Roth, eds., *After-Words: Post Holocaust Struggles with Forgiveness, Reconciliation, and Justice* (Seattle and London: University of Washington Press, 2004), 104.

21. H. Paul Santmire, *Ritualizing Nature: Renewing Christian Liturgy in a Time of Crisis* (Minneapolis: Fortress Press, 2008), 216–44.

22. Ibid., xiii.

23. See Michael Walzer, *Spheres of Justice: A Defense of Pluralism and Equality* (New York: Basic, 1983), 312–21.

24. *Global Mission in the Twenty-first Century: A Vision of Evangelical Faithfulness in God's Mission* (Chicago: Evangelical Lutheran Church in America, 1999), 6–20, 29–34. http://archive.elca.org/GlobalMission/policy/gm21full.pdf, July 22, 2009.

25. Ibid., 5.

26. Andres R. Edwards, *The Sustainability Revolution: Portrait of a Paradigm Shift* (Gabriola Island, B.C.: New Society, 2005), 97–112.

27. Craig L. Nessan, "Orthopraxis," in *Cambridge Dictionary of Theology*, ed. Ian McFarland et al. (Cambridge: Cambridge University Press, 2010).

28. Cf. Norma Cook Everist and Craig L. Nessan, *Transforming Leadership: New Vision for a Church in Mission* (Minneapolis: Fortress Press, 2008), 40–42.

29. Philip D. W. Krey and Peter D. S. Krey, eds. and trans., *Luther's Spirituality* (New York: Paulist, 2007), 30.

30. Dennis A. Jacobsen, *Doing Justice: Congregations and Community Organizing* (Minneapolis: Fortress Press, 2001), 27.

31. For this and the following description of the principles of community organizing, see Jacobsen, *Doing Justice*, 25–28.

32. William T. Cavanaugh, *Torture and Eucharist: Theology, Politics, and the Body of Christ* (Oxford: Blackwell, 1998), 271.

33. For this and the following quotation, see ibid., 279.

34. Ibid., 281.

Conclusion

1. So Diana Eck, *A New Religious America: How a "Christian Country" Has Become the World's Most Religiously Diverse Nation* (San Francisco: HarperSanFrancisco, 2001).

2. Hans Küng and Karl-Josef Kuschel, eds., *A Global Ethic: The Declaration of the Parliament of the World's Religions*, trans. John Bowden (New York: Continuum, 1993), pp. 14-15.

3. Hans Küng, ed., *Yes to a Global Ethic*, trans. John Bowden (New York: Continuum, 1996), 2.

4. Ibid.

5. The final text of the Earth Charter was approved at a meeting of the Earth Charter Commission at the United Nations Educational, Scientific, and Cultural Organization (UNESCO) headquarters in Paris in March 2000. The document is from Andres R. Edwards, *The Sustainability Revolution: Portrait of a Paradigm Shift* (Gabriola Island, BC: New Society, 2005), 42-45. The quote is on p. 42.

6. The first three questions are adaptations of the World Council of Churches, *Baptism, Eucharist and Ministry* (Geneva: World Council of Churches, 1982), x. The fourth question is the author's own formulation.

7. These ideas were first explored in Craig L. Nessan, "After the Deconstruction of Christendom: Toward a Theological Paradigm for the Global Era," *Mission Studies* 18, No. 1-35(2001):78–96.

8. Paul Knitter, *One Earth, Many Religions: Multifaith Dialogue and Global Responsibility* (Maryknoll: Orbis, 1995), 178–79.

NAMES INDEX

SUBJECT INDEX

SCRIPTURE INDEX